New Moral Natures in Tourism

How do we understand human-nature relationships in tourism or determine the consequences of these relationships to be "good," "bad," "right," "wrong," "fair," or "just"? What theoretical and philosophical perspectives can usefully orient us in the production and consumption of tourism towards living and enacting the "good life" with the more-than-human world?

This book addresses such questions by investigating relationships between nature and morality in tourism contexts. Recognizing that morality, much like nature, is embedded in histories and landscapes of power, the book engages with diverse theoretical and philosophical perspectives to critically review, appraise, and advance dialogue on the moral dimensions of natures. Contributing authors explore the very foundations of how we make sense of nature in tourism and leisure contexts – and how we might make sense of it differently.

The book will be essential reading for researchers, students, and practitioners grappling with questions about the moral values, frameworks, or practices best suited to mobilizing tourism natures. What will the future of tourism hold in terms of sustainability, justice, resilience, health, and well-being?

Bryan S. R. Grimwood is Associate Professor in the Department of Recreation and Leisure Studies at the University of Waterloo. His research analyzes human-nature relationships and advocates social justice and sustainability in contexts of tourism, leisure, and livelihoods.

Kellee Caton is Associate Professor of Tourism Studies at Thompson Rivers University and co-chair of the Critical Tourism Studies international network. Her work explores how we come to know tourism as a sociocultural phenomenon, and how we come to know and reshape the world through tourism.

Lisa Cooke is Associate Professor of Cultural Anthropology at Thompson Rivers University. Her research and teaching focus on Indigenous-Settler relations in the territory now most dominantly known as Canada and the ways that contemporary settler colonial cultural forms work to reconstitute particular relations of domination and dispossession.

Routledge Ethics of Tourism
Series edited by Professor David Fennell

This series seeks to engage with key debates surrounding ethical issues in tourism from a range of interdisciplinary perspectives across the social sciences and humanities. Contributions explore ethical debates across socio-cultural, ecological, and economic lines on topics such as: climate, resource consumption, ecotourism and nature-based tourism, sustainability, responsible tourism, the use of animals, politics, international relations, violence, tourism labour, sex tourism, exploitation, displacement, marginalisation, authenticity, slum tourism, Indigenous People, communities, rights, justice, and equity. This series has a global geographic coverage and offers new theoretical insights in the form of authored and edited collections to reflect the wealth of research being undertaken in this sub-field.

Animals, Food and Tourism
Edited by Carol Kline

Tourism Experiences and Animal Consumption: Contested Values, Morality and Ethics
Edited by Carol Kline

Wild Animals and Leisure: Rights and Wellbeing
Edited by Neil Carr and Janette Young

Domestic Animals, Humans, and Leisure: Rights, Welfare, and Wellbeing
Edited by Janette Young and Neil Carr

New Moral Natures in Tourism
Edited by Bryan S. R. Grimwood, Kellee Caton, and Lisa Cooke

For a full list of titles in this series, please visit www.routledge.com/Routledge-Ethics-of-Tourism-Series/book-series/RET

New Moral Natures in Tourism

Edited by
Bryan S. R. Grimwood,
Kellee Caton, and Lisa Cooke

LONDON AND NEW YORK

First published 2018
by Routledge

2 Park Square, Milton Park, Abingdon, Oxfordshire OX14 4RN
52 Vanderbilt Avenue, New York, NY 10017

Routledge is an imprint of the Taylor & Francis Group, an informa business

First issued in paperback 2020

British Library Cataloguing-in-Publication Data
A catalogue record for this book is available from the British Library

Library of Congress Cataloging-in-Publication Data
A catalog record has been requested for this book

ISBN: 978-1-138-29170-6 (hbk)
ISBN: 978-0-367-59126-7 (pbk)

Typeset in Times New Roman
by Apex CoVantage, LLC

For all of our life companions.

Contents

Figures

Contributors

Skye Akbar is Research Associate the University of South Australia. Skye has a strong focus on applying her skills and experience to improve outcomes for those who experience disadvantage and vulnerabilities. Growing up on the Eyre Peninsula with family in primary production and being of the Waljen group of the Wongutha Peoples of the North-Eastern Goldfields of Western Australia established her understanding of remote life, communities, and economies. Her passion is for research that supports self-determined community economic development and well-being for local peoples. Skye aims to continue research in this area, as it is of considerable importance to people in these communities and to the wider community.

Giovanna Bertella is Associate Professor at UiT the Arctic University of Norway in the School of Business and Economics in Tromsø (Norway). Her research interests focus broadly on tourism planning and development. Topics covered in her research include rural tourism, tourism networking and innovation, tourism entrepreneurship, nature-based tourism, animals in tourism, and sustainability. The geographical and cultural settings investigated in her research include northern Norway and Italy.

Neil Carr is Associate Professor and Head of the Department of Tourism at the University of Otago, New Zealand, as well as the Editor of *Annals of Leisure Research*. His research focuses on understanding behaviour within tourism and leisure experiences, with a particular emphasis on animals, children and families, and sex. His recent publications include *Dogs in the Leisure Experience*. Wallingford, UK: CABI (2014) and an edited book entitled *Domestic Animals and Leisure*. Basingstoke, UK: Palgrave Macmillan (2015).

Kellee Caton is Associate Professor of Tourism Studies at Thompson Rivers University in Canada. She holds a PhD from the University of Illinois. Her research focuses on how we come to know tourism as a sociocultural phenomenon and also on how we come to know and reshape the world through tourism – in particular, she is interested in the moral dimensions of these two epistemic processes. She co-chairs the Critical Tourism Studies network and its new North American chapter, sits on the editorial boards of *Annals of Tourism*

Research, *Tourism Analysis*, and the *Journal of China Tourism Research*, and serves on the executive of the Tourism Education Futures Initiative.

Thomas Colas is a graduate of Sciences Po Paris and Sorbonne University and currently conducts research at the Ecole Normale Supérieure for a master's degree. He specialises in Science and Technology Studies and in Fundamental Physics. His academic interests range from environmental and climate change history to cosmology and particle physics. His current fields of study are transnational history of knowledge and historiographical views of the scientific revolutions.

Lisa Cooke is Associate Professor of Anthropology at Thompson Rivers University in Canada. She is a cultural anthropologist specialising in Indigenous studies. Her research interests revolve around examining Indigenous-Settler relations in Canada as they play out in, through, and between places. She has found ethnographic examinations of tourism and the production of touristic spaces a great entry point to exploring contemporary colonial cultural forms and the ways that Indigenous-Settler relations shape or are shaped by them. Earlier work conducted in Whitehorse and Dawson City in Canada's Yukon Territory informs her current examination of Indigenous-Settler relations as they play out in the southern interior of British Columbia.

Bruce Erickson is Assistant Professor in Environment and Geography at the University of Manitoba. His work examines the cultural politics of outdoor recreation and nature tourism, asking how the spheres of leisure and recreation form an integral part of our interactions with the social and bio-physical world. Drawing from cultural geography, political ecology, environmental history, psychoanalysis, leisure studies, and critical theory, his scholarship aims to highlight how recreational activities are a useful starting place for understanding our complicated relationships to nature. He has a PhD in Environmental Studies from York University. He is the author of *Canoe Nation: Nature, Race and the Making of a Canadian Icon* and is the co-editor of *Queer Ecologies: Sex, Nature, Politics, Desire*.

Adrian Franklin trained as an anthropologist in the UK and has held professorial positions at the University of Bristol, UK, the University of Oslo, Norway, and the University of Tasmania, Hobart, Australia. He is currently Professor of Sociology at the University of South Australia. His research interests span the sociology of the 21st century: human relations with non-humans; posthumanism; the sociology of travel and tourism; the contemporary social bond; loneliness and contemporary life; the sociology of successful cities; and material cultures. His books include *Animals and Modern Cultures* (1999); *Nature and Social Theory* (2003); *Tourism* (2005); *Animal Nation: The True Story of Animals and Australia* (2007); *A Collector's Year* (2009); *Collecting the Twentieth Century* (2010); *City Life* (2010); *Retro: A Guide to the Mid-Twentieth Century Design Revival* (2011); and *The Making of MONA* (2014). His new book is *Animal Theory* for Sydney University Press.

Bryan S. R. Grimwood is Associate Professor in the Department of Recreation and Leisure Studies at the University of Waterloo in Canada. Trained as a human geographer and engaged scholar, Bryan specialises in tourism and Indigenous Peoples, tourism ethics and responsibility, northern landscapes, and outdoor experiential education. His research is informed theoretically by relational perspectives of nature and morality and draws on diverse qualitative methodologies and principles of community-based and participatory research. He sits on the editorial boards of *Leisure Sciences* and the *Journal of Ecotourism* and co-chairs the North American chapter of the Critical Tourism Studies network.

Freya Higgins-Desbiolles is Senior Lecturer in the School of Management at the University of South Australia. Freya worked previously in development, development education, and university teaching in international relations. Freya has been a lecturer in tourism with the School of Management of the University of South Australia since 2001. She serves on the Advisory Board of Trinet, is an affiliate of Equality in Tourism, is a co-founder of the Tourism Advocacy and Action Forum, and is a co-convenor of the Peace Tourism Commission of the International Peace Research Association. Freya's research is focused on projects that deliver new insights into the tourism phenomenon and that advocate a more just and sustainable tourism future.

Carol Kline is Associate Professor of Hospitality and Tourism Management at Appalachian State University in the Department of Management. Her research interests focus broadly on tourism planning and development and tourism sustainability but cover a range of topics such as foodie segmentation, craft beverages, agritourism, wildlife-based tourism, animal welfare in tourism, tourism entrepreneurship, niche tourism markets, and tourism impacts to communities.

Gregory Lowan-Trudeau, PhD, is a Métis scholar and educator with interests in Indigenous environmental education and activism. He is currently Associate Professor in the Werklund School of Education at the University of Calgary and Adjunct Professor in First Nations Studies at the University of Northern British Columbia, Canada. Greg is the author of *From Bricolage to Métissage: Rethinking Intercultural Approaches to Indigenous Environmental Education and Research* (Peter Lang).

Kevin Markwell is Associate Professor in the School of Business and Tourism at Southern Cross University, Australia. He has utilised social construction theory to understand the complex and often contradictory relationships between tourism, leisure, and nature and has published on a range of related topics, including ecotourism attraction systems, artificial reefs and sustainable diving, nature interpretation, tourism constructions of nature, and human-animal relations. His latest book is the edited collection *Animals and Tourism: Understanding Complex Relationships* (2015, Channel View Publications).

Philip M. Mullins is Associate Professor of Outdoor Recreation and Tourism Management in the Ecosystem Science and Management Program at the

University of Northern British Columbia in Canada. His research aims to encourage ecologically sustainable and socially just communities and environments through sound collaborative research, critical analysis, and innovative practice in recreation, leisure, and tourism.

Arianne Reis is Senior Lecturer in the School of Science and Health at Western Sydney University. Her areas of research interest are diverse and span from nature-based recreation and tourism to active leisure pursuits and sport events. Within these broad areas of interest, her focus has increasingly been on matters of social and environmental justice as they relate to active leisure and tourism practices. Theoretically, Arianne draws from the Marxist and Critical Theory traditions, with a keen interest in environmental philosophy to produce critiques of the relationships of tourists and nature-based recreationists with nature and non-human animals. With respect to issues of social justice, these have become more prominent in her current work on mega sport events and their impacts on communities. Within this area, her interests lie on the social consequences of neoliberal practices on those who are in the margins of society, a theoretical basis that also overlaps with her work on non-human animals' (non)place and agency in leisure practices.

Jillian M. Rickly is Associate Professor of Tourism Marketing and Management at the University of Nottingham. She is a tourism geographer with interests in authenticity/alienation in tourism motivation and experience, the ethics of sustainability, and mobilities and well-being. Her PhD is in geography from Indiana University (2012). Her work has been published in the *Annals of Tourism Research*, *Journal of Sustainable Tourism*, *Tourist Studies*, and *Mobilities*, along with many other journals. She is also co-author of *Tourism, Performance, and Place: A Geographic Perspective* (Ashgate, 2014) and co-editor of *Tourism & Leisure Mobilities: Politics, Work, and Play* (Routledge, 2016), *Events Mobilities: Politics, Place and Performance* (Routledge, 2016), and *Authenticity & Tourism: Materialities, Perceptions, Experiences* (Emerald, forthcoming 2018).

R. Cody Rusher is a graduate student in the Industrial-Organizational Psychology and Human Resource Management program at Appalachian State University. Born and raised in a town of less than 1,000 people, he considers himself entrenched with passion for community involvement, diversity, and sustainability. His current research interests revolve around work-family balance, focusing particularly on the relationship between one's work and one's home life among non-traditional family types.

Eric J. Shelton, PhD, is an independent researcher and trustee on the Yellow-eyed Penguin Trust, an environmental NGO operating from Dunedin, New Zealand, and working across the natural range of this bird to produce protected whole-of-ecosystem habitat for a range of sea birds and other endemic and native flora and fauna. Arianne Reis and Eric presented *The Nature of Tourism Studies* (2011) to help clarify various ideas on how, in such settings, tourism relates to nature. Eric writes also about the politics of conservation and nature within neoliberalism and the place of nature-based tourism, culminating in a volume co-edited with Mary Mostafanezhad, Roger Norris, and Anna Carr entitled *Political Ecology of Tourism* (2016). Eric's thinking embraces the uncertainties of poststructuralism, the postcolonial, and, here, the implications of the associated moral relativism.

Mick Smith is jointly appointed between the School of Environmental Studies and the Department of Philosophy at Queen's University. He has published widely on topics of environmental philosophy, emotions, and ecological community. His books include *An Ethics of Place: Radical Ecology, Postmodernity, and Social Theory* (SUNY); *Against Ecological Sovereignty: Ethics, Biopolitics and Saving the Natural World* (University of Minnesota); and, with Rosaleen Duffy, *The Ethics of Tourism Development* (Routledge).

Soile Veijola is an internationally renowned sociologist and feminist theorist working in the area of tourism cultural studies at the University of Lapland, Finland. Her research and teaching focuses on ethical epistemologies of tourism studies, social production of knowledge, gender and embodiment, tourism as work, the tourist dwelling, silent communities, and the ethics of neighbouring, hospitality, and care. Her publications include several articles and books co-authored with Eeva Jokinen, beginning with *The Body in Tourism* (1994) to the most recent, *Time to Hostess: Reflections on Borderless Care* (2012). Her latest book is *Disruptive Tourism and Its Untidy Guests: Alternative Ontologies for Future Hospitalities* (Palgrave 2014), co-authored with Jennie Germann Molz, Olli Pyyhtinen, Emily Höckert, and Alexander Grit.

Foreword

One of the unexpected outcomes from a research project I conducted about 20 years ago, during which I interviewed tourists after they had arrived home from a three week "nature-tourism" experience on the island of Borneo, was that quite a few of them considered their "local natures" to be less interesting and appealing than they had prior to their trip. Their local natures were just not "spectacular enough" to quote one of the participants. After all, they had climbed the cloud-clad summit of the highest mountain in South-East Asia, Mt Kinabalu, explored the subterranean depths of Niah Caves, and watched in wonderment as semi-wild orangutans playfully chased each other at Sepilok Orang Utan Sanctuary. The natures that made up their local, everyday landscapes hardly stood up to the extravagant natures they had experienced on their tour. This finding placed in stark relief for me how the discursive and material structures and practices of the tourism industry framed, presented, and mediated nature, in effect constructing specific "tourism natures" for touristic consumption. It also taught me, early on in my career, to "expect the unexpected" when it comes to trying to understand tourist experiences of nature. It is the complex and often contradictory relationships that exist between tourism and nature scrutinised via the lenses of morality and ethics that are the focus of this excellent book, *New Moral Natures in Tourism*.

"Nature," as the editors point out, is a difficult and slippery concept to grapple with philosophically and ontologically. Our understandings of it and the meanings that we attach to it are contested and vary across time, space, and culture. Nature is arguably as much a product of history and culture as it is a product of biophysical and ecological processes. However, this book's central concern is not so much on definition but, importantly, on the "moral terrains" across which tourism and nature traverse, intersect, and overlap. How can tourism-nature relationships become more just and fair, taking into account the interests not just of tourists and the industry, but the more-than-human actors involved?

Tourism has a long-standing relationship with nature. Regardless of whether "mass tourism," "ecotourism," or somewhere in between, tourism harnesses, subdues, domesticates, exploits, co-creates, appropriates, and (re)configures nature in myriad ways. Destinations utilise nature, whether entire ecosystems, such as Australia's Great Barrier Reef, or individual elements, such as a single tree, as tourist attractions, which subsequently drive tourism demand. Romantic, perhaps nostalgic discourses of pristine Edenic natures, seemingly devoid of any influences of humanity, permeate destination marketing, thereby papering over ancient, intimate relationships that have existed and continue to exist between Indigenous Peoples and their lands. The tourism industry is an agent of change that can drastically affect nature and the ecological and social processes and systems that it comprises.

Concern for the effects of tourism on nature can be detected in the literature from the late 1970s. In 1976, the then Director General of the International Union for the Conservation of Nature, Gerardo Budowski, published an article in the journal, *Environmental Conservation*, in which he articulated relationships – which he termed co-existence, conflict, and symbiosis – between tourism and environmental conservation. He was generally optimistic in his outlook, arguing that tourism could develop a symbiotic relationship with nature conservation provided that appropriate planning and sound management practices were rigorously applied and that proper consideration be given to ecological processes which must guide resource use. In 1978, Erik Cohen published an article in *Annals of Tourism Research* that presented the first comprehensive analysis of the environmental impacts caused by tourism, while in 1982, Alister Mathieson and Geoff Wall published their book, *Tourism: Economic, Physical and Social Impacts*, which explored the tourism-environment relationship. Later in the decade came the first publications on ecotourism and sustainable tourism, which began to draw attention to the relationships between tourism and nature in a more critical and nuanced way, and which laid the foundation for a considerable amount of scholarship on ecologically sustainable tourism. As the editors of this volume point out, however, little attention was being given to ethics and morality at that stage.

The tourism industry and associated structures has also recognised the implications of tourism on nature and the environment. The UN World Tourism Organisation (WTO) has a dedicated focus on the sustainable development of tourism and heads up the 10 Year Framework of Programmes for Sustainable Tourism Development, launched in London in 2014. WTO is also actively engaged in programs on climate change and biodiversity conservation. The International Civil Aviation Organisation and the International Air Transport Association has set in place targets to reduce carbon emissions derived from aircraft through greater fuel efficiencies, with the latter also keenly interested in alternative fuels and carbon offsetting programs. And, within the accommodation sector, global hotel chains and individual owner-operators are implementing strategies to reduce carbon emissions from their properties.

But, as the contributors to this book clearly show, there is a raft of more fundamental questions that must be explored if we are to properly address the outcomes of tourism-nature relationships. How can we create tourisms that respect nature? How does tourism embrace moralities in regards to environmentalism, animal ethics, and Indigenous understandings of nature? How do we encourage and facilitate dialogues between scholars, practitioners, and tourists themselves to actively engage in moral questions about the nature of tourism and its relationships with nature? The editors have curated a diverse set of chapters that explore the contested moral terrains upon which tourism and its intersections with nature are embedded. Surely, the tourism industry's response to the impending spasm of extinctions of species and ecosystems has to be more than simply the creation of "last-chance tourism"? What are the moral obligations of the tourism industry, and of the tourists the industry serves, towards nature?

We are facing a crisis in global biodiversity brought about by a plethora of factors but accelerated by global climate change. Biologist Eugene Stoermer began using the term "Anthropocene" in the 1980s to refer to the impact that human-induced change was having on the earth, and, in 2000, he and Nobel Prize-winning Dutch atmospheric chemist Paul Crutzer published a paper defining the Anthropocene as the current geological epoch in which human interventions in the environment are having profound and globally significant impacts. These impacts include global climate change, the diversion or other significant interruptions to most of the world's major rivers, the transformation of large swaths of the world's land surface, and the removal of about a third of the ocean's productivity per year.

The Anthropocene marks a new relationship between nature and humanity, to be sure. It signals the pervasive impact that humanity is having on global ecosystems, and it also marks a new understanding of the relationships between the human and non-human, including non-human animals, as well as plants, water, soils, and the atmosphere. Humans are now agents of environmental change at a global scale and at a geological time scale. And tourism structures and practices are well and truly implicated in these environmental changes.

Those of us in the social sciences must be willing to find common ground with our colleagues in the natural sciences and only through new intellectual and theoretical hybridities will resolutions be found to our most serious crises affecting nature. We must break down the silos that have tended to separate the natural sciences from the social sciences and aim for a much more genuine inter-disciplinarity. We must be willing to be open to learning from the natural scientists as much as we need to share our understandings and insights with them. Such creative collaborations must also be nurtured and strengthened with Indigenous Peoples and based on genuine respect for Indigenous knowledges. Indigenous cultures, lands, and livelihoods have so often been compromised, to say the least, by the tourism industry's use of nature.

The theoretical and empirical insights that this book presents make a valuable contribution to the small but growing literature on the intersections of morality, tourism, and nature, and the book itself provides a way forward to the growing "moral turn" in tourism scholarship. The editors ask us to consider the "philosophical and theoretical perspectives [that] can usefully orient us in living and enacting better human-nature relationships through tourism" and the "opportunities and challenges" that tourism offers us in "relating more ethically to the more-than-human world." The contributing authors take up such questions and explore what a socially and environmentally "just" tourism might look like. In doing so, the book challenges readers to interrogate their own touristic behaviours. There are, of course, uncomfortable implications and difficult challenges of such scrutiny, but such challenges must be faced if we are to work towards a more ethical and morally justifiable relationship between tourism and nature.

Kevin Markwell
Southern Cross University, Australia

Acknowledgements

This book came together because of the good energies, efforts, and support of several individuals. We are especially grateful to the contributing authors for sharing their thoughtful scholarship and working with us to bring this project to life. Special thanks to Kevin Markwell and Soile Veijola for their respective foreword and afterword contributions, which situate the book wonderfully in past, present, and future trajectories of knowing and relating to natures through tourism. Thanks to David Fennell and Faye Leerink for their assistance and encouragement early on with the book proposal. We are forever thankful to the people and places and critters that have inspired our learning, values, responsibilities, and lives. Gratitude.

Introduction

Tourism, nature, morality

Bryan S. R. Grimwood, Kellee Caton, and Lisa Cooke

On the surface, this book is about human-nature relationships in tourism. It is broadly concerned, in other words, with investigating tourism as a context that facilitates interactions between what is typically differentiated in Western thought as the human social world and the non-human (or more-than-human) natural world. Clearly, such interactions are not exclusive to tourism; humans and natures collide in all sorts of interesting and consequential ways through science, agriculture, resource extraction, education, politics, religion, sport, technology, among other domains. Tourism is, indeed, just one of countless contexts through which human-nature relationships are given shape, made meaningful, and explored.

But it is a rather significant one at that.

Tourism has become a world-making force that interacts with the more-than-human world in multifaceted and dynamic ways. Some of these interactions are decisively material and ecological and can affect life-sustaining systems upon which we all depend, the most extreme example being the role tourism has played over time in the anthropogenic global changes now depicted as part of the Anthropocene (Gren & Huijbens, 2016). To access the beach in the sun, for instance, many of us have contributed to the carbon emissions associated with air and automobile travel and helping to power climatic changes that intensify hurricanes or accelerate glacier melt. Several among us hope to offset or mitigate any pending apocalyptic futures by spending our tourism dollars and energies in ways that support nature conservation, whether that is at the scale of a landscape or individual species (Fennell, 2015). Here, our practices of ethical tourism consumption are intended to support the integrity of ecological systems and their diverse components, so essential to our being-in-the-world.

Other tourism-nature relationships are associated with contested values, meanings, and discourses that shape how people perceive or experience a particular nature place or more-than-human encounter. The gendered ideologies that script how tourists are intended to view polar bears through the lens of their digital cameras are a case in point. As Yudina and Grimwood (2016) expose, the promotion and representational capture of polar bears as wildlife "spectacles" reproduces not only anthropocentric and instrumental valuing of non-humans, but also the masculine systems of rationality upon which such valuing is contingent. Such contested values and meanings do not simply circulate at levels of abstraction.

They also become embedded in the making of tourism places, an observation that underpins Cooke's (2017) reading of Skwelkwek'welt/Sun Peaks. While this alpine place in interior British Columbia is at once part of the unceded ancestral lands of Secwěpemc First Nations and the corporate site of Canada's first ski resort municipality, it is the latter that yields the economic, political, and discursive power to naturalize it for touristic purposes and disappear Indigenous relations and claims (Cooke, 2017). When we escape to find pleasure in nature, we do so with social-cultural baggage and effects in stow.

So, if these sort of issues, interactions, and consequences lie at the surface of this book, what then are our core intentions? What deeper aims captivate the more than a dozen scholars from different geographies and career stages who devoted their intellectual riches towards the preparation of the chapters in this collection? Well, as the book title implies, nature and morality have something to do with it. And, clearly, so does tourism. Accordingly – and in the spirit of keeping things straightforward – let's affirm that we have gathered this collection of papers with the purpose of examining relationships between nature and morality in tourism. In so doing, the book invites exploration into several questions that we feel are largely untapped in tourism studies: how do we understand and value tourism-nature relationships, or determine the consequences of these relationships to be "good," "bad," "right," "wrong," "fair," "just," or "unjust"? What philosophical and theoretical perspectives can usefully orient us in living and enacting better human-nature relationships through tourism? What opportunities and challenges does tourism present for relating more ethically to the more-than-human world? What tourism natures ought we be working to craft and create? This is complex territory that can be accessed from several different points of departure.

For now, let's begin with the premise that "nature" is both contested and promiscuous in an ontological sense (i.e., the reality of nature is hardly as obvious or static as we often make it out to be). This is an affront to contemporary popular discourses that conceptualize nature in one of three typical ways (Castree, 2001; Demeritt, 2002). *External* nature refers to what is perceived to be the original and inherent material aspects of the world – the self-evident and so-called natural environment, inclusive of non-living and living (albeit non-human) components. In this view, nature is raw and pristine, autonomous from society, and associated with conventional distinctions like rural/urban, country/city, and wilderness/civilization. *Intrinsic* nature refers to an unchanging essential quality or attribute that is more or less discernable in some thing or some being. This conception of nature finds expression in references to the inherent characteristics of an entity, such as human nature, or an event, such as a hurricane or earthquake, which tend to be cited as natural disasters dictated by physical processes. The third common meaning, *universal* nature, implies that nature is a holistic and integrated force guiding worldly processes. In this meaning, nature refers to the "natural" order of things and is represented in notions like "the laws of nature" or James Lovelock's widely debated Gaia hypothesis (Castree, 2001).

While the widespread use and familiarity of these contemporary meanings is not likely to fade, scholars from across the social sciences and humanities concur that nature is not a timeless or universal idea, nor is it a politically innocent one. Indeed, scholars have traced how meanings of nature change over time, evolve from or are performed within particular contexts, and enact a great deal of worldly effects (e.g., Castree, 2005; Franklin, 2002; Glacken, 1967). For instance, the idea of nature as strictly biophysical space, which in its most pristine state stands for "wilderness," is widely regarded as a product of Western Enlightenment tendencies to categorically distinguish human society from other environmental phenomena. Martin Heidegger provides some of the philosophical basis on this front. In his essay *The Question Concerning Technology*, Heidegger (1993) frames how the natural world is often experienced, encountered, or revealed to us as a "standing-reserve," a tap of resources that humans draw on and from to serve our practical needs (Cooper, 2005). Nature, in this sense, is valued as a means for satisfying human ends. This instrumental relationship is not inherent to our being-in-the-world, according to Heidegger, but rather a function of epistemological establishments dating back to Rene Descartes that privilege knowledge in the "spectator sense." As Cooper (2005) elaborates, this is a particular type of human understanding obtained through detached, objective observation and analysis and which leads to theoretical abstraction. It inevitably construes nature as "an objective, material realm standing over against us spectating subjects" (Cooper, p. 341). Our task, if we are to follow Ingold's (2011) reading of Heidegger, is to rethink and renew how we inhabit the world such that "every thing or being is a certain gathering together of the threads of life" (xviii). Inhabiting in this way requires that we eschew those knowledge frameworks with entrenched divisions between object and subject and which underpin, and enable, human exploitation of the natural world.

Several trajectories of scholarship attend to this critical task of re-configuring conceptualizations of nature and our place within it. Much work has followed in the wake of Cronon's (1995a) provocative essay, which effectively established the study of nature as a phenomenon that is inescapably social, cultural, and historical in its production. Broadly conceived as the social construction of nature, or as a *social nature* orientation, this body of literature attracts and incorporates various feminist, poststructural, postcolonial, Marxist, phenomenological, and relational perspectives (Castree & Braun, 2001; Cronon, 1995b; Fitzsimmons, 1989). Common amongst these theoretically informed accounts is a skeptical insistence that things are not as clear as they seem, "that what we once accepted as self-evidently pre-ordained and inevitable is in fact contingent and might conceivably be remade in some other way, if only we would try" (Demeritt, 2002, p. 776). Proponents thus identify with social nature for opening up analytical and political possibilities for a radical environmentalism (see, e.g., Latour, 2004; Smith, 2011). They find social nature useful because it implies that humans have the capacity to improve current environmental circumstances by understanding, producing, and practicing different versions of nature and in ways that are more responsible and socially just (Braun, 2002; Cronon, 1995a).

While such deliberations of nature are well developed within disciplinary domains of Geography, Sociology, Anthropology, and Environmental Philosophy, their relevance to tourism studies has really only materialized in the last decade or so, a function perhaps of how in tourism we adopt and adapt knowledge from our disciplinary parents, or perhaps how tourism research has often leaned commitments towards satisfying industry interests. Several years ago, Franklin and Crang (2001) observed that in much tourism research, nature was "uncritically confused or conflated with 'environment'" (p. 16) and that "both the object of 'nature' and the desire for 'nature'" were taken up quite unproblematically and uncritically (p. 16). These tendencies were mirrors of those broader conventions and popular thought that situate nature as something static, universal, and purely external to social-cultural practices, ideologies, and values.

More recent accounts in tourism have helped destabilize hegemonic views of nature and fashion nature-society in non-dualistic, or relational, terms. There's been some uptake on, and extension from, Franklin and Crang's (2001) call to get more critical and get with the hybrids. In particular, tourism scholars have engaged metaphors – dwelling, production, hybridity, performance, multiplicity, networks, to name a few – that help articulate tourism natures in terms of emergent activity, social-material entanglements, and creative possibility (see, e.g., Cloke and Perkins, 2005; Grimwood & Doubleday, 2013; Mullins, 2009; Reis & Shelton, 2011; van der Duim, Ren, & Jóhannesson, 2013; Waitt & Cook, 2007). To borrow from Castree (2014), these projects have evinced the notion that " 'nature' is not a given, waiting to be analysed, experienced or interacted with" (p. 34) through tourism. Rather – and using Waitt and Cook's (2007) phrasing here – they have drawn attention in tourism studies to "how the human and the non-human worlds are always open to transformation, or in other words, an ontology of always being in a mode of becoming" (pp. 536–537).

If tourism natures are "in-the-making", and these configurations are contingent upon human agency (at least in part), then it follows that we'd be wise to invest energy into thinking deeply about the natures we want, and how natures are represented, both to us and by us. Of interest to us in this book are the moral issues, perspectives, and opportunities that arise when we mull about, or aim collectively to bring into being, transformations necessary for just and sustainable tourism natures. In other words, we are less concerned in this book with asking what nature in tourism *is* and more in what nature *is considered to be*, or *ought to be*, as well as what the effects of these renderings are (Castree, 2014).

When it comes to nature and morality, tourism researchers and professionals often look to environmental ethics, an applied ethics that emerged in the 1970s with the tides of awareness about modernity's environmental atrocities (Jamieson, 2008), including, no doubt, the impacts of tourism (Cohen, 1978). Environmental ethics is concerned with understanding humanity's relationship to nature and defining human obligations and responsibilities to the environment. Holden's (2003, 2014) attention to environmental ethics in tourism captures several fundamental issues and perspectives, including the range anthropocentric and non-anthropocentric orientations (the former implying an instrumental value of nature and the latter an intrinsic value in nature). As Holden observes, environmental ethicists are often concerned with constructing a non-anthropocentric ethics based on a suitable theory of intrinsic value, theories such as ethical sentientism, autopoietic or life-based ethics, ecocentrism, or cosmic purpose ethics (see, e.g., Fox, 1990; Fennell, 2006). Debates between pluralistic and monistic environmental ethics have also been prominent – for example, in the works of Oelschlaeger (1994) and Callicott (1994), respectively – while more recent attention has focused on operationalizing a relational environmental ethics based on relational values (see, e.g., Chan et al., 2016; Figueroa & Waitt, 2008; Grimwood, 2015). Central to most points within these debates is the recognized need to articulate an enlarged conception of humanity's moral vision, something that Leopold (1966) was alert to in his eminent articulation of the "land ethic" and that we see finding form in tourism literature on animal ethics (Fennell, 2012) and ecofeminism (Yudina & Grimwood, 2016).

If, however, we are attentive to the sort of social, cultural, and critical theorizations of nature noted above, environmental ethics as conventionally put to use in tourism studies (as per Holden, 2003) is likely to be unhelpful. As Castree (2003) explains, most competing perspectives in environmental ethics (e.g., instrumental vs. intrinsic values, anthropocentrism vs. ecocentrism) start from that divisive ontology that distinguishes nature from society or a deterministic ontology that collapses society into nature or subscribes to natural realism. Furthermore, as Whatmore (2002) argues, the ruling class of moral extensionist and ecocentric perspectives in environmental ethics are underscored by cognitive, linguistic, and rationalist competences as the basis for fashioning ethical subjectivity. They therefore tend to overlook and exclude corporeal embeddedness, intersubjectivity, and practical engagement in the world as dimensions in our moral complexion (Whatmore, 2002).

Recognizing that morality, much like nature, is embedded in histories, lived experiences in places, and landscapes of power (Mostafanezhad & Hannam, 2014), we are reminded of Smith's (2009) perspective that:

> ethics are not just socially imposed norms, they are also ways of composing who we are. . . [Ethics] provides a basis for questioning the way things are, informs how we might relate to others, and is a mode of being in which we exercise our individual responsibilities in concert, though not necessarily agreement, with others.
>
> (pp. 270–271)

Perhaps the ethics we need in relation to tourism natures is not so much about following prescribed standards as it is about consciously reflecting on our moral beliefs and learning to perceive ourselves as responsible agents always seeking possibilities for individual, social, and ecological betterment (Smith, 2009). We might begin to think of this as a process of *becoming otherwise*; of taking the "moral turn" in tourism (Caton, 2012) to consistently imagine and craft our relations among self, collective, and world *anew*. Our hope with this book is to invite epistemological and experiential movements in this direction by compiling papers that critically review, appraise, and advance dialogue on the moral dimensions of natures enacted in and through tourism. Contributing authors have been tasked with addressing moral values, frameworks, or practices best suited to mobilizing tourism natures towards futures characterized by sustainability, justice, resilience, and health and well-being. We hope this book prompts students of tourism to grapple similarly with the very foundations of how we make sense of nature in tourism – and how we might make sense of it differently, and to what moral ends.

Storylines of the book

While organizing the substance of this book, we chose not to subdivide chapters into thematic sections. We appreciate how this common practice of partitioning creates useful structure, scope, and direction for navigating the multitude of perspectives and approaches that edited volumes such as this invariably contain. And there is no doubt that our own ideas and scholarship are products of the sort of tidy, rational logics that value the sort of ordering of knowledge and world that comes with thematic classifications. In the case of this book, however, separating chapters into more or less discrete sections never felt right. Every time we tried, the sections we identified seemed rather arbitrary (even when situated within related literatures), or they privileged a limited and uncomfortable reading of the complexities, controversies, or connections across chapters. They undermined a more holistic, collective narrative on moral natures in tourism that we found being animated by the various contributors to this book.

This broader narrative that emerged is one that seems to pivot along three main storylines. The first is reflected by the notion of *moral terrains*, which has been used elsewhere as a metaphor to convey the multitude of possible values or ethical orientations entangled within, or overlaying, a particular nature space (Grimwood, 2011; Proctor, 1995). Importantly, as Figueroa and Waitt (2008) suggest, prevailing and especially powerful webs of value are layered over tourism places. Not only do these establish behavioural norms and authorize who and what belongs, they also become "inscribed onto bodies through affective responses to touring," which in turn, "enable people to come to know and build or negate relationships with other human body-selves as well as non-human entities" (Figueroa & Waitt, 2008, p. 328). Several chapters in this book, especially those presented early on, work both to expose the moral terrains of tourism natures and to show how situated practices and performances resist or affirm prevailing value systems.

In Chapter 1, Freya Higgins-Desbiolles and Skye Akbar consider the moral terrains of engagement in Indigenous tourism in Australia. Recognizing that Indigenous Australian tourism development practices often do not live up to their purported benefits for Indigenous individuals and communities, Freya and Skye investigate how advancements in Indigenous rights support greater self-determination among Indigenous Peoples over the use, assertion, and protection of culture and country through tourism. Their analysis shifts across scales – from global declarations and guidelines to the case of Lirrwi Yolngu Tourism Aboriginal Corporation's Tourism Masterplan – to pinpoint policy contexts that set the stage for a thriving Indigenous Australian tourism sector based on Indigenous control and cultural knowledge and responsibilities. Freya and Skye argue that enacting these foundations will reduce exploitation and invite into the moral terrains of Indigenous tourism improved collaborations between Indigenous and non-Indigenous stakeholders, more responsible tourist engagement, and deeper relations to country.

Chapter 2 and Chapter 3 marshal critical awareness of the settler colonial and racialized discourses that pervade the moral terrains of tourism natures. Lisa Cooke takes us north to the Yukon Territory, Canada, where wilderness and frontier imaginaries collide with – or come into view through – the windshields of RVs and a Walmart parking lot. The apparent irony of these encounters exists only at the surface according to Lisa, and her ethnographic reading exposes how entirely logical these assemblages (i.e., of road, vehicles, multinational corporation, eagles, trees, tourists, northerners) are as derivatives of the cultural matrix that is contemporary settler colonial Canada. Along the way, we learn from Lisa how "forces converge and meanings congeal" upon this terrain to (re)produce frontier mentalities which transform everything – from toilet paper to birds perched treetop – into consumable commodities. This grounded analysis is nicely augmented by Bruce Erickson's interrogation of the relationship between race and nature, and how these often get conflated in structuring touristic desires to experience difference. Bruce establishes whiteness as an organizing discourse that disciplines how we view and experience modern nature tourism, including the "exotic" places and peoples encountered. He goes on to show these racial logics at work: first, in tourist attempts to overcome modernity's shortfalls by engaging with anachronistic others; and, second, in tourist investments in risk and persevering through danger. The critique effectively situates the pleasures associated with nature tourism within the moral terrains that produce and privilege whiteness, prompting the need for deliberate thinking and action that undermines, or steps outside of, such landscapes of power.

That our movements through, and attachments to, particular tourism natures give shape to our everyday behaviours, habits, and ethical orientations comes into focus in Chapter 4. Here, Jillian Rickly draws on her research into the hypermobilities of lifestyle rock climbers to explore relationships between lifestyle choice and the "good life", citizenship, personal and social responsibilities, and sense of belonging and freedom. What Jillian lays out is an ethics of lifestyle climbing that is deeply contextual and varied, but which consists of an individual's pursuit of pleasure and their commitment to contributing positively to certain social collectives and rejection of others. Jillian's analysis reveals rather clearly how the moral terrains of tourism are not simply visited; rather, they can move with and through us and become etched into our varied mobile ways of being.

In Chapter 5, the moral terrains storyline bleeds into the book's second storyline, *human-animal relationships*. Here, the book begins making connections to recent developments in the study of animals in tourism (Carr, 2009; Kline, 2018; Markwell, 2015), including work on animal ethics and welfare (Fennell, 2012, 2013). Arianne Reis and Eric Shelton consider the power of discourse to position non-human animals in ways that legitimate human agendas. Through an extended example of the positioning of the domestic dog in Aotearoa/New Zealand, Arianne and Eric explore the dog's objectification by humans, who discursively construct it as predator, pet, or companion. They contextualize tourism as one driver of this process, as national economic agendas are looped into species management projects via ecotourism; in the case of their example, dogs become predators when they threaten penguins, an endangered species that draws tourists to the area. Tourists thus have a responsibility to be critically aware of the interests of the various animals they encounter, as visitors are bound up in Aotearoa/New Zealand's eco-politics, whether they desire to be or not.

Both Chapter 6 and Chapter 7 explore the use of animals as food in tourism contexts. Giovanna Bertella (Chapter 6) considers the power of food tourism entrepreneurs to enact institutional change in regard to the use of animal products. Drawing on vegetarian ecofeminism as a theoretical framework, Giovanna interviews entrepreneurs active on Italy's food tourism scene who embrace vegetarian ecofeminism's premise of the intrinsic value of animals. This is a difficult business climate for such views, as notions of food authenticity in the Italian context run counter to vegetarianism, but Giovanna finds that entrepreneurs who align their business practices with their personal belief systems can still be successful and ultimately perhaps spur change in their institutional field. Carol Kline and Cody Rusher's complementary study (Chapter 7) explores perceptions of eating meat in a tourism context among members of the Millennial demographic, a generation with comparatively strong interest in ethical consumerism and relatively high rates of vegetarianism. Through interviews with university students, who have been asked to consider a series of vignettes requiring ethical reasoning, Carol and Cody consider the question of why attitudes and beliefs relating to animal ethics sometimes translate into action and sometimes don't, particularly during travel. They conclude that travel can alter one's ordinary habits due to necessity, convenience, social pressure, or curiosity. Thus, ethical reasoning about the eating of animals is complex and contextual.

In Chapter 8, Neil Carr offers a broad discussion of the interaction between humans and animals in a tourism context. He explores various moral positions humans can take toward animals, from instrumentalism through a strong animal rights approach. Locating his own position as one which views animals as sentient beings with value that goes beyond their usefulness to humans, Neil argues for an obligation on the part of tourism operators to ensure animal welfare. However, in pursuing this approach, he argues, we must critically examine our underlying motivations. In conceptualizing animal welfare, we must be sure that we are not merely pursuing our own human-centric needs (whether they be economic or guilt-ridding), but that we are instead always striving to view our obligations from an animal-centric perspective.

The third storyline, *values-engaged scholarship*, weaves throughout the book but picks up steam in the later chapters. To borrow from Tribe and Liburd (2016), this storyline is about harnessing "the importance of values and meaningful interpretation. It engages human qualities and dispositions, authentic presence and meaningful participation in the context of world making" (p. 50). Complementing the other tourism research in this vein, which remains rather limited, contributions to this book seek to open up collaborative and experimental spaces where tourism natures as conventionally conceived are undone and reframed.

In Chapter 9, Adrian Franklin and Thomas Colas examine the moral (and settler colonial) investments made in ideas of nature's "pureness" as they trouble ideals of "native" species and ecologies in Australia's wildlife tourism industry. They highlight the ways that native species become folded into, and deployed in the service of, political and cultural agendas as they are held up as symbols of national identity. "Feral" species – that is, introduced flora and fauna – are discursively placed as binary opposites. Adrian and Thomas argue that feral species are both an inevitable and at times critical component of any ecological landscape, but suggest that the ideals and discursive production of native natures work to erase feral invasions, implications, and impacts. As Adrian and Thomas conclude, rather than working to maintain a false and problematic dichotomy between native (pure) and feral (contaminated) natures, nature tourism in Australia has an opportunity to embrace the hybrid complexities of these dynamic ecosystems for what they are and can do.

In Chapter 10, Philip Mullins examines the limitations and potential damaging consequences of the "Leave No Trace" (LNT) movement and campaign. Philip highlights the ways that the LNT ethic generates problematic boundaries between society and nature, where humans are seen as transient, isolated visitors within a pristine, "peopleless" nature. He also calls into question the LNT's assumption that leaving no human trace is an achievable outcome, or one that is in the best interests of either nature or society. As an alternative, Philip suggests the need for a more participatory ethic to being with (rather than in) the natures we desire and experience. This model is one that acknowledges the possibility of positive engagements with nature that allow humans to shape landscapes and in turn be shaped by them through recreation, education, and tourism. Not only does this approach make space for humans in the worlds that we inhabit, it acknowledges non-Western ways of knowing and being as equally resonate sets of relationships with the physical world.

Chapter 11 by Mick Smith expands on the role of geological tourism, specifically in regards to fossil encounters, and investigates its ability to decenter humanity as the primary agent in the creation of time and space. Geotourism is often concerned with preserving the past while also contributing educationally and economically to the present. However, Mick suggests that encounters with fossils have the potential to do much much more. Specifically, he articulates how a fossil's residual agency can help situate humans in a larger context, one where we are forced to understand the linkages between past and present, and then between the present and our undetermined future. According to Mick, fossils have the power to challenge human exceptionalism and reorient our thinking in a way that provokes us to act responsibly and in resistance to the Anthropocene.

Gregory Lowan-Trudeau's Chapter 12 investigates how Indigenous and Western methodologies can come together in respectful ways to produce hybrid perspectives and practices for the study of tourism and environment. Using Homi

Bhabha's "Third Space" as a conceptual starting point, Gregory works through the productive, uneven, and uneasy ways that Indigenous and Western methodologies come together. By way of a beautiful range of examples of different methodological approaches, readers are challenged to consider research methodologies as political interventions that shape not just how we come to understand the world but how we generate the terms and impacts of those understandings. Gregory's chapter reminds us that we are responsible to the ways that power relations are reconstituted or challenged through the research questions we ask about nature, land, and country and the approaches we deploy to answer these.

The concluding chapter by Kellee Caton takes readers on a stroll through the metaphorical forest of learning and moral reflection prompted by the collection of chapters in this book. With Kellee, we revisit recurrent themes and make connections to knowledges within and beyond tourism studies that expand our sense of the paths we have tramped and the many possible trails that lie before us. In taking up new moral natures in tourism, we are reminded that our moral gaze can and must intrinsically appreciate the diverse mysteries and teachings of otherness. This is an ethics of welcoming and relating, of renewing our individual selves and dreaming with others about what could be.

References

Braun, B. (2002). *The intemperate rainforest: Nature, culture, and power on Canada's west coast*. Minneapolis, MN: University of Minnesota Press.

Callicott, J. B. (1994). *Earth's insights: A multicultural survey of ecological ethics from the Mediterranean Basin to the Australian outback*. Los Angeles, CA: University of California Press.

Carr, N. (2009). Animals in the tourism and leisure experience. *Current Issues in Tourism*, *12*(5–6), 409–411.

Castree, N. (2001). Socializing nature: Theory, practice, and politics. In N. Castree & B. Braun (Eds.), *Social nature: Theory, practice, and politics* (pp. 1–21). Malden, MA: Blackwell Publishing Ltd.

Castree, N. (2003). A post-environmental ethics? *Ethics, Place & Environment*, *6*(1), 3–12.

Castree, N. (2005). *Nature*. New York: Routledge.

Castree, N. (2014). *Making sense of nature*. New York: Routledge.

Castree, N., & Braun, B. (Eds.). (2001). *Social nature: Theory, practice, and politics*. Malden, MA: Blackwell Publishing Ltd.

Caton, K. (2012). Taking the moral turn in tourism studies. *Annals of Tourism Research*, *39*(4), 1906–1928.

Chan, K. M. A., Balvanera, P., Benessaiah, K., Chapman, M., Díaz, S., Gómez-Baggethun, E. . . . Turner, N. (2016). Why protect nature? Rethinking values and the environment. *PNAS*, *113*(6), 1462–1465.

Cloke, P., & Perkins, H. C. (2005). Cetacean performance and tourism in Kaikoura, New Zealand. *Environment and Planning D: Society and Space*, *23*, 903–924.

Cohen, E. (1978). The impact of tourism on the physical environment. *Annals of Tourism Research*, *5*(2), 215–237.

Cooke, L. (2017). Carving "turns" and unsettling the ground under our feet (and skis): A reading of Sun Peaks Resort as a settler colonial moral terrain. *Tourist Studies*, *17*(1), 36–53.

Cooper, D. E. (2005). Heidegger on nature. *Environmental Values, 14*(3), 339–351.
Cronon, W. (1995a). The trouble with wilderness; or, getting back to the wrong nature. In W. Cronon (Ed.), *Uncommon ground: Rethinking the place in nature* (pp. 69–90). New York: W.W. Norton & Company.
Cronon, W. (Ed.). (1995b). *Uncommon ground: Rethinking the place in nature*. New York: W.W. Norton & Company.
Demeritt, D. (2002). What is the 'social construction of nature'? A typology and sympathetic critique. *Progress in Human Geography, 26*(6), 767–790.
Fennell, D. A. (2006). *Tourism ethics*. Toronto, ON: Channel View Publications.
Fennell, D. A. (2012). *Tourism and animal ethics*. New York: Routledge.
Fennell, D. A. (2013). Tourism and animal welfare. *Tourism Recreation Research, 38*(3), 325–340.
Fennell, D. A. (2015). *Ecotourism* (4th ed.). New York: Routledge.
Figueroa, R. M., & Waitt, G. (2008). Cracks in the mirror: (Un)covering the moral terrains of environmental justice at Uluru-Kata Tjuta National Park. *Ethics, Place and Environment, 11*(3), 327–349.
Fitzsimmons, M. (1989). The matter of nature. *Antipode, 21*(2), 106–120.
Fox, W. (1990). The most widely recognized approaches in ecophilosophy. In *Toward a transpersonal ecology: Developing new foundations for environmentalism* (pp. 149–196). Boston, MA: Shambhala Publications, Inc.
Franklin, A. (2002). *Nature and social theory*. Thousand Oaks, CA: SAGE.
Franklin, A., & Crang, M. A. (2001). The trouble with tourism and travel theory? *Tourist Studies, 1*, 5–22.
Glacken, C. (1967). *Traces on a Rhodian shore: Nature and culture in western thought from ancient times to the end of the eighteenth century*. Berkeley, CA: University of California Press.
Gren, M., & Huijbens, E. H. (2016). *Tourism and the anthropocene*. New York: Routledge.
Grimwood, B. S. R. (2011). "Thinking outside the gunnels": Considering natures and the moral terrains of recreational canoe travel. *Leisure/Loisir, 35*(1), 49–69.
Grimwood, B. S. R. (2015). Advancing tourism's moral morphology: Relational metaphors for just and sustainable Arctic tourism. *Tourist Studies, 15*(1), 3–26.
Grimwood, B. S. R., & Doubleday, N. C. (2013). Illuminating traces: Enactments of responsibility in practices of Arctic river tourists and inhabitants. *Journal of Ecotourism, 12*(2), 53–74.
Heidegger, M. (1993). The question of technology. In D. F. Krell (Ed.), *Basic writings from being and time (1927) and the task of thinking (1964)* (pp. 307–341). Toronto, ON: Harper Perennial.
Holden, A. (2003). In need of new environmental ethics for tourism. *Annals of Tourism Research, 30*(1), 94–108.
Holden, A. (2014). The evolution of environmental ethics: Reflections on tourism consumption. In C. Weeden & K. Boluk (Eds.), *Managing ethical consumption in tourism* (pp. 70–80). New York: Routledge.
Ingold, T. (2011). *The perception of the environment: Essays in livelihood, dwelling and skill* (re-issued). New York: Routledge.
Jamieson, D. (2008). *Ethics and the environment: An introduction*. New York: Cambridge University Press.
Kline, C. (Ed.). (2018). *Tourism experiences and animal consumption: Contested values, morality and ethics*. New York: Routledge.
Latour, B. (2004). *Politics of nature: How to bring the sciences into democracy*. Cambridge, MA: Harvard University Press.

Leopold, A. (1966). *A sand county almanac: With essays on conservation from Round River*. New York: Ballantine Books.
Markwell, K. (Ed.). (2015). *Animals and tourism: Understanding diverse relationships*. Toronto: Channel View Publications.
Mostafanezhad, M., & Hannam, K. (Eds.). (2014). *Moral encounters in tourism*. Burlington, VT: Ashgate.
Mullins, P. M. (2009). Living stories of the landscape: Perception of place through canoeing in Canada's North. *Tourism Geographies*, *11*(2), 233–255.
Oelschlaeger, M. (1994). *Caring for creation: An ecumenical approach to the environmental crisis*. New Haven, CT: Yale University Press.
Proctor, J. D. (1995). Whose nature? The contested moral terrain of ancient forests. In W. Cronon (Ed.), *Uncommon ground: Rethinking the human place in nature* (pp. 269–297). New York: W. W. Norton & Company, Inc.
Reis, A., & Shelton, E. (2011). The nature of tourism studies. *Tourism Analysis*, *16*(3), 375–384.
Smith, M. (2009). Development and its discontents: Ego-tripping without ethics or idea(l)s? In J. Tribe (Ed.), *Philosophical issues in tourism* (pp. 261–277). Toronto, ON: Channel View Publications.
Smith, M. (2011). *Against ecological sovereignty: Ethics, biopolitics, and saving the natural world*. Minneapolis, MN: University of Minnesota Press.
Tribe, J., & Liburd, J. J. (2016). The tourism knowledge system. *Annals of Tourism Research*, *57*, 44–61.
van der Duim, R., Ren, C., & Jóhannesson, G. T. (2013). Ordering, materiality, and multiplicity: Enacting actor-network theory in tourism. *Tourist Studies*, *13*(1), 3–20.
Waitt, G., & Cook, L. (2007). Leaving nothing but ripples on the water: Performing ecotourism natures. *Social and Cultural Geography*, *8*(4), 535–550.
Whatmore, S. (2002). *Hybrid geographies: Natures, cultures, spaces*. Thousand Oaks, CA: SAGE.
Yudina, O., & Grimwood, B. S. R. (2016). Situating the wildlife spectacle: Ecofeminism, representation, and polar bear tourism. *Journal of Sustainable Tourism*, *24*(5), 715–734.

1 We will present ourselves in our ways

Indigenous Australian tourism

Freya Higgins-Desbiolles and Skye Akbar

Introduction

Indigenous tourism has become a trendy niche ever since the "new tourists" (Poon, 1993) developed a taste for the exotic offerings of ethnic cultural tourism experiences. Simultaneously, neoliberal pressures have seen Indigenous Australian tourism operators encouraged to enter the tourism market to cater to this lucrative tourist demand and thereby free governments of their social and developmental obligations for these dispossessed and disadvantaged communities and peoples. Using a critical lens, we interrogate the ethics of current Indigenous Australian tourism development and marketing practices and question the purported economic benefits offered to Indigenous Australians who attempt to engage in this opportunity. With years of instability experienced by those working at the operational levels, it is worth asking: whose interests are being served?

Following an Indigenous rights approach, we investigate how developments in Indigenous rights over cultural knowledge may support Indigenous Australian individuals and communities to participate in cultural industries, such as tourism, in more self-determined ways. Beginning with the United Nations Declaration on the Rights of Indigenous Peoples (United Nations, 2008), we also investigate the opportunities to assert, present, and protect cultural knowledge in tourism through Indigenous local laws and protocols, declarations, guidelines, and regulatory means, including the recent developments of the Larrakia Declaration and the formation of the World Indigenous Tourism Alliance. Additionally, we present a case study of Lirrwi Tourism and the Lirrwi Yolngu Tourism Aboriginal Corporation's Tourism Masterplan (2014). Our findings suggest it is only when Indigenous Australian cultural knowledge holders are empowered to offer cultural tourism experiences in a way that meets their cultural responsibilities can a thriving cultural tourism sector result. Such a foundation allows for collaborations between Indigenous and non-Indigenous stakeholders on a footing of ethical and responsible engagement, thus improving benefits and reducing instances of exploitation. More importantly, though, Indigenous tourism conducted on Indigenous terms exposes a different moral space where people, culture, and country all sustain each other, and this invites tourists and tourism to experience a different moral universe. Mostefanezhad and Hannam (2014) have discussed multiple moralities in tourism encounters; this chapter narrates a moral terrain of engagement through Indigenous Australian tourism and thereby exposes a possibility for peoples to enter into dialogues across difference.

Background

Understanding Indigenous Australia[1] engagement with tourism is complex for a number of reasons, not least of which is the great diversity which characterises Indigenous nations. Indigenous Australia is comprised of two main groupings (Aboriginal and Torres Strait Islander Peoples) who are quite different. These main groups are subdivided into hundreds of individual nations with distinct languages, protocols and cultures. The Sydney Olympic Games of 2000 were a major catalyst to the development of the contemporary Indigenous Australian tourism industry. Concerted efforts were made at all levels of government to develop, train, and support an Indigenous Australian tourism sector that would cater to the tourists the Olympics was anticipated to attract in subsequent years. The results of these efforts were the development of a variety of Indigenous Australian tourism ventures across the country that offered outstanding cultural, ecological, and adventure tourism experiences. These ventures gained a high profile, and tourism academics have studied these enterprises to illuminate a great variety of models, approaches, and motivations (e.g., Bennett, 2005; Dyer, Aberdeen, & Schuler, 2003; Higgins-Desbiolles, Trevorrow, & Sparrow, 2014; Nielsen, 2010). Such cases made it clear that some businesses were addressing the tensions between Indigenous Australian cultural values and the demands of Western tourism business practices. Debates ensued about the role of culture in tourism businesses (Miller, 2000) and whether stereotypes of traditions used in marketing were damaging Indigenous Australian tourism opportunities and negatively affecting Indigenous Australians. Particular concerns were raised about how Indigenous Australians were depicted as "primitive" and failed to show the great diversity of these nations (Ahoy, 2000; see also Waitt, 1999).

It is also important to note that the Royal Commission into Aboriginal Deaths in Custody (1991) was a contributing catalyst to efforts to use tourism to build Indigenous Australian self-esteem and to offer economic opportunities for well-being and thriving. Indigenous Australian tourism occurs against a backdrop of profound Indigenous Australian disadvantage resulting from legacies and ongoing manifestations of invasion, colonisation, and dispossession. Indigenous Australians are over-represented in negative indicators of health and well-being, and Australian governments at all levels have long promised, and also long failed, to develop policies and actions that meaningfully address the "gap" in Indigenous Australian disadvantage. In terms of Indigenous Australian tourism, government support was developed according to precepts of economic rationalism, which some suggest may actually limit tourism's role in addressing Indigenous disadvantage in Australia (Whitford, Bell, & Watkins, 2001).

Indigenous Australian tourism businesses are typically small-to-medium-sized enterprises; however, their operational models vary. Some businesses are solely owned and operated by an Indigenous Australian person or their family; some are owned by community groups and managed by an Indigenous Australian; some are owned by Indigenous Australian people and managed by non-Indigenous People; and some businesses are owned by Indigenous Australian people and operated by separate non-Indigenous organisations. Also, some Indigenous Australians work for non-Indigenous organisations to provide Indigenous Australian content for broader tourism products and services. This diversity in business structure reflects the diversity of Indigenous Australia and the contexts within the industry.

Recent statistics suggest Indigenous Australian tourism is not a healthy economic sector. During 2010, there were 306,000 domestic overnight Indigenous Australian tourism trips, which generated 2.5 million visitor nights and $490 million in expenditure. Relative to 2009 numbers, these represent declines of 17%, 19%, and 23% in each category, respectively (TRA, 2011). Moreover, since 2006, decreases in domestic Indigenous Australian tourism has resulted in 19% annual reductions in overnight trips, 23% annual reduction in visitor nights, and total expenditure reductions averaging 21% per year (TRA, 2011). Domestic overnight Indigenous Australian tourism has registered a more rapid decline than the total domestic market for the same period (TRA, 2011). In 2010, Tourism Research Australia (TRA, 2010) found that Indigenous Australian tourism was lagging behind other Australian experiences, such as beach holidays and city breaks, in both appeal and participation for domestic consumers.

With such economic indicators suggesting decline, the progression and assertion of Indigenous rights into Indigenous tourism contexts presents an opportunity for re-invigorating and re-positioning Indigenous Australian tourism. Indeed, this chapter argues that an Indigenous rights orientation has offered an opportunity to re-draw frameworks so that Indigenous Australian cultural tourism is strengthened at its core and may thus be more attractive and sustainable. A brief literature review follows to underpin this analysis.

Literature review

In recent years, a number of scholars have argued that tourism can contribute positive social impacts, foster social change, and even regenerate the social conscience of a people (e.g., McGehee & Santos, 2005; Higgins-Desbiolles, 2003, 2006; Hollinshead & Jamal, 2001). There is growing literature demonstrating that Indigenous Australian tourism is a space where such outcomes are possible and important. In her analysis of Indigenous Australian tourism as a tool for reconciliation, Higgins-Desbiolles (2003) presented a case study of Camp Coorong to demonstrate how educational tourism can change social relations. Galliford (2010) explored further the possibilities of reconciliation through tourism and found "it is in the moments of dialogue and engagement on cultural tours between tourists and Aboriginal people that transversals are happening" (p. 241). Galliford's work showed that Indigenous Australians subvert the stereotypes and cultural impositions of tourism, and tourists may use these opportunities to transform their understandings of their national identities. In their research on tourists visits to Uluru-Kata Tjuta National Park, Waitt, Figueroa, and McGee (2007) explored "whether the embodied knowledge derived from travelling, witnessing, climbing, walking, touching and being touched by Uluru opens moral gateways between indigenous and non-Indigenous People" (p. 248). Their findings showed that some tourists have their "moral gateways" closed off to learning from or about Indigenous knowledges at the Park (due largely to a mind-set of enlightenment rationalism and a nationalism evident in tourist behaviours and attitudes). But importantly for this chapter, Waitt et al. found that "only those tourists who admit to the experience of shame, through making felt the invisible qualities of indigenous culture, suggest the possibilities of living together-in-difference. In these cases, moral gateways operate to assist the process of reconciliation" (p. 261). These arguments are critical to the analysis of the impacts of Indigenous Australian tourism on transforming social relations in a context of settler-colonial histories.

It is recognised, however, that ensuring Indigenous participation in the tourism industry is not, in itself, a recipe for positive social change. Bunten (2010), for instance, has observed arguments suggesting that for Indigenous Peoples to undertake business opportunities (so often premised on Western ideologies), they must compromise cultural values and risk changes to their position within their own society. Notzke (1999) noted similar concerns in Arctic contexts where a lack of control over culture and knowledge can exist for Indigenous tourism hosts. Notzke grappled with how such information can be controlled once it has been shared? These analyses indicate that ambiguity, uncertainty, and contested values exist when tourism opportunities are pursued by groups such as Indigenous Australians. The moral terrains of tourism (Grimwood, 2015), in other words, are clearly exposed.

The drivers of Indigenous Australian economic participation (Altman & Finlayson, 2003), combined with the multiple agendas set for all Indigenous tourism (Higgins-Desbiolles, 2003), mean that there are many stakeholders in Indigenous Australian tourism. Interested parties include Indigenous Australian cultural knowledge holders, business owners, local communities, Indigenous Australian tourism bodies, as well as local, state, and federal government authorities. This multitude of stakeholders, each with their own motivations and priorities, means that individual operators have extensive webs of relationships to manage and engage. Adding to the complexity of such operations is the fact that interactions among stakeholders occur on uneven terrains of power. As Higgins-Desbiolles, Trevorrow, and Sparrow (2014) demonstrated in their analysis of the Coorong Wilderness Lodge, these terrains of stakeholder interactions often result in considerable difficulties for Indigenous Australian tourism operators and a general ambivalence among Indigenous Australians about engaging with the tourism industry.

However, a shift towards ideals of rights and self-determination may empower some Indigenous Australians to identify opportunities and rethink participation in the industry, including through community participation, individual or family-run tourism ventures, and in joint-venture partnerships with non-Indigenous partners. Ryan and Huyton (2000) found that a broad range of factors appear to be important prerequisites for successful and sustainable Indigenous Australian participation in tourism. These include Indigenous Australian control, market realism for Indigenous Australian participants, appropriate corporate structures and scale of enterprise, accommodation of cultural and social factors, and educating the industry and consumers (Ryan & Huyton, 2000). With these factors in place, can tourism provide Indigenous Australians with opportunities to: remain on or connected to country; to maintain, revive, or renew cultural practices; create intergenerational opportunities and well-being; and support self-determining futures (Bennett, 2005; Higgins-Desbiolles, 2003)? The critical issue to address is what is required to attain such ideal circumstances where tourism can offer such profound positive social impacts when indeed the politics and moral terrains where Indigenous ad non-Indigenous Australians meet is not improving. To highlight a pathway forward, we have offered a brief critical analysis of the state of Indigenous Australian tourism and the factors that have led to this state above. We now follow this with the critical challenge to analyse the core of this phenomenon by asking: what is Indigenous Australian tourism, and who is it for? What have been the challenges of the past, and how do we overcome them to support a successful industry? Key to this critique will be the consideration of the progress of Indigenous rights, how these impact Indigenous People, and how they extend to this industry.

Definitions as a point of power

One task to undertake in order to understand the power and ethical implications of tourism is to address the diverse definitions of Indigenous tourism in order to illuminate the recognition these definitions afford and the agency they allow. Hinch and Butler's (1996) definition is the most widely used; they defined Indigenous tourism broadly as "tourism activities in which Indigenous People are directly involved either through control and/or by having their culture serve as the essence of the attraction" (p. 10). Hinch and Butler provided a matrix to classify categories of Indigenous tourism by assessing the level of Indigenous control and the cultural content of the product offering. This matrix demonstrates that Indigenous tourism may involve varying levels of Indigenous ownership, management, and cultural content and that it can exist without Indigenous involvement at all. This model therefore demonstrates the capacity for some forms of "Indigenous tourism" to dispossess Indigenous Peoples through tourism, taking their cultures and exploiting them for non-Indigenous benefit.

Peters and Higgins-Desbiolles (2012) outlined a scheme for Indigenous tourism which worked to better illuminate the challenging question of who benefits. These authors suggested Indigenous tourism has been viewed in various ways, including as:

- A cultural product associated with Indigenous People;
- A cultural product desired by tourists who want Indigenous experiences;
- A niche sector that enhances mainstream tourism products;

- A marketing tool to "brand" a destination; and
- A tourism product owned and/or controlled by Indigenous Peoples.

Bunten (2010) described a phenomenon almost thrust upon Indigenous tourism operators, stating that tourists come expecting some or all of the following:

- The greeting;
- The guide;
- Demonstrated use of the heritage language;
- Traditional architecture;
- A performance;
- A gift shop or souvenirs for sale and often demonstrations of traditional native crafts; and
- Sometimes a Westernized native feast, such as the Hawaiian lū'au or Maori hangi meal.

Bunten noted that such expectations allow little opportunity "for a deeply personalised encounter" (p. 294–295) and that new models are emerging to satisfy new generations of Indigenous entrepreneurs who want more Indigenous approaches to business respected.

Difficulties of definitions certainly extend to the Australian context. For instance, the Australian Commonwealth government provides a list of activities which Indigenous tourists may undertake. Importantly, this may include activities that do not have any involvement of Indigenous Australian people. Tourists seeking an Indigenous Australian tourism experience may:

- See Aboriginal art, craft, or cultural displays;
- Visit an Aboriginal gallery;
- Visit an Aboriginal cultural centre;
- Attend an Aboriginal dance or theatre performance;
- Purchase Aboriginal art/craft or souvenirs;
- See an Aboriginal site or community;
- Go on a tour with an Aboriginal guide;
- Attend an Aboriginal festival;
- Stay in Aboriginal accommodation; and
- Some other interaction with Aboriginal people (TRA, 2014).

Activities such as "seeing an Aboriginal art piece" or "some other interaction with Aboriginal people" being described as Indigenous Australian tourism in this government definition results in the collation of misleading industry statistics and inhibits meaningful analysis of secondary data. This not only undermines the business decision-making of Indigenous Australian tourism operators; it also acts in a way to allow non-Indigenous People to exploit tourists' interests in Indigenous Australian tourism experiences and undermine the ability of Indigenous Australians to prosper from and control the interface with tourism. Such acts of marginalisation and exploitation underscore the need for Indigenous-led approaches.

Indigenous-led approaches

This situation of Indigenous invisibility, exploitation, and disempowerment is now being challenged and Indigenous-led approaches are beginning to overturn long-standing practices, including in domains like tourism. Key to this transformation is the development of the United Nations Declaration on the Rights of Indigenous Peoples (UNDRIP) after decades of work and leadership by the Working Group on Indigenous Populations. Since its adoption by the United Nations in 2007, UNDRIP has become a catalyst to advancing the human rights of Indigenous Peoples around the world and continues to impact the interface between Indigenous Peoples and the tourism industry.

Article 11.1 of UNDRIP states that:

> Indigenous Peoples have the right to practise and revitalize their cultural traditions and customs. This includes the right to maintain, protect and develop the past, present and future manifestations of their cultures, such as archaeological and historical sites, artefacts, designs, ceremonies, technologies and visual and performing arts and literature.
>
> (UN, 2008, p. 6)

In addition to this, Article 31.1 states that:

> Indigenous Peoples have the right to maintain, control, protect and develop their cultural heritage, traditional knowledge and traditional cultural expressions, as well as the manifestations of their sciences, technologies and cultures, including human and genetic resources, seeds, medicines, knowledge of the properties of fauna and flora, oral traditions, literatures, designs, sports and traditional games and visual and performing arts. They also have the right to maintain, control, protect and develop their intellectual property over such cultural heritage, traditional knowledge, and traditional cultural expressions.
>
> (UN, 2008, p. 11)

These two articles support the rights of Indigenous Peoples to their own knowledge and sites of significance. When considering the tourism context, this can be interpreted to mean that:

- Indigenous Peoples should have control over how their culture is portrayed and how physical sites of significance are interacted with, including in all for-profit contexts;
- Indigenous Peoples should have the right to decline to include any tangible and intangible aspects of culture in their own and other's tourism products;

- And Indigenous Peoples should have the right to call for intervention when any of these rights are violated.

Article 3 states that "Indigenous Peoples have the right to self-determination. By virtue of that right they freely determine their political status and freely pursue their economic, social and cultural development" (UN, 2008, p. 4). In addition to this, Article 23 states that:

> Indigenous Peoples have the right to determine and develop priorities and strategies for exercising their right to development. In particular, Indigenous Peoples have the right to be actively involved in developing and determining health, housing and other economic and social programmes affecting them and, as far as possible, to administer such programmes through their own institutions.
> (UN, 2008, p. 9)

These two articles support the rights of Indigenous Peoples to a self-determined economic and social contribution to their societies. They highlight the empowerment of Indigenous control and argue that Indigenous Peoples have the capacity to undertake economic and social contribution on their own terms. When considering the tourism context, this can be interpreted to mean that:

- Indigenous Peoples should have control over commercialisation of their culture, including ensuring that social and financial benefit for contributing communities is secured.

This declaration has been key to the transformation of tourism as Indigenous Peoples use it to assert their rights. However, the implementation of UNDRIP principles in the tourism industry requires non-Indigenous tourism stakeholders to engage with Indigenous perspectives and respect these rights. Both Johnston (2000) and Higgins-Desbiolles (2007) have analysed UNDRIP's potential impacts on the operations of the tourism industry with a view to examining how this intervention might allow Indigenous Peoples to pursue more self-determining futures through tourism.

More recently, the Larrakia Declaration of 2012 emerged from a conference in Darwin, Australia, and applied UNDRIP principles to the tourism industry (PAITC, 2012). Behind this initiative were 191 delegates from 16 countries representing Indigenous communities, government agencies, the tourism industry, and supporting bodies. It was clearly established to overturn the exploitative nature of past Indigenous tourism and to use the impetus of UNDRIP to turn things around through Indigenous-led intervention. The Declaration's opening principles declared the positive grounds for this intervention:

- Recognising that for Indigenous tourism to be successful and sustainable, Indigenous tourism needs to be based on traditional knowledge, cultures, and practices, and it must contribute to the well-being of Indigenous communities and the environment.

- Recognising that Indigenous tourism provides a strong vehicle for cultural understanding, social interaction, and peace.
- Recognising that universal Indigenous values underpin intergenerational stewardship of cultural resources and understanding, social interaction, and peace (PAITC, 2012, no page number).

The Larrakia Declaration declares that "respect for customary law and lore, land and water, traditional knowledge, traditional cultural expressions, cultural heritage . . . will underpin all tourism decisions" (PAITC, 2012, no page number). This statement places Indigenous engagement with tourism on the sound cultural footing of Indigenous law and protocols and thus is seeking to overturn previous exploitative conditions. Additionally, the Larrakia Declaration demands that "Indigenous culture and the land and waters on which it is based, will be protected and promoted through well-managed tourism practices and appropriate interpretation" (PAITC, 2012, no page number). This statement recognises the custodial responsibilities of Indigenous Peoples for culture, country, and all of its beings and turns tourism to respect for these as the ground rules for future engagement.

The Larrakia Declaration also acknowledges the challenges that tourism presents for some Indigenous individuals and communities and seeks to overturn the previously imposed and exploitative ways of tourism. It asserts:

> Indigenous Peoples will determine the extent and nature and organisational arrangements for their participation in tourism and that governments and multilateral agencies will support the empowerment of Indigenous People.
>
> (PAITC, 2012, no page number)

This principle asserts the right to self-determination including the right to block tourism, control access, limit it (geographically or seasonally), and control the organisation and organisational processes through which tourism is pursued.

The next principles address the powerful stakeholders of governments and the tourism industry. The Larrakia Declaration states that "governments have a duty to consult and accommodate Indigenous Peoples before undertaking decisions on public policy and programs designed to foster the development of Indigenous tourism" (PAITC, 2012, no page number). It then turns to the tourism industry, with its power to overturn exploitation and enact more respectful engagement:

> The tourism industry will respect Indigenous intellectual property rights, cultures and traditional practices, the need for sustainable and equitable business partnerships and the proper care of the environment and communities that support them.
>
> (PAITC, 2012, no page number)

This demonstrates the essential nature of Indigenous knowledges in Indigenous tourism and shows an effort to invite the tourism industry into a more respectful engagement. The final principle offers a reciprocal return for such a transformation to a partnership approach:

> That equitable partnerships between the tourism industry and Indigenous People will include the sharing of cultural awareness and skills development which support the well-being of communities and enable enhancement of individual livelihoods.
>
> (PAITC, 2012, no page number).

The Larrakia Declaration now provides an Indigenous-led framework to ensure Indigenous inclusion and benefit from Indigenous tourism. The final segment of this declaration recognises the launch of the World Indigenous Tourism Alliance chartered to "facilitate, advocate and network with each affiliated Indigenous tourism body and with industry, governments and multilateral agencies" (PAITC, 2012, no page number). While declarations such as UNDRIP and the Larrakia Declaration are components of soft law and, therefore, are not currently enforceable, they do possess moral authority and can be turned to for assertions of Indigenous Peoples' rights. Additionally, the principles found in these declarations have been paralleled in the real-world activities and leadership of some Indigenous Australian tourism enterprises.

Case study

The significance of Indigenous-led approaches is arguably best illustrated through a case study that demonstrates how some of these principles inform real world tourism ventures. One of the most recent developments in Indigenous Australian tourism is the development of Lirrwi Tourism in the Northern Territory. We offer this as a case study of Indigenous tourism, built on Indigenous values, and demonstrating Indigenous self-determination through tourism. Lirrwi Tourism

> was established in 2010 to develop, support and promote Yolngu tourism in Arnhem Land [a region of Australia's Northern Territory in which the Yolngu Peoples live] . . . Lirrwi's main objective is to create a new economy for Yolngu people in Arnhem Land through tourism. It does this by bringing people together to share Yolngu culture, connecting Aboriginal and non-Aboriginal people.
>
> (About Lirrwi Tourism, n.d.)

The Yolngu Peoples have shown extraordinary leadership in Australia and are known for initiatives such as the 1963 Bark Petition (considered a turning point in recognition of Indigenous rights in Australia) and more recently the Garma Festival, which is "recognised as the nation's premier forum for discussion of Indigenous affairs" (ABC News, 2015). Now the Yolngu are showing leadership in community-initiated and community-controlled tourism with this Lirrwi Tourism venture and its supporting Yolngu Tourism Masterplan.

The Lirrwi Yolngu Tourism Aboriginal Corporation's Tourism Masterplan features Yolngu values at its centre. It states:

> Lirrwi is a powerful Yolngu word which means "charcoal". Lirrwi defines the layers of charcoal, which go deep into the earth and deep into the past. It is the place where Yolngu people always return to, in life and beyond life. A single piece of charcoal cannot burn brightly on its own. It takes many pieces. So too with the people and the culture. In the Yolngu world everything is connected, the country, the people, the plants and the animals, even the sky and the world above.
>
> (Lirrwi Yolngu Tourism Aboriginal Corporation, 2014, p. 10)

In fact, Yolngu moral ecologies are demonstrated through this plan, as people and people's responsibilities for country are placed front and centre in the planning.

The guiding principles put forward for Lirrwi Tourism are organised under headings: the country, tourism business, people, culture and respect. These are worth providing in full:

The country

- Arnhem Land has been the home of Yolngu people since the beginning of time; they have always been there, and this must be acknowledged and respected.
- Yolngu have a responsibility to care for country.
- Tourism should never control what happens on country.

Tourism business

- Yolngu must have the right to say who can and who cannot visit the country.
- Yolngu wish to share knowledge with people from other places.
- The marketing and promotion of Arnhem Land must embrace all these values.
- The tourism calendar must synchronise with the Yolngu calendar.
- Yolngu should partner with Balanda [the Yolngu name for white person or European, Yolngu Matha Dictionary, n.d.] but not depend on Balanda.
- Tourism must be flexible and fit in with Yolngu culture, not control it.
- Infrastructure must be not overdone and kept in harmony with the country.
- Finances are only an instrumental means for achieving success and will never be considered an end in themselves: maximising profit will never be the number one business objective.

People

- Recognition that Yolngu are "farmers and custodians", not nomads.
- Visitors must recognise that Arnhem Land is a place to be slow and steady.

- Yolngu wish to be inclusive for all Australians.
- Tourism should be a positive influence on Yolngu to provide value.
- Tourism should be a source of pride for Yolngu.
- Yolngu will be open to mentoring.
- Tourism must recognise "Mulwat" – value.

Culture

- Yolngu will have the right to decide how much and what information to share.
- Surface information is enough for sharing.
- Ceremony takes precedence over tourism.
- External stakeholders must learn Yolngu culture and system.

Respect

- The land, and all it contains, needs to be recognised for its significance to Yolngu people.
- Sacred sites must be respected by everyone.
- History must be revised through tourism to recognise the Yolngu people as the first people of Arnhem Land.
- The environment will be respected at all times.
- Respect is a key requirement for all visitors.

(Lirrwi Yolngu Tourism Aboriginal Corporation, 2014, p. 6)

These guiding principles suggest how Indigenous-led approaches might engage and alter the moral terrains of tourism. The basis of everything is the land and it is treated first in these principles. The opening three sentences assert the Yolngu responsibility to care for country, the ongoing duties and connections the people hold, and how tourism and tourists must respect these as the foundation for any tourism engagement. These principles also assert relationships and protocols that bring visitors and the tourism industry into a Yolngu moral framework so that respectful and positive relationships can be built and sustained. Yolngu call upon all visitors to enter into the Yolngu cultural space open to difference and receptive to the spirit and experience is being shared (as opposed to demanding things as paying tourists for instance). When principles assert "external stakeholders must learn Yolngu culture and system", the tourism industry is, in effect, invited to change its praxis from one of exploitation to one of *learning with*. Specifically, Yolngu values must be the basis of all tourism practices with Yolngu on Yolngu country. These include right to access sites and experiences, respect for Yolngu priorities and timing, and Yolngu valuations of tourism purpose and significance. These principles also indicate that Lirrwi tourism expects visitors and other tourism stakeholders to listen deeply to Yolngu worldviews when engaging with them in tourism; understand Yolngu history ("always been here", "first people of Arnhem Land"); recognise Yolngu views and perceptions of identity and culture (not wandering nomads but "farmers and custodians"); and value Yolngu moral ecologies ("Tourism must recognise 'Mulwat' – value"). With these principles, Lirrwi Tourism and Yolngu Peoples create a Yolngu-led basis from which to host tourists and engage with the wider tourism industry on their terms. Imposed terms for tourism development that tend towards assimilation, homogenisation, and exploitation are resisted.

This case study provides a meaningful demonstration of what an Indigenous-led approach to tourism embodies, as the values of the particular Indigenous community hosting tourists shape the nature of the experiences offered and the encounters they lead to. This values-based approach to tourism also calls on the tourism industry to be willing to transform its approaches so that engagement and reciprocal benefit can occur while "living in difference" (Waitt et al., 2007, p. 261). Mostefanezhad and Hannam (2014) have discussed multiple moralities in tourism encounters, and here we see an Indigenous Australian moral terrain where people, culture, and country are interconnected and tourists and the tourism industry are required to adapt to this different moral paradigm. This might be a risky endeavour, as current tourism dynamics pressure for subservience to tourists' desires. However, as highlighted here, the Indigenous rights approach to tourism inspires Indigenous operators to assert their cultural obligations in their engagement with tourism, and it places the engagement with tourists and tourism on a different moral footing from other forms of tourism. As the Lirrwi case study demonstrates, the Yolngu use their strategic plan and their tourism enterprise to communicate Yolngu values, assert their vision for morally encountering culture and country, and invite others to learn from this opportunity. This opens up a space for dialogue across difference and to engage in different ways of being, valuing, and relating to a moral universe. Thus, tourism becomes more than a mere commercial exchange and can bring diverse peoples into conversation on good living.

Conclusion

This chapter has sought to illuminate a moral terrain of engagement through tourism and expose changing patterns of tourism planning and practice within the context of one Indigenous-led case study. A niche of Indigenous Australian tourism products and experiences have been developed for a variety of benign and exploitative reasons – some entirely devoid of Indigenous Australian engagement – and this has led to some of the difficulties recounted above in this chapter. Undeterred, a number of Indigenous Australian entrepreneurs, families, and communities have seized the opportunity of tourism to develop world class tourism offerings to try to build positive futures for themselves. However, with the recent developments of UNDRIP and the Larrakia Declaration, Indigenous Australia-led and self-determining initiatives are of increasing importance. The Lirrwi tourism project of the Yolngu Peoples provides a living example of a tourism offering that invites tourists to learn from Yolngu people about their moral worlds and appreciate what thousands of years of living on country has taught them as a people. Experiencing Indigenous Australian tourism under conditions of Indigenous rights and

Indigenous authority offers tourists a chance for a moral encounter with the potential to transform their worldviews and stands in stark contrast to tourism where Indigenous rights and authority are marginalised. Ultimately, our analysis suggests that the moral terrains of tourism are full of transformative potentials when all of its agents engage in a spirit of respect and openness to the different values and views of others. When Indigenous rights serve as the backbone of planning and implementing tourism, self-determination is more likely to be fostered within contexts of uneven power relationships. Under such circumstances, the historically marginalised worldviews, cultures, and value systems of Indigenous Peoples can be brought respectfully into dialogue with others, and the tourism encounter can provide possibilities for mutual growth and understanding.

Note

1 The terminology for the Indigenous Peoples of Australia has been subject to change and is also contested. This chapter uses the term "Indigenous Australians" to refer to the collective description of all of Australia's Indigenous Peoples; equally suitable are terms such as Aboriginal and Torres Strait Islander people, and frequently, the term "Aboriginal people" is used in terms of Australian Indigenous tourism products and experiences. When citing the work of others, we utilise the terminology that was originally used by the author/s of that work. Also following respectful practice, when referring to a specific nation, we utilise the specific name of that nation and people rather than a generic term such as Aboriginal or Indigenous. When the term "Indigenous People/s" is used, it refers to the wider community of Indigenous Peoples and their concerns.

References

ABC News. (2015, July 31). Garma festival 2015: What is it, where is it, who goes, and what should we expect this year? Retrieved December 5, 2016, from www.abc.net.au/news/2015-07-31/garma-festival-2015-premier-forum-for-indigenous-affairs/6659372.

About Lirrwi Tourism. (n.d.). Retrieved December 3, 2016, from www.lirrwitourism. com.au/about-us/.

Ahoy, L. (2000). Promotion vs product. In *Tourism – the Indigenous opportunity: National Indigenous tourism forum proceedings report*, Sydney, June 3–4, pp. 59–65.

Altman, J., & Finlayson, J. (2003). Aborigines, tourism and sustainable development. *Journal of Tourism Studies*, *14*(1), 78–91.

Bennett, J. (2005). *Indigenous entrepreneurship, social capital and tourism enterprise development: Lessons from Cape York*. Unpublished PhD thesis, LaTrobe University.

Bunten, A. C. (2010). More like ourselves: Indigenous capitalism through tourism. *The American Indian Quarterly*, *34*(3), 285–311.

Dyer, P., Aberdeen, L., & Schuler, S. (2003). Tourism impacts on an Australian Indigenous community: A Djabugay case study. *Tourism Management*, *24*, 83–95.

Galliford, M. (2010). Touring 'country', sharing 'home': Aboriginal tourism, Australian tourists and the possibilities for cultural transversality. *Tourist Studies*, *10*(3), 227–244.

Grimwood, B. S. R. (2015). Advancing tourism's moral morphology: Relational metaphors for just and sustainable Arctic tourism. *Tourist Studies*, *15*(1), 3–26.

Higgins-Desbiolles, F. (2003). Reconciliation tourism: Tourism healing divided societies! *Tourism Recreation Research, 28*(3), 35–44.
Higgins-Desbiolles, F. (2006). More than an industry: Tourism as a social force. *Tourism Management, 27*(6), 1192–1208.
Higgins-Desbiolles, F. (2007). Taming tourism: Indigenous rights as a check to unbridled tourism. In P. Burns & M. Novelli (Eds.), *Tourism and politics: Global frameworks and local realities* (pp. 83–107). Amsterdam: Elsevier.
Higgins-Desbiolles, F., Trevorrow, G., & Sparrow, S. (2014). The Coorong Wilderness Lodge: A case study of planning failures in Indigenous tourism. *Tourism Management, 44*, 46–57.
Hinch, T., & Butler, R. (1996). Indigenous tourism: A common ground for discussion. In R. Butler & T. Hinch (Eds.), *Tourism and Indigenous Peoples* (pp. 3–19). London: International Thomson Business Press.
Hollinshead, K., & Jamal, T. (2001). Delving into discourse: Excavating the inbuilt power-logic (s) of tourism. *Tourism Analysis, 6*(1), 61–73.
Johnston, A. (2000). Indigenous Peoples and ecotourism: Bringing Indigenous knowledge and rights into the sustainability equation. *Tourism Recreation Research, 25*(2), 89–96.
Lirrwi Yolngu Tourism Aboriginal Corporation. (2014). *Yolngu tourism masterplan Arnhem land 2014–2032*. Retrieved December 3, 2016, from www.lirrwitourism.com. au/tourism-masterplan/.
McGehee, N. G., & Santos, C. A. (2005). Social change, discourse and volunteer tourism. *Annals of Tourism Research, 32*(3), 760–779.
Miller, G. (2000). Is it culture or is it business? *Tourism – the Indigenous opportunity: National Indigenous tourism forum proceedings report*, Sydney, June 3–4, pp. 92–94.
Mostefanezhad, M., & Hannam, K. (2014). *Moral encounters in tourism*. Farnham: Ashgate.
Nielsen, N. R. (2010). *Strengths, support and self-determination: Indigenous tourism planning and the Biamie Dreaming Cooperative*. Unpublished PhD thesis, Southern Cross University.
Notzke, C. (1999). Indigenous tourism development in the Arctic. *Annals of Tourism Research, 26*(1), 55–76.
PAITC. (2012). *The Larrakia declaration on the development of Indigenous tourism*. Darwin. Retrieved January 20, 2017, from www.winta.org/the-larrakia-declaration/.
Peters, A., & Higgins-Desbiolles, F. (2012). De-marginalising tourism research: Indigenous Australians as tourists. *Journal of Hospitality and Tourism Management, 19*(6), 76–84.
Poon, A. (1993). A global transformation. In A. Poon, *Tourism, technology and competitive strategies* (pp. 85–92). Wallingford: CAB International.
Royal Commission into Aboriginal Deaths in Custody. (1991). *Report of the Royal Commission into aboriginal deaths in custody*. Retrieved 3 June 2016, from www.naa.gov.au/collection/fact-sheets/fs112.aspx.
Ryan, C., & Huyton, J. (2000). Who is interested in Aboriginal tourism in the Northern Territory, Australia? A cluster analysis. *Journal of Sustainable Tourism, 8*(1), 53–88.
TRA. (2010). *Indigenous tourism in Australia: Profiling the domestic market, Tourism Research Australia*. Retreieved January 1, 2017, from http://sustain.pata.org/wp-content/uploads/2014/12/TRA-Indigenous-Tourism-in-Australia1.pdf.
TRA. (2011). *Snapshots 2011: Indigenous tourism visitors in Australia* [Fact sheet]. Retrieved from www.tra.gov.au/Research/View-all-publications/All-Publications/snapshots-2011-indigenous-tourism-visitors-in-australia.

TRA. (2014). *National visitor survey*. Retrieved December 25, 2016, from www.tra.gov.au/documents/nvs/Travel_by_Australians_March_2014_results_of_the_National_Visitor_Survey.html.

United Nations. (2008). *United Nations declaration on the rights of Indigenous Peoples*. Retrieved October 24, 2017, from www.un.org/esa/socdev/unpfii/documents/DRIPS_en.pdf

Waitt, G. (1999). Naturalizing the "primitive": A critique of marketing Australia's Indigenous Peoples as "hunter-gatherers". *Tourism Geographies*, *1*(2), 142–163.

Waitt, G., Figueroa, R., & McGee, L. (2007). Fissures in the rock: Rethinking pride and shame in the moral terrains of Uluru. *Transactions of the Institute of British Geographers*, *32*(2), 248–263.

Whitford, M., Bell, B., & Watkins, M. (2001). Indigenous tourism policy in Australia: 25 years of rhetoric and economic rationalism. *Current Issues in Tourism*, *4*(2–4), 151–181.

Yolngu Matha Dictionary. (n.d.). *Balanda*. Retrieved August 7, 2017, from http://yolngudictionary.cdu.edu.au/word_details.php?id=105.

2 Windshields, wilderness, and Walmart

Cultural logics of the frontier in Yukon, Canada

Lisa Cooke

The view from the parking lot

I pulled into the Walmart parking lot in Whitehorse, Yukon, Canada and parked behind a large motor home one warm July Evening. Walmart offers free camping in the parking lots of many of their stores. Every night of every summer, dozens of RV travellers passing through Whitehorse take them up on this offer (Figure 2.1). Early evening was a good time to visit the parking lot, as campers were often out and about and, having finished dinner, were willing to chat with me.[1] My interest in RV traveller experiences of their trips North to Yukon and Alaska were not limited to this parking lot. I was interested more broadly in how ideas of North figure in Canadian national-cultural imaginaries, and how the imaginative capacities of these imaginaries drew people North – through the layers of meaning, history, politics, and power that come together in both the material and discursive production of actualized places called North. I have spent countless hours travelling the highways of Yukon, tagging along on tours, and chatting with people along the way.

For the first several months of my fieldwork, I passed by Walmart almost every day on my way to tourist sites. I noticed the rows of campers in the parking lot every evening, but was not paying very close attention to what was going on there. One evening, as I drove past Walmart on my way home, a coyote darted across the road in front of me and wove his/her way through neatly organized motor homes lining the parking lot. I let my gaze follow Coyote and the wild nature he/she signalled. Everywhere I went on this ethnographic journey, people talked about being drawn North by a desire to experience nature and wilderness. "We've come for the wilderness and the nature" were words I heard repeated time and again. Following Coyote's lead, I started to hang out more at Walmart. The image of him/her darting through RVs in the Walmart parking lot was shot through with a dialect complexity that demanded my attention.

On this particular evening, looking up from getting myself organized in the car, I was struck by the scene on the back of the RV parked in front of me (Figure 2.2). The custom design had two loons swimming with chicks at their sides in a peaceful looking lake. Artistically written above the picture were the words "The Call of the Wild." This moment gave me pause as a complicated assemblage of politics, meanings, histories, and power congealed around me.

Figure 2.1 Walmart parking lot in Whitehorse, Yukon, Canada, June 2006.
Photo by the author.

Figure 2.2 An RV in the Walmart parking lot in Whitehorse, Yukon, July 2007.
Photo by the author.

As a cultural anthropologist, I scan landscapes for these very moments – moments where complexes of cultural logics and processes come together, assemble, and make themselves visible. Sitting in my car on this night, I asked myself: can "The Call of the Wild" be answered at Walmart? And if it can, does that mean that wilderness, like toilet paper, dish soap, cat litter, and frying pans, is available at Walmart? And if the answer is yes, and wilderness, as a particular version of wild space, is available here, alongside the other items of the everyday, what does the view from here suggest about the relationship between Walmart, the roads that get us here, the windshields that frame the view, and the moral dimensions built into the production and consumption of this space called "North" as wilderness in settler colonial Canada?

Settler colonial ironies and logic

Ironies run across the surface of the parking lot. I encountered them every day as I sat and talked with people about why they wanted to travel North, what they imagined and anticipated, and what they were experiencing. Time and again I listened as people talk about "the wilderness," the "adventure," and "great outdoors." This is not only what they imagined; it is what they were experiencing. In the words of one traveller, Eric,[2] who I met at Walmart on a warm July evening: "It's the trip of a lifetime. I mean the wilderness. Look at this place!"

Looking around as he spoke these words, what I saw was the glowing blue and white sign perched over the entrance of Walmart. He saw something else. He perceived, felt, and appreciated wilderness in this place. My first instinct was to dwell in the apparent ironies of it all. The thing is, my sense of irony says more about my own ethnocentric settler colonial notions of nature and wilderness than anything else. I have an idea of what wilderness is – the same wilderness that Cronon (1996) so eloquently refers to as historically produced out of a complex of modernity and colonialism that turns nature spaces into wilderness places. Coyote – the one that darted past me – unsettled this ethnocentric, settler-privileged sense of irony. The thing with dialectical images is that they shatter irony, and in doing so reveal the fragments of history, power, and complexity that come together to produce surface views of things (Cooke, 2016; Pensky, 2004). Coyote short circuits this surface-level irony, making visible my own biased positionality situated precisely at the intersection of modernity and colonialism, which creates the contemporary settler colonial terrain of coloniality[3] upon which Walmart, ideas of North in Canadian national-cultural imaginaries, Coyote, RV travellers, and myself come together in a parking lot in Whitehorse.

By examining the forces and flows that come together at this site, what comes into view is a scene that is entirely culturally logical. Why not camp at Walmart? It's free, convenient, feels safe, and makes sense. What is for sale in tourist brochures filled with images of lone motor homes traveling along scenic roadways is the view of Yukon spaces from the road. This parking lot is an articulation of the same system of automobility paved out of visions of northward expansion of and on the frontier. Out of this entire matrix of cultural systems – capitalism, colonialism, modernity – the road and the parking lot emerge as central in both the production and experience of Yukon spaces as tourist destination *and* wilderness-scape. Just like Coyote, the road and the parking lot are part of this place, not apart from it. Their presence makes sense, albeit somewhat uncomfortable sense to those of us who want to hold on to ideas of wildness as sacred, special, and pristine. It is in this discomfort that the moral dimensions of this conversation come into view. This chapter is a contemplation of how I got here, discursively and physically, to this place called North, in the parking lot of a multinational corporation that has changed the metabolism of globalized late capitalism (Fishman, 2006). Experiencing a nature produced as quintessential to a settler Canadian national-cultural imaginary on Kwanlin Dün and Ta'an Kwäch'än Council territory my attention is drawn to the values inscribed onto, into, and through this complex landscape of settler colonial/touristic/capitalist desire.

North to the frontier

This journey North requires a little conceptual context. The terrain of encounter upon which Coyote, Walmart, and I came together emerged out of my own fascination with ideas of North in Canada. What do I mean by North? In Canadian national-cultural imaginaries, ideas of North come together in complex ways to produce a discursive and material scape upon which settler colonial narratives are inscribed (Grace, 2001; Shields, 1991). Think about it (especially if you are Canadian): what does the idea of North conjure? A space of wild nature? A barren frozen wasteland? A resource-rich hinterland? Sweeping unpeopled vistas of big mountains and wild rivers? A central node of national identity? The frontier? Chances are it is some complex configuration of all of these ideas. This is what makes North so fascinating as an imaginative form. It is shifting, elusive, and often magnetic in its draw.

Let's pause for a moment on the idea of the frontier. I would argue that North, as a shifting constellation of meanings, desires, and spaces comes into view in Canada largely out of the imaginative capacities of the frontier. Imagined as resource rich hinterland and/or pristine wilderness-scape, North is a space on the edge – a fluid edge that has less to do with direction or physical geography than it does with where "civilization" is thought to end and wildness begins. Just as historian Frederick Jackson Turner (1935) suggested of the westwarding of the American frontier through that country's national expansion, North emerges in Canada out of the frontier's northward migration. In both cases, the frontier is colonial and capitalist – it transforms occupied places into emptied spaces "free for the taking."

What comes to mind when you think of a/the frontier? Unpeopled wild spaces waiting to be discovered and explored? A space on the edge? As Anna Tsing (2005) suggested:

> A frontier is an edge of space and time: a zone of not yet – not yet mapped, not yet regulated. It is a zone of unmapping: even in its planning, a frontier is imagined as unplanned. Frontiers aren't just discovered at the edge; they are

> projects in making geographical and temporal experience . . . Frontiers make wildness, entangling visions and vines and violence; their wildness is *both* material and imaginative . . . Frontiers energize old fantasies, even as they embody their impossibilities.
>
> (p. 28–29)

For Tsing, the frontier is not "a place or even a process but an imaginative project capable of molding both places and processes" (p. 32). The frontier is an imaginative project made as unmade; planned as unplanned. Frontiers are cultural projects where politics, history, and economics converge to produce both the edges to be discovered and the terms by which that discovery is allowable. In these terms, the frontier produces space upon which national (colonial/capitalist) narratives of expansion and "progress" can be inscribed. Again, this is an imaginative project that sees capitalist economic desires turning space into resources while colonial arrogance and power erases Indigenous Peoples and being from land. Land comes into view as uninhabited, resource rich, and waiting to be "discovered" and claimed.

Through the imaginative capacities of the frontier, North is constructed as a space on the edge. Frontiers are imaginative projects that simultaneously energize the fantasies of their own making – their promise, possibilities, potentials – while embodying the impossibilities and inherent contradictions of these same fantasies. The edges are shifty. Through touristic framing and the comfortable distances granted by modernity, resource-rich hinterlands are transformed into pristine wilderness spaces and harsh unforgiving frontier-scapes become spaces of natural beauty and personal freedom and renewal. The logic of the frontier folds back on itself, opening up new spaces, resources, and visions to be exploited. Where capitalist desires turn space into resources for extraction on the frontier, these same forces take hold of new visions of wild nature turned wilderness and turn it into a touristic commodity to be marketed, sold, and appreciated at Walmart.

In Yukon and Alaska, the frontier, produced as a pre-commercial, yet-to-be-discovered space has been packaged, marketed, and sold by tourism branding efforts (Hogan & Pursell, 2008). The (surface) irony is obvious here. The frontier is impossibly pre-commercial. It is a commercial, capitalist project at its core. In fact, these cultural complexes establish the very logic and operations of the concept of frontier. The forces that work in and through the frontier run quickly across its surface, grabbing hold of "things," and turning them into marketable commodities. In its making the frontier embodies its own impossibilities, as the very terms that constitute it perform and predict its immediate reversals, "forming productive confusions and becoming models for other frontiers" (Tsing, 2005, p. 33). The logic of the commodity cuts deeply into either vision of the frontier – resource-rich or pristine wilderness – and operates the same way on each.

Walmart saw us coming. Discourses of tourism marketing joined forces with the logics of the market and tourists have become a resource on this frontier. New frontiers have been discovered. New sources of untapped resources have come into view. A highway lined with motor homes in search of wild nature and northern adventure is one such resource. Once seen as wild space to be claimed, tamed and conquered by colonial ambition, governments and businesses now construct, brand, market, and sell Yukon spaces as untouched, magical natural places. Travel Yukon (2017), the official Yukon Government Tourism office invites visitors to "Come to our wild northern playground," bundling experiences into three sections: Water, Northern Lights Viewing, and Land. As Alexander Wilson (1991) cautions, "[w]hen our physical surroundings are sold to us as 'natural' . . . we should pay close attention" (p. 12). I agree. As Bruce Braun (2002) aptly notes, nature is "artifactual" (p. 3). On this frontier called Yukon, in the Walmart parking lot in Whitehorse, a form of nature emerges as an artifact of touristic and market relations that produce ways of interpreting the physical world in selected, commoditized ways. Braun goes on to take up the matter of nature as a site of power. He draws our attention to those spaces where nature becomes visible and knowable *as* nature. Braun insists that "[w]hat must be brought into thought is not nature per se but the construction of *spaces of visibility* in which nature – and our economic and political investments *in* nature – is constituted" (p. 16). The Walmart parking lot in Whitehorse is one such space of visibility.

The call of the wild

On the same evening that I parked my car behind the motor home featuring "The Call of the Wild" mural of mountains and loons, I met Florence and Conrad.[4] A small group of people gathered at the edge of the parking lot overlooking the Yukon River. As I approached, I could see that they were excitedly looking at something on the other side of the road. It was a bald eagle perched on top of a tree beside the river. Several had cameras out and were busy snapping pictures. "What a sight!" Florence exclaimed as Conrad took a notebook out of his shirt pocket and carefully wrote something down.

I later asked the couple about their trip. Having travelled from Florida to Alaska (I met them on their return trip), they had made a point of documenting every time they saw "wildlife" in a log. As we talked about their trip, Florence explained: "We are real nature lovers so every time we see a wild animal we just have to make a note of it. It's why we did this trip, to Alaska, to see the nature . . . that and the scenery of course." Entering this event in his log of "nature" sightings, Conrad wrote: "Bald Eagle. 7PM. Walmart in Whitehorse, Yukon, Canada."

For Florence and Conrad, nature is available at Walmart, and this nature is no different from any other point along the road. For these travellers admiring the bald eagle at Walmart, "nature" was the "wild" animals they could see from their motor home as they travelled down the road or were parked in the Walmart parking lot. "The scenery" was something else – not nature itself but the backdrop against which "nature" occurred.

Let's think about the scenery for a moment and the kinds of nature that count as nature in this parking lot. Here, in the Walmart parking lot in Whitehorse, nature *takes place*. It becomes visible. That visibility is enabled by a context of settler colonial legacies (past and present), national imaginings (both American and

Canadian), late-capitalist globalization, and selected, sanitized, marketable, touristic notions of "wild" spaces that are woven into the broader imaginative project of the frontier. However, in the space of visibility opened up at Walmart by the converging forces and forms assembled here, only certain natures can *take place* as nature (bald eagles), while the "scenery" (a Walmart parking lot) is naturalized out of sight. This is precisely why it took me tracking Coyote into the parking lot for me to notice it.

In response to my question, "what brought you North?" a couple from Texas, whom I met outside their motor home in the Walmart parking lot, responded: "Oh, the nature! We are real outdoors people and have always wanted to see the wilderness of the north – so here we are!"[5] So here we are! – At Walmart. I heard similar responses over and over. Visitors talked at length about their love of nature and their lifelong imaginings of "true northern wilderness." In the words of an Ontario woman I met at Walmart:

> I have been dreaming about northern wilderness since I was a girl. You know, real wilderness. Not Southern Ontario wilderness, but real, vast, untouched nature. This trip is like a dream for me. I can't believe that I am actually here. And that it is so beautiful. Miles and miles of wilderness, as far as the eye can see. It's so awesome.[6]

These were two conversations among many that I had at Walmart that revolved around people's narratives of "northern adventure" and "nature" appreciation without ever a mention that we were having these conversations in a Walmart parking lot. Walmart is so deeply embedded in the landscape and consciousness of the everyday that it disappeared out of these conversations. These travellers were not talking about Walmart when they made comments about being "here." "Here" meant North, on this trip that they had been anticipating for years.

As a cultural anthropologist, I am always interested in those moments where bundles of cultural values come together in taken-for-granted ways that allow them to escape questioning – something being called "natural" surely flags such a moment. What is particularly interesting about these encounters at Walmart is not just what counts as nature here, but that the cultural logics of colonialism, capitalism, and modernity are so deeply embedded into this landscape of everydayness that they completely disappear from view. It is through this matrix of coloniality – whereby colonial practices and structures, guided by narratives of modernity and progress (Mignolo, 2007) – that Walmart comes into view and experience as "natural." The settler colonial structures of the dispossession of Indigenous Peoples and epistemologies from land are literally paved into the ground (Cooke, 2016, 2017) and then camped on in large motor homes, appreciable as wilderness nature.

What makes this process so power-full is the imaginative capacity to produce terrains upon which moral values about wilderness and nature as personally renewing and virtuous can be inscribed on the back of colonial and settler colonial violence and ongoing dispossession. This requires careful discursive handling whereby space comes into being as nature, nature into view as wild, and this wild-ness, appealing (as a touristic commodity) *and* morally virtuous (for the personal renewal it grants). This process demands a careful negotiation between "wilding" and "taming." Nature needs to be perceived as wild enough to be appreciated for its wild-ness, but tamed enough that this wild-ness can be apprehended for such appreciation. Capturing this process of wilding-taming perfectly, The Yukon Vacation Planner (2017), published by the Yukon Government, reads as one of its headings "Tame the wild and run free" (p. 11). This is the business of the frontier – as imaginative project (Tsing, 2005) through the matrix of coloniality (Mignolo, 2007). Nature on the frontier needs to be smoothed, paved over to be appreciable and consumed for its wildness. At the same time, what cannot infiltrate the space of visibility opened up by this process are the settler colonial violences, erasures, dispossessions, and denials that make this space "available" at all. The road offers a way to do this – materially and symbolically.

The Yukon Vacation Planner (2017) declares that in Yukon visitors will "Discover that every road is the scenic route" (p. 15). Yukon wilderness, as it is produced, marketed, and sold to tourists is a touristic commodity that can be safely enjoyed from the road. A comment in the guest book at the Whitehorse Visitors Centre reads: "It's fantastic to drive through Canada and Alaska and make a look for the nature."[7] Another reads: "Wilderness we're coming!!!"[8]

This wilderness and the road are inextricably linked. The former is not possible without the latter. The former – as experience, destination, commodity – is a product of the latter. Of the process of exploring the North by road, travel writer Geoffrey Roy (2000) writes:

> Traveling through pristine wilderness by road is one of the great joys of the Yukon . . . This wilderness teems with wildlife and you will have as much chance of seeing it from the side of the road as you will stalking it through the bush.
>
> (p. 155)

In this passage, Roy suggests that one is as able to experience Yukon "wilderness" as "pristine" as easily and authentically from inside a vehicle as from walking through "the bush." Note Roy's use of the terms "wilderness" and "the bush." Wilderness is what we can admire from the road. The word conjures feelings of majestic beauty. "The bush," on the other hand, is more often perceived as a space of work and danger. For Roy, wilderness is nature as it is seeable from the road. We would have to "stalk" wildlife to see it in "the bush." Not only is there no need to leave the car to experience "pristine wilderness." If you leave the road, it will no longer be wilderness. Once off the road you will find yourself in "the bush" – a very different kind of nature space.

The interconnected relationship between constructions of wilderness, the automobile, and the road is reflected in Roy's comments. Yukon can only exist as wilderness because of the road that gets us there and from which we can admire the view. Cars and roads grant access to those places deemed far enough away from civilization to be considered wilderness. They provide the safe vantage point from which wilderness can be admired *as* wilderness. Of this, Lucy Lippard (1999, p. 139) writes:

> The view, or the scenic overlook, is a ready-made photograph waiting to be snapped . . . We go to a place only to stare off into another place where we can't or won't go . . . the scenic overlook is a substitute for exertion . . . They are controlled views of landscape – itself already something of a controlled abstraction.

Scenic outlooks along the road open a space of visibility where nature, produced in Yukon as wilderness, can be gazed upon. To experience Yukon's wilderness, for many travellers, is to look at it. And looking at it is most often done through the windshield, or at most from just outside your vehicle at the side of the road.

I met up with two couples travelling together, in separate RVs, at a roadside pull-out on the Alaska Highway between Whitehorse and Haines Junction, Yukon. As we talked, we admired a cluster of wild flowers at the edge of the gravel pull-out. One of the women said: "Aren't they lovely. It is such a treat to get to see so many wild flowers just growing naturally right here at the side of the road."[9] The other woman chimed in: "If they aren't at the side of the road, we don't see them." Exploring the relationship between automobiles and national parks in Washington State, David Louter writes that once through the gates of the park, we enter

> a landscape for the car in nature. It is a landscape that seems pristine. The road travels through a dark forest, passes through meadows, and gradually ascends the mountain in the long series of turns that, like stanzas in a poem, reveal an unfolding panorama of glaciers, rock, and sky. Conforming to the topography and edged with guard walls of stone, the road seems to belong to the landscape. It frames our view. It is how we see the park. It is how we know nature in this place.
>
> (2006, p. 3)

This passage could have been written about travelling North by road. North, an imagescape often synonymous with nature itself (Grace, 2001), is essentially a road-side experience for many that travel to Yukon. The windshield and road frame this North-as-wilderness.

One warm summer evening, I found myself sitting in the passenger seat of an RV as the owner of the "rig" climbed in the Captain's chair. He grabbed onto the steering wheel, looked at me with a smile, and said:

> It's awesome how much you can see from up here. Important to keep it [the windshield] clean, so you can always see the picture clearly. Incredible ain't it? Wall to wall glass – just like a big screen TV with a great picture.[10]

Perched in the front seats of his RV, we talked about his trip. He told stories of things he and his wife had seen and places they had stopped. As he talked, he gazed out the windshield often – remembering, imagining. I found myself gazing out with him, trying to see what he was imagining. The view, however, from the windshield on this day was of the front door of Walmart.

Road systems inscribe a particular visual structure to the ways in which landscapes can be read and experienced. The windshield creates a particular frame through which this reading and experiencing occurs. John Urry (2005) suggests that this visual structure is guided by discursive processes that transform "land" into "landscapes." Complexes of meaning and power translate the physical world into readable cultural texts. In Yukon, physical space (what Urry calls "land") is most often transcribed into the touristic imagination as wilderness landscapes. This process of transcription occurs by way of the intersections of various discursive forces creating "the visual economy of nature" (Urry, 2005, p. 81).

This visual economy of nature is also located within, and structured by, the broader discursive complexes of tourism, which themselves are ordered by logics of late-capitalist consumption. Within these complexes of meaning, select versions of wild nature spaces come into view as wilderness from the road, and are framed by the windshield. In Canada, the writing of this entire visual economy is predicated on settler colonial structures that have erased, displaced, and dispossessed Indigenous Peoples and ways of knowing and being out of sight. These processes are not events, but rather, ongoing processes of dispossession and denial.

As my roadside pull-out conversation with the two couples from Texas that I mentioned earlier progressed, we went on to talk about some of the highlights of their trip. Both couples were driving large RVs towing SUV vehicles that they used for day trips. At one point on their trip, the group decided to leave the motor homes at a campground and all pile into one of the SUVs for a day trip to the Alaskan Coast. Recalling this decision one of the woman said:

> It was a terrible idea. The women got stuck in the back seat and we could hardly see a thing. When you're riding in the motor home you have that huge window to see everything through. It's like a big screen television. You're up high and can see everything. From the back seat of the stupid car we couldn't hardly see a thing. We will not do that again. Even if you can get more places with the car than with the motor home it isn't worth it if you can't see anything.[11]

Again, "the view" from the car comes up as a key feature of people's experiences of Yukon, North, and nature. As illustrated in the words of these road travellers, being able to "get" somewhere differs greatly from being able to "see" it. For these travellers, the view from inside the vehicle on the road is central to the visual consumption of places. To see a place (through the window) is to experience it. If you can't see it, or the view is obscured, why go?

Urry (2005) writes that "[t]he pleasure of such [toured] places derives from the consumption of goods and services that somehow stand for or signify that place"

(p. 79). In Yukon, the "goods" are nature, wilderness, and wildlife. Experiencing Yukon means consuming nature, and this consumption is framed as morally virtuous. In the film *As the Crow Flies* (Chapman, 1997), which plays throughout the day at the Visitor's Information Centre in Whitehorse, a woman's voice in the opening segment of the film says: "The Yukon experience – the wilderness experience – it can only be character building." Right away visitors to the territory are told that "The Yukon experience" is synonymous with "the wilderness experience" and that there is something inherently character building about it. Images of people hiking, fishing, gazing out over mountain vistas frame these words. The conflation of Yukon and wilderness acquires currency with these visually appealing images. No one in the film is seen swatting away black flies, getting lost, or being caught out in the rain. This conflation speaks to the affective investments made in ideas of nature as a source of personal renewal well beyond the purely visual.

Nurturing this kind of affective and moral association between Yukon, wilderness, and personal renewal requires careful framing. A broad political economy of display and consumption that revolves around road travel frames Yukon landscapes as touristic commodities in ways that disappear the road itself. We aren't asked to think about carbon footprints or emissions as we travel thousands of kilometres by road to experience this nature. The road, our vehicles, and the consumer impacts of this travel is bracketed out. Nor are we asked to consider the ways that these same roads North grant(ed) access to colonial administrators and facilitated the "claiming" of northern territories into the Dominion of Canada. These roads allowed permanent routes in for the enforcement of colonial and settler colonial policies that include(ed) taking Indigenous children into the Residential School and child welfare systems, the introduction of wage labour that permanently impacted Indigenous economies, and the relocation of Indigenous settlements along the roads (Nadasdy, 2004). To be sure, the impacts on Indigenous Peoples of roads as technologies of mobility have not been exclusively negative. My point here, rather, is to highlight that some of the impacts, and legacies left in their wake, have been permanent routes of settler colonial domination and dispossession – material manifestations of settler colonialism as structure, not event (Wolfe, 2006). And moreover, these are not the parts of the "roads as scenic routes" highlighted in their framing as tourist destinations. Instead, Yukon Government Department of Environment (2007) writes in a brochure titled *Where to find RV dump stations in the Yukon*: "Yukon wilderness: untamed, unspoiled. Travelers have unparalleled access to nature's majesty, right outside their RV doors. It is a magical place." As geographer Bruce Braun (2002) suggests, "The material and the discursive do not just co-exist" along and through Yukon roads on this moral settler colonial capitalist touristic terrain, but "implode in knots of extraordinary density" (p. 19).

Back in the parking lot

My encounters at Walmart signal this implosion. Camping at Walmart naturally articulates within the flows of assembled forces at work in making both this place (in all its multiplicities as North, nature, the frontier, and Walmart) and people's experiences of it. The choice to camp at Walmart and admire and appreciate nature from the parking lot and through the windshield along the road that drew people here speaks to the broader discursive complexes of modern productions of nature, tourism marketing, and late-capitalist consumption on this frontier.

Walmart is a familiar site of everydayness. That is an understatement. Walmart is perhaps the most pervasive symbol of the everyday in contemporary North American popular and consumer culture. Charles Fishman (2006) notes that ninety percent of all Americans live within fifteen miles of a Walmart. The store will have approximately 7.2 billion visits this year. The earth's population is only 6.5 billion. Walmart is hyperbolic. It is super-sized capitalism and such a dominant force in the landscape of the everyday that more than the entire world's population passes through the doors each year in search of banal everyday items – toilet paper, shampoo, diapers.

As I visited Walmart almost daily for three consecutive summers, I witnessed many scenes of the everyday playing out in the parking lot. On a warm summer evening, a woman gave her husband a haircut in a chair outside their motorhome. Young boys played catch in the spaces between RVs. A gentleman sat in his lawn chair and read the paper. At dinnertime, people fired up portable barbeques and prepared meals. They walked their dogs along the grass patches that line the parking lot. They parked their shopping carts beside their RVs having delivered a load of supplies and left them as if to return for more tomorrow. In the evenings, men busied themselves pulling out collapsible ladders to meticulously wash the windshields and windows of the RVs.

This is a site where tourism and everyday life are indistinguishable from each other. Scott McCabe (2002) suggests that tourism has become so entrenched in everyday life and consumption that "[t]ourism creates a world for a person that is not separate from everyday life, but intrinsic to it" (p. 73). In this parking lot, the forces that shape both tourism and everyday life assemble, converge, and congeal.

Closer to the parking lot entrance, a steady stream of vehicles pulls in and out. Yukon residents also shop here. Walmart specializes in the whatnots of the everyday: toilet paper, dish soap, dog food, diapers. A yellow smiling face stickered to the storefront window assures shoppers of the "everyday low price guarantee."

This scene, or collection of scenes playing out constantly, is all as *natural* as an eagle perched on a tree by the river. This is the ecosystem of contemporary daily life lived in settler colonial Canada. This is the terrain upon which forces converge and meanings congeal. And in a strange and logical way, it all makes uncomfortable sense. The logic of the frontier turns everything into a commodity – toilet paper, bald eagles, wilderness-scapes, and Yukon. Yukon as wilderness is a consumable commodity, and road travellers lining the highway and parking lot an exploitable resource on this frontier.

The road, like the parking lot, is part of this assemblage of meanings and logics. Through the windshield, from the road, Yukon spaces are enjoyable as wilderness places for those whom I met at Walmart. The pleasures of wilderness experiences need to be contained, anxieties and discomforts mediated. The historical conditions that make the production of wilderness as touristic experience possible frame how the windshield serves as the lens through which travellers interpret as pleasurable their encounters with Yukon's wild nature. That Walmart disappears out of view in actual lived Yukon "wilderness experiences" speaks to the logic at work in the production of this complicated constellation of assembled forces. Walmart and wilderness are products of the same historical conditions. People travel to both as part of the same journeying North. Experiencing each is shot through by the other.

Notes

1 The research presented in this chapter was conducted between May 2006 and August 2008 in Whitehorse and Dawson City, Yukon, under Yukon-Canada Scientists and Explorers Act Research Licenses #06–02S&E and #07–27S&E. Participant observation, informal conversations, and semi-structured interviews formed the central methodological tools. While the primary research presented here was conducted some time ago, as I write this in 2017, the parking lot in Whitehorse remains full of RV campers most summer evenings.
2 All the names of research participants whose words are quoted throughout this chapter have been changed.
3 The concept of coloniality draws our attention to the relationship between colonialism and narratives of modernity flagging these inextricable cultural projects as inseparable "sides of the same coin" (Mignolo, 2007; Quijano, 2007). I am using the concept here in this way.
4 Interview by author, Whitehorse, Yukon, August 16, 2007.
5 Interview by author, Whitehorse, Yukon, June 18, 2008.
6 Interview by author, Whitehorse, Yukon, August 22, 2008.
7 Comment in Guest Book at the Visitor Information Centre, Whitehorse Yukon, July 21, 2008.
8 Comment in Guest Book at the Visitor Information Centre, Whitehorse Yukon, July 9, 2008.
9 Interview with author, along the Alaska Highway, Yukon, July 2008.
10 Interview with author, Whitehorse, Yukon, August 19, 2007.
11 Interview with author, along the Alaska Highway, Yukon, July 2008.

References

Braun, B. (2002). *The intermperate rainforest: Nature, culture, and power on Canada's west coast.* Minneapolis, MN: Minnesota University Press.

Chapman, R. (1997). *As the crow flies.* Canada: Whitehorse Visitor's Centre, Whitehorse, Yukon.

Cooke, L. (2016). 'Skwelkwek' welt is what we call this place': Indigenous-settler relations and the othered side of British Columbia's Sun Peaks Resort. In S. Nepal & J. Saarinen (Eds.), *Political ecology and tourism* (pp. 225–238). New York: Routledge.

Cooke, L. (2017). Unsettling the ground under our feet (and skis): A reading of Sun Peaks Resort as a settler colonial moral terrain. *Tourist Studies, 17*(1), 36–53.

Cronon, W. (1996). The trouble with wilderness; or getting back to the wrong nature. In W. Cronon (Ed.), *Uncommon ground: Rethinking the human place in nature* (pp. 69–90). New York: W. W. Norton & Company.

Fishman, C. (2006). *The Wal-Mart effect: How the world's most powerful company really works – and how it's transforming the American economy.* New York: Penguin Books.

Grace, S. (2001). *Canada and the idea of the North*. Montreal and Kingston: McGill-Queen's University Press.
Hogan, M. P., & Pursell, T. (2008). The "real Alaskan" in the "last frontier." *Men and Masculinity, 11*, 63–85.
Lippard, L. R. (1999). *On the beaten track: Tourism, art, and place*. New York: The New Press.
Louter, D. (2006). *Windshield wilderness: Cars, roads, and nature in Washington's National Parks*. Seattle, WA: University of Washington Press.
McCabe, S. (2002). The tourist experience and everyday life. In G. M. S. Dann (Ed.), *The tourist as a metaphor of the social world* (pp. 61–75). New York: CABI Publishing.
Mignolo, W. (2007). Delinking: The rhetoric of modernity, the logic of coloniality and the grammar of de-coloniality. *Cultural Studies, 21*(2), 449–514.
Nadasdy, P. (2004). *Hunters and bureaucrats: Power, knowledge, and aboriginal-state relations in Southwest Yukon*. Vancouver: University of British Columbia Press.
Pensky, M. (2004). Method and time: Benjamin's dialectical images. In D. Ferris (Ed.), *The Cambridge companion to Walter Benjamin* (pp. 177–198). Cambridge: Cambridge University Press.
Quijano, A. (2007). Coloniality and modernity/rationality. *Cultural Studies, 21*(2), 168–178.
Roy, G. (2000). *North Canada: Yukon, Northwest territories, Nunavut*. Bucks: Bradt Publications.
Shields, R. (1991). *Places on the margin*. London: Routledge.
Travel Yukon. (2017). Retrieved June 15, 2017, from www.travelyukon.com.
Tsing, A. (2005). *Friction: An ethnography of global connection*. Princeton, NJ: Princeton University Press.
Turner, F. J. (1935). *The frontier in American history*. New York: Henry Holt and Company.
Urry, J. (2005). The place of emotions within place. In J. Davidson, L. Bondi, & M. Smith (Eds.), *Emotional geographies* (pp. 77–83). Hampshire: Ashgate.
Wilson, A. (1991). *The culture of nature: North American landscape from Disney to the Exxon Valdez*. Toronto: Between the Lines.
Wolfe, P. (2006). Settler colonialism and the elimination of the native. *Journal of Genocide Research, 8*(4), 307–409.
Yukon Territorial Government (YTG). (2007). *Where to find RV dump stations in the Yukon* print brochure. Whitehorse, Yukon: Department of Environment.
Yukon Vacation Planner. (2017). Retrieved September 30, 2017, from www.yumpu.com/en/document /view/58149701/ yukonvacationplanner-2017.

3 Anachronistic others and embedded dangers

Race and the logic of whiteness in nature tourism

Bruce Erickson

It is a bit of a cliché to say that the exotic has long been a feature of tourism. From the early "Grand Tours" of Europe to the rise of ecotourism in the late 20th century, tourists are motivated by an encounter with difference. In his influential discussion of tourism as a feature of modernity, Dean MacCannell (1976) argues that a search for authenticity motivates the modern tourist. This authenticity is located most predominantly in "pre-modern" spaces: "in other historical periods and other cultures, in purer, simpler lifestyles" (MacCannell, 1976, p. 3). Similarly, John Urry's (1990) discussion of the tourist gaze highlights the way in which tourism demands an experience outside of the everyday. This demand, in his analysis, reshapes urban centres throughout the world, but also contributes to the commodification of difference and the production of race and ethnicity as a spectacle to be consumed (see also Buzinde, Santos, & Smith, 2006; Wood, 1998; Zhihong, 2007).

The interest and investment in difference within the field of tourism is no surprise, but we should be reminded that it says more about the identity of the tourist than it does of the places and peoples being toured. In his analysis of Orientalism as both a field of knowledge throughout the 18th, 19th and 20th centuries and as a field of power that structures the relationship between Europe and the broadly defined (and misrepresented) "Orient," Edward Said (1978) suggests that the discourse of Orientalism was productive of not just an understanding of the East, but also the West itself. Because Orientalism was so entrenched in a need to affirm the distinction between the Orient and the Occident – that is, because of Orientalism's thorough ethnocentrism – it has been deemed a worldview built out of the ideas about the Occident. If the Orient was backward and eccentric, it was Europe and the West who were forward and rational (and could therefore straighten out the Orient). This perspective results in a constant, if very flexible, support for European (and American) superiority that was woven through political power as well as the cultural lens of European identity itself.

In this chapter, I will argue that a similar process happens in touristic encounters with race, whereby the differences encountered (and deemed an ethically valuable feature of tourism) are structured by a discourse of whiteness even before the tour begins. This is a process that can be identified in the relationship between nature and race, which are often conflated together in the desire to visit the exotic.

Whiteness, within tourism, has long held the position of dominance not by virtue of the demographic of tourists, but through the establishment of difference as being significant. It is whiteness, as the assumed "blank slate" of race, that sets up the tourist gaze and makes legible the differences that are valuable in tourism. In my argument, whiteness is not a subject position or a simple racial classification, but rather, an organizing discourse for the way that we see race itself – it is a lens through which we understand what race is. Within that lens, whiteness is privileged as the pure original position of the human subject. In this way, it is whiteness (as a form of racial logic) that makes these differences pleasurable as they affirm ones' position within the world. Further, the racial logic of modern tourism is sutured onto the landscape in such a way that the whiteness of tourism is affirmed not just through the bodies of tourists and their hosts, but also by the meanings given to the landscapes visited. By looking at two broad genres of encountering difference through race and nature – as anachronistic others and as embedded dangers – I illustrate the importance of understanding whiteness as a discourse that structures much of modern nature tourism, including its moral undertones and positionings.

Whiteness and tourism

Within arenas of tourism and nature, difference is not something that is feared by whiteness (as it might be within White Supremacy). Rather, difference offers whiteness a moral position from which to claim a global citizenship, a position that is foreclosed to "othered" subjects. To understand this, we can look at Said's discussion of the difference between the European subject and its socially constructed Arab other. By focusing not just upon the academic view of the Orient but also on the way in which the figure of the Orient is weaved through European popular culture, Said's analysis highlights how European culture is produced through a complicated incorporation of that represented non-European difference. Thus, the European colonial identity, as Homi Bhabha (1994) argues, is established not through a simple separation between "us and them" but through an ambivalent hybridity on both sides, in which we are them, and they are us. Tourism certainly illustrates this ambivalence and incorporation, in which the Western traveller finds moments of difference (in food, in rituals, in comfort levels, in privileges) but situates those differences with the drive to self-actualization that is focused upon being a part of a "global culture." Cara Aitchison (2001) describes this as the paradox of cultural tourism: "While crossing national boundaries the global tourism industry simultaneously serves to reinforce the otherness of cultures" (p. 140).

What I am arguing here is not just that racial difference (which is socially and culturally constructed) is fundamental to how tourism operates, but that tourism's investment in otherness affirms whiteness as the hegemonic logic that makes racial difference visible (Seshadri-Crooks, 2002). Whiteness, as a form of racial discourse, demands that racial difference be produced and made visible. In tourism contexts, whiteness demands that these differences be made enjoyable and economically productive (and indeed, that enjoying and selling difference are ethically valuable activities). Within this framework, we can see how race still dominates our experiences of otherness, even as many people disavow race as an object of importance. While racism, or white supremacy, promotes discrimination based upon racial features, the logic of race supported by whiteness in tourism may argue against racism but still maintain the importance of, and fascination with, racial differences. Race becomes a morally desired feature of diversity, but as Said argues, the enumeration and fascination with this difference is established by placing an invisible whiteness as the core of the human subject.

For example, writing about the hippie rave tourist culture in Goa, India, Arun Saldanha (2007) argues that whiteness is established "from continually drawing from others what it needs to surpass itself" (p. 18). For Saldanha, whiteness comes to know itself by adopting and integrating exoticism at the same time as it defines those features as exotic and different. Tourists in Goa draw upon Indian culture, nature, and spirituality in a way that helps them go beyond their provincial European lives and become more universal or global. However, at the heart of this tourist identity is a steady core of white bodies that are bonded together by the commitment to knowing themselves beyond the limited modern world. Thus, hippie culture in Goa is particularly about whiteness not by virtue of an exclusive whiteness (there are brown and black bodies within the culture), but by the attempts to use the exotic life of Goan raves to affirm white privilege. In this form of white privilege, whiteness is considered different from other racial identities because it can become the other even as it maintains its own identity. Whiteness can become global whereas other groups are fixed within their provinciality, their geography.

This pattern is not exactly new, especially in the colonial context (whether it is in India or North America), where the frontier, the exotic and the savage have all been used by colonial subjects to define whiteness. On one side, whiteness is that which is opposite to the savage, but on the other side, white subjects are also presented as being able to incorporate the other as a sign of strength. Indian masquerade, anti-modernism, and romanticism all encounter difference in the landscape as a means to surpass the limits of what they see as a stagnant whiteness, only to be re-invented as an invigorated and stronger white subject (see Slotkin, 1973; Lears, 1981; Erickson, 2013). This ingestion of others within the production of a racial identity, whether through tourism, conquest, or racial cross-dressing suggests that whiteness is not simply based upon skin colour, but upon a system of racial meaning that ascribes classification based upon a predetermined logic of race that is flexible yet anchored. For Saldanha (2007), hippies in Goa both used Indian culture *and* distanced themselves from Indian people through rhythms and patterns. These patterns included their diet, drug use, and parties (e.g., whiteness dominated the dance floors in Goa, especially in the early morning).

Saldanha's (2007) analysis of the Goan rave scene illustrates the function of the exotic for whiteness: exotic otherness affirms the centrality of difference to the human experience and places whiteness as the organizing principle of it all. It is exotic if it is not white, but whiteness is the link that connects, or incorporates, the different cultures of the world together. In this logic of whiteness, racial differences are constructed and enabled to exist because they help anchor whiteness as the universal space of non-difference. Learning about differences then becomes pleasurable because they affirm whiteness as the pure human subject, the "non-different" centre of the world.

Importantly for tourism, especially for understanding the geography of tourism, the racial logic of whiteness extends the visibility of race not just to bodies, but also to landscapes. Along with the temporal and spatial patterns of the subjects themselves, racial logic dictates what kinds of landscapes are racialized, whereby hotels, cafes, and airports are not, and villages, mosques, and jungles are. For example, Michelle Christian (2013) illustrates how Costa Rica's tourism industry is built upon a white exceptionalism that differentiates Costa Rica from the rest of Latin America. In the eyes of tourism promoters in Costa Rica, the country exists as a white exception to a racialized Latin America. This exception is established in part by the Costa Rican natural landscape that was predominantly left out of the exploitative colonial period, leaving behind a "pure" landscape for the enjoyment of white tourists. Combined with a tradition of rural democracy that has led to a more peaceful and cohesive political system, Costa Rica embodies a landscape playground for the white traveller. Democracy and conservation codes Costa Rica as a white space in the tourist industry (see also Rivers-Moore, 2007).

Anachronistic others

Costa Rica also offers insight into the first genre of experience that flows from this racial logic of whiteness – that racial bodies are a signal of a past that is now accessible through tourism. In her analysis of the "No Artificial Ingredients" campaign by the Costa Rican ministry of tourism, Meagan Rivers-Moore (2007) argues that "bodies of colour in Costa Rican tourism are simultaneously invisible within discourses of the nation and hypervisible as both atavistic relics of a historic past and as spatially segregated, exotic tourist attraction in the present" (p. 341). In the marketing of Costa Rica to the global north, the campaign focuses upon the experience of the country as a safe, modern white landscape. Indigenous Peoples and Afro-Costa Rican communities on the southern Atlantic coast are either left out of tourism promotion or included only as an exotic, if perhaps "dangerous," attraction for more adventurous tourists (Christian, 2013). They hold "ancient cultures" that are of interest to the tourist, but the tourist representations offer them limited influence on the present national culture. These communities are held as part of the national story only in their ability to represent the national past, embodying and selling what Anne McClintock (1995) calls anachronistic space.

As McClintock (1995) illustrates, one of the central tenets of modernity is the linear progression of time, in which the history of the world moves forward towards a progressively more and more advanced and civilized society. Anachronistic spaces are those landscapes that are presented as being outside of this progress of modernity. These spaces are at a disjuncture with the modern world, left behind and outside civilization, where "geographic difference across *space* is figured as a historical difference across *time*" (McClintock, 1995, p. 40). For McClintock, Africa in the colonial period was the model of anachronistic space, and to travel from Europe to Africa was to travel back in time.

Similar patterns are found through the colonial landscape of the 20th century. Writing about early 20th century "sportsman's" search for wilderness in Ontario's Temagami region, Jocelyn Thorpe (2012) argues that Temagami offered an experience of the past, especially in the interaction with Indigenous guides that hosted and facilitated the hunting and fishing experience. In the rhetoric that promoted tourism in Temagami, the Indigenous guides excelled in wilderness, which was "the hunting grounds their forefathers once called home" (1905 Advertisement quoted in Thorpe, 2012, p. 65), but was adrift in the modern world. The wilderness existed outside of this modern world as a last vestige of the past that would soon disappear. This past was signalled by a combination of the natural landscape and Indigenous presence. The resultant narrative served the colonial dispossession of the landscape from the Teme-Augama Anishnabai who still claim rights to Temagami. In Thorpe's (2012) words, the idea "of the forest as part of the past and "the Indian" as part of the forest displaced the Teme-Augama Anishnabai *in time*" (p. 64). Being of the past, the Teme-Augama Anishnabai were dismissed from having control of the land in the present and the future, a position they have vigorously disputed.

Similar experiences of the past can be found elsewhere within contemporary tourism in Canada. Bruce Braun (2002), in his discussion on tourism and forestry in Clayoquat Sound, British Columbia, argues that ecotourism functions through the lens of "modernity-as-loss" (p. 134), where tourists are drawn to experiences of anachronistic spaces as an affirmation of the progress of modernity. Through an analysis of a sea kayaking tour in Clayoquat Sound, Braun describes how the tour produces an experience of the landscape as a pre-modern space. The route of the trip stays close to undisturbed parts of the Sound, including campsites that are located with no visual contact of any other campers or modern developments and day hikes into breathtaking temperate rainforests. As if to emphasize the anachronism of the landscape, the tour encountered old markers of human impacts – an old Nuu-Chah-nulth longhouse and old markers of preindustrial logging – only to find them overtaken by the lush forest, swallowed by the timelessness of the vegetation. Despite celebrating the power of the wilderness, Braun reminds us that, in the ecotourist's gaze, the power of the forest to survive these pre-industrial impacts is nothing compared to the ever-encroaching power of modernity to eliminate the forest (or nature in a broader sense) itself. For the tourists, Clayoquat Sound was an escape, an island within a sea of modernization that threatened the landscape. The tourists were there to glimpse this pre-modern and "pristine" landscape not in order to replicate it throughout the rest of their lives, but in order to return to the modern world re-invigorated by nature and ready to work. Modernism, from the ecotourist lens, takes pleasure and draws inspiration from witnessing the loss of pre-modern nature, peoples, and lifestyles. Indeed, Braun (2002) illustrates how ecotours are designed to both enhance the pre-modern experience (in the route and the construction of a scenic landscape) and not disrupt modern life (for example, tours are built into the standard work-week schedule). The connection to environmentalism highlights the moral dimensions of this interest in the anachronistic past, as the primitive life, or the connection to nature it is supposed to embody, is heralded as an ethical position for many urban environmentalists (Braun, 2002; Erickson, 2013).

Like the relegation of the Teme-Augama Anishnabai into the past, the Clayoquat Sound tours place the influence of the Nuu-Chah-nulth people in the past. The experience of modernity-as-loss eclipses the real loss of land faced by Indigenous Peoples that are pushed aside by modernism. Ecotourism "stages a spatial encounter where the "non-West" becomes (yet again) the terrain for the remaking of Western subjects" (Braun, 2002, p. 139). Whiteness becomes reinvigorated, even as it mourns what it is witnessing. The value of the temperate rainforest, the Temagami wilderness, or other iconic wilderness/natural landscapes comes from the belief (often quite justified) that these landscapes are threatened and therefore ethically valuable within an increasing industrialized world. Importantly, whiteness positions itself as both the centre of modernity, and as the problem of modernism. Civilized spaces are white landscapes, yet they depend upon those landscapes over-written by modernity for meaning and innovation.

Take, for example, the non-ecotourism experience of Disney's Animal Kingdom, in which we find similar divisions between white spaces of modernity and non-white anachronistic spaces that affirm the need for whiteness to extend beyond itself to answer the problems of modernity. This racial logic comes out in the differences between the Asia, Africa, and DinoLand U.S.A. exhibits. Asia and Africa, as Stephanie Rutherford (2011) illustrates, are landscapes teaming with nature and wildlife, while Dinoland highlights dead nature.

> A visit to Africa or Asia is a visit back in time . . . rooted in a prior era where nature was lush, fecund, and abundant. As time has moved on in the United States, so too has nature, leaving DinoLand U.S.A. rife with death.
>
> (Rutherford, 2011, p. 71)

These landscapes are not just about nature, as the production of a generalized Africa and Asia rely upon (stereotyped) social landscapes that Disney's "Imagineers" use to produce an "authentic" nature: an African market, an Asian village, and the actors paid to play the locals within them. Thus, African and Asian bodies are put on display as part of the anachronistic landscape of abundant nature (which Disney will also show as being threatened by those same non-white bodies through illegal logging or poaching), whereas modern DinoLand is stereotypically white. For Rutherford, the result of this is that guests can inhabit their modern identities and learn from the anachronistic others to save the eventual demise of nature through consumption and capitalist investment. Enlightened and ethical modern subjects learn from both science and anachronistic cultures (including Native Americans in a *Pocahantas* performance) to save the Earth. While the focus of the entertainment cum education at Disney is on our ability to both harm and heal the natural world, the geographic narrative used to convey this message also locates modern environmentalism within the global north.

As should be clear, it is not hard to find examples of anachronistic spaces within tourism. These spaces are often produced to confirm the superiority of Western cultures, in the manner of classic Orientalism, but they can also present a more liberal story in which there is much to learn from the anachronistic other, who perhaps leads a purer life. Yet, even within these celebrations of the primitive past, what becomes affirmed is the progression of history towards our contemporary world and beyond. These stories are made meaningful by a racial logic that locates whiteness as the central position of the modern subject. The differences of anachronistic space, whether used to illustrate the height of modern civilization or to illustrate the downfall of industrialization, are understood only in so much as they deviate from the white ideal: a rational, enlightened, productive subject. Again, this is not the logic of purity, in which only white bodies are allowed to be productive, rational, or enlightened. Whiteness is not a specific subject position that one holds, rather it is an ideology that one strives for. Ecotourists, Disney fans, and Goan hippies all operate within this logic of race through their attempts to overcome the failings of modernity by engaging with an anachronistic other while still maintaining a distinction between us and them.

Embedded dangers

This analysis of anachronistic spaces suggests that whiteness depends upon interaction and contact with others in order to affirm the power and potential of whiteness. Tourism has become a central feature of that relationship, as it provides the perfect template for the encounter with difference. In some cases, the anachronism functions not just as a difference, but also a danger the white subject needs to overcome. For example, in 2005, *Outside* magazine carried a feature article on a "First Contact" tour with an un-contacted tribe in Indonesia. As an extreme example of anachronistic tourism, this tour highlights one of the narrative functions that these encounters provide; namely, the ability for white subjects to overcome limits in ways that non-white subjects cannot. These limits are often experienced as threats to the tourist subject.

In 2003, Kelly Woolford started operating First Contact tours in New Guinea, claiming to provide Western tourists the opportunity to meet face-to-face with an un-contacted Indigenous group that he described as a "stone age tribe" (Woolford, quoted in Behar, 2005, p. 98). In the article for *Outside*, Michael Behar follows Woolford into the jungle for one of these encounters and returns somewhat sceptical. The article starts:

> I'm somewhere in a godforsaken rainforest on the north coast of West Papua, Indonesia, and I'm ready to get the hell out of here. I'm five days into a three-week jungle trek . . . and things have gotten both weird and dangerous. Now I'm scared and confused, and I've lost all faith in my guide.
>
> (Behar, 2005, p. 96)

They had just encountered "bow-and-arrow wielding bushmen who were so angry that they charged our camp, lobbing three arrows high above our heads" (Behar, p. 96). After a few more brief encounters with the bushmen, with fewer arrows but still quite antagonistic, Behar and the tour return out of the jungle and back to the United States, leaving Behar to ponder whether the encounters were real or staged. Although he consulted with several anthropologists who are unconvinced by the footage he has captured, Behar finds one feature that makes him believe that perhaps the encounters were not staged for him: the local guides hired by Woolford looked genuinely scared by their encounters. Fear of the dangerous encounter with the other offers Behar (2005) the access to an authentic experience, even as the evidence is strong that it was set up.

Similar questions about the authenticity and ethics of "first contact" tours reign in media accounts (Anstice, 2006), and most discussions of these types of tours roundly condemn them. Either the tour operators are fraudsters that are deceiving the tourists, or this is truly a first contact experience that dismisses the safety, exclusion, and sovereignty of the tribe in order to sell entertainment. The issue of authenticity, as the *Outside* feature illustrates, is not simply about the ethics of the encounter, or even the immediate pleasure of the experience, rather it is about distinction. Being a careful consumer of authentic tourist experiences is one of the status markers of tourism. As MacCannell (1976) correctly asserts, "Tourists dislike tourists" (p. 10). That is, tourists will assert a particular identity upon being the right kind of tourist. "Touristic shame is not based upon being a tourist, but on not being tourist enough, on a failure to see everything the way it 'ought' to be seen" (MacCannell, 1976, p. 10). Thus, Behar's worth as a tourist, and a travel writer, is based upon his ability to see through the gimmick and see what is really there. MacCannell argues that this obsession with authenticity within tourism is a symptom of modernity, in which our everyday lives have lost the social context for ascertaining truth and authenticity. Grasping what is real and staged is, consequently, deemed a form of cultural competency that shows off one's taste as a marker of status. The type of tourist that you are, often described as the distinction between the tourist and the traveller, signals not just the type of experience that you desire, but your ability to understand the world for what it really is. This is an ethical judgment that signals your worth as a traveller and as a modern subject, making it a significant terrain upon which moral values are positioned.

Behar's (2005) validation of the danger of his experience through the faces of the local guides places violence within the tourist frame, where real violence is part of the unmediated experience of the local. Being in danger provides the traveller a distinction from the tourist, but as Kristin Lozanski (2014) argues, it also anchors a distinction between the traveller and the local. Even though they might actively seek out dangerous situations, as Behar had, travellers implicitly and materially expect protection in most of those situations. As Lozanski (2014) writes,

> although danger may be knit into Western travellers' rationale for travel as a marker of difference from much of the Western context, the transformation

> of danger – insomuch as danger reflects threat or possibility of harm – into material harm is inconsistent with travel discourse.
>
> (p. 42)

This is certainly logical, as we do not expect people to voluntarily put themselves into landscapes they know *will* injure them. However, the desire to work on the edge of this distinction between danger and harm in the context of cultural tourism often means that while, in the mind of the tourist, it is not logical for the Western tourist to be harmed, it is accepted that locals have risky everyday lives that may lead to material harm. Thus, tourists in Palestine assume that they will not be caught within the line of fire of the Israeli army, but are routinely told stories by locals of when that happens to Palestinians.

The distinction established through nearly manifested violence provides the authenticity to the trip, making it real, powerful, and desirable. In the first contact tours, danger becomes embedded within the experience, and enhances the learning and change that comes from it. For Behar (2005), even with the possibility that the experience was set up, he is desperate to get back and experience it again. The readers of his article are meant to believe the dangerous primitive in the encounter is authentic because of the harm possible to the tourist and allows Behar to make normalizing claims about the value of such experiences. In the same way that a particular river run is more dangerous and, therefore, more coveted in the field of whitewater kayaking, the primitive other of the first contact tour becomes an embedded danger within the landscape. Thus, while the jungle itself is dangerous [Behar describes nearly stepping on a death adder, "one of the deadliest snakes in Papua" (p. 98)] the real danger of the landscape is the unknown, racialized other. This flows from the anachronistic landscape as the racialized other is seen to only exist within that space, not as a subject of modernity that has the same mobility of the tourist.

Take for example a controversial rock climbing trip to Kyrgyzstan that ended up with the kidnapping of prominent American climbers by a rebel military group. In the wake of the rescue (in which the climbers pushed one of their captors off a cliff), a controversy stirred over the ethics of the climbers being in an area of potential armed conflict (Erickson, 2005). As I have argued elsewhere, the danger and violence within this controversy is made legible through the discourse of whiteness, which makes the white tourist able to engage with danger as a form of entertainment (and indeed, sponsorship). Within this controversy, the local soldiers became part of the landscape as just another danger the climbers needed to negotiate. Controversy over climbing ethics, like the distinction between travellers and tourists, are fundamental to climbing culture and similarly provides climbers with distinction based upon their actions. In the parallels made between the style of climbing (roped or unroped, bolted or not) and the decision to climb in a volatile political region, the white climbers become mobile subjects in control of their destiny, one which is affirmed in their ability to survive natural and cultural dangers. The dangerous others of the volatile region became part of the landscape and the decision to interact with them was read not just as a miscalculation but an invitation of risk that is foundational to the distinction of the climber (Erickson, 2005). Similar to Behar's (2005) appreciation of the danger of the first contact tour, the potentially violent others become an embedded danger that provides a distinction for this trip over others.

The Kyrgyz climbing trip is an extreme example, yet we can see this logic of engaging danger or deprivation as a form of distinction throughout adventure travel. Lozanski (2011) reminds us that poverty and suffering are a marker of "road status" for travellers who try to distance themselves from simple tourists, through which they "mirror the lives of ostensibly authentic others, others whose authenticity is often marked by their poverty" (p. 474). This relationship to the other is not one of solidarity, but a kind of consumption, in which the traveller uses the status of the other to gain cultural capital. Mobility becomes the significant difference as the traveller's experience of poverty and hardship is temporary, while the local's experience is unending. Both conditions (of material excess on the part of the traveller at home and of actual poverty on the part of the local) are a requirement for the traveller's experience. Indeed, the traveller often uses these experiences not just as entertainment, but self-development, in which the hardship provided by temporarily engaging either with dangerous others or the dangers of other's lives, provides the traveller with a better understanding of themselves (Lozanski, 2011).

In these stories, the key to understanding the experience of the travellers, and their investment in the risk of travel is how the ability to persevere through danger and deprivation affirms the logic of whiteness. Importantly, it does so not simply through a discourse of strength (that the white subjects are stronger therefore can endure the danger better), but through a moral position in which the encounter with danger highlights the value of the white subject through its differentiation from the local. The dangers of the other are intertwined with the landscape in such a fashion that the other has no opportunity for mobility, nor any real desire for it. In the Kyrgyzstan kidnappings, the concern expressed by the climbing community was not for an area torn by an unstable government and armed rebellions, but for travellers who end up there. Similarly, in the travel industry, tourist worries about pickpockets, violent theft, or sexual assault are most often worries about the tourist bodies, not about the acts themselves. It is assumed that tourists are going to be the targets of such acts, are more deserving of concern when they do, and that the prevalence of those acts in the landscape are part of the culture. When tourist behaviours do put locals at risk, it is assumed that their bodies are accustomed to such risks. Behar (2005) sees the fear on the faces of his guides not as an ethical dilemma in which he is responsible for their well-being, but a marker of the success of their trip.

Resisting whiteness?

What I have shown here is that tourism mobilizes a discourse of whiteness as an organizing logic for understanding the modern world. It is not a discourse that allows only white people to engage in tourism, but one which situates the pleasures of tourism within a moral sphere that affirms the universality of whiteness as the globally desired subject of humanity. Non-white subjects are allowed to participate, but their presence does little to the overall logic of exoticism that seeks to find and consume exoticism as a central pleasure of tourism. While tourism studies in general have done much to criticize and illustrate the ethnocentric approach to tourism, looking at the role of race in nature tourism reminds us that whiteness can be affirmed through a celebration of difference.

Nature tourism also allows us to think about the kind of impositions the logic of whiteness makes on communities that are trying to step outside of their assigned roles in tourism. For example, in writing about Maasai cultural tourism in Kenya, Edward Bruner (2001) documents three different types of performances. The first is a stereotypically anachronistic tour that is an emblematic form of imperialist nostalgia, "fixing Maasai people in a frozen past, representing them as primitive, denying their humanity, and glorifying the British colonialism that enslaved them" (Bruner, 2001, p. 886). The second is a nationalist performance within the urban centre that celebrates the cultural creativity of the Maasai and other cultures within Kenya for a nationalist audience. The third, which is the most elite tourist spectacle, is a tented camp experience that involves flying tourists in for a safari in the Serengeti. Maasai performances at this camp draw from a Hollywood perspective where Maasai sing and dance "African" songs that are familiar to Western audiences and take them for a tour of the landscape. As Bruner describes it, "the colonial image of the Maasai has been transformed in a postmodern era so that the Maasai become the pleasant primitives, the human equivalent of the Lion King, the benign animal king who behaves in human ways" (p. 894). Importantly, unlike the other tours Bruner describes, this tour is produced not as a cultural tour, but as a nature tour, where tourists are shuttled across the Kenya/Tanzania border to different safari sights – the object of the tour is the Serengeti, of which the Maasai are nature part.

Another unique aspect of the Safari tour is that Maasai are part owners of the resort, they are employees in all levels of the resort and they receive part of the fee from the surrounding nature reserve. However, despite this involvement and investment in the tourist operation, their control is limited by two features (Bruner, 2001). First, of course is the influence of global pop culture on what counts as Maasai culture. The songs that they sing are influenced by both the popularity of the Disney film *The Lion King* and the pseudo-ethnography of *National Geographic*. The songs are a performance for the tourist, and the Maasai know this, but are still subject to its demands. Second, the involvement of Maasai as Maasai is limited to their cultural roles in the performance (Bruner, 2001). When they work outside of the performance, as waiters or as managers for example, they are perceived by tourists not as Maasai, but just Kenyans. While they can be partners, this partnership is circumscribed to promote the idea that Maasai culture is still pure, implicitly suggesting that if Maasai were to be waiters, it would be a fallen position, a degradation of their culture. As an example of this, Bruner points to how the manipulation of the performance is outwardly produced by the Maasai – the tourists get gifts from the Maasai to take home with them, the entry fee is collected by the chief, and the Maasai offer explanation of their dance and culture. These aspects promote a kind of authenticity to the interaction that is belied by the reality that the tour company carefully makes those decisions to appeal to the tourists. Even within local control, the demand for authenticity privileges the racial logic of whiteness, and local groups will often acquiesce in order to access the material gains of tourism.

Margeret Werry (2011) similarly writes about the control of tourist operations by local groups, discussing the involvement of Maori in tourism. In addition to some of the (Maori-owned) cultural tours that performs a pre-contact Maori culture, Werry discusses the rise of urban Maori tours which focus on "the urban Maori experience – the kinds of lives that Indigenous Maori people . . . live in a city like Auckland." (p. 174). In their attempt to provide contemporary visibility for Maori people in the nation, these tours still face the challenge of selling difference to their consumers. As such, there is a challenge for the tour operators to provide both enough intimacy to the tourists to make the tour engaging and entertaining while at the same coding that intimacy in ways that limit discomfort or resistance. In practice, this means offering insight into particular historical events that contain spiritual significance (e.g., ceremonies in particular landscapes or tours of art galleries) but not touch too much into political and economic difficulties (e.g., discussions of social housing or Maori resistance movements). Tour guides provide the experience of indigeneity in the landscape as the commodity, making contemporary Maori life a tourist product itself.

The tour guides, as Werry (2011) makes clear, are conscious of the problems caused by such a commodification (and de-politicizization) of their identity. Their discomfort is partly about a loss of control, but also about the kind of logic that tourists often approach these tours with. Unlike, say, a tour of British culture in New York City, the urban Maori tour is pleasurable to the tourists because it provides an exception to the belief that Indigenous cultures cannot modernize. There is an implicit amazement on the part of the tourists – exemplified by their interests in population size, life expectancy, and education levels of Maori in Auckland (Werry, 2011) – at the modernization of Maori life. This modernization is mediated through the tours by paying special attention to the natural landscape available to Maori in Auckland, places that hold significance outside of their urban form. In this way, as Werry argues, "indigeneity entails for the tourists the experience of an . . . attachment to place and people" (p. 176). For the tourist, Maori hold a bond to the landscape that persists despite the urban form, not through it, and the intimacy of the tour transfers that bond to the tourist.

In both of these examples, the tour operators come up against the discourse of whiteness that is mobilized through tourism. The tour operators and local communities find an opportunity for material benefits through cultural tours. These tours can also provide some forms of cultural benefits, like the maintenance of language or increased visibility within the city. These benefits however are negotiated through the logic of tourism that necessarily (in order to achieve those material benefits) follows a script of racial difference that situates whiteness as the organizing principle for the global world. This is a difficult contradiction to negotiate, and my analysis should not be taken as criticism of the choices made by these tour providers. Instead, what we need to do is be conscious of the organizing structures of tourism that facilitate this logic and to start experimenting with ways of undermining the centrality of whiteness to the tourist experience.

References

Aitchison, C. (2001). Theorizing other discourses of tourism, gender and culture: Can the subaltern speak (in tourism)? *Tourist Studies*, *1*(2), 133–147.

Anstice, M. (2006). *First contact* (Motion picture) BBC4: Indus Films.

Behar, M. (2005, February). Selling the last savage. *Outside*, 96–113.

Bhabha, H. (1994). *The location of culture*. New York: Routledge.

Braun, B. (2002). *The intemperate rainforest: Nature, culture, and power on Canada's West Coast*. Minneapolis, MN: University of Minnesota.

Bruner, E. (2001). The Maasai and the Lion King: Authenticity, nationalism, and globalization in African tourism. *American Ethnologist*, *28*(4), 881–908.

Buzinde, C. N., Santos, C. A., & Smith, S. L. (2006). Ethnic representations: Destination imagery. *Annals of Tourism Research*, *33*(3), 707–728.

Christian, M. (2013). ' . . . Latin America without the downside': Racial exceptionalism and global tourism in Costa Rica. *Ethnic and Racial Studies*, *36*(10), 1599–1618.

Erickson, B. (2005). Style matters: Explorations of bodies, whiteness, and identity in rock climbing. *Sociology of Sport Journal*, *22*(3), 373–396.

Erickson, B. (2013). *Canoe nation: Nature and race in the making of a national icon*. Vancouver: UBC Press.

Lears, T. J. (1981). *No place of grace: Antimodernism and the transformation of American culture, 1880–1920*. Chicago: University of Chicago Press.

Lozanski, K. (2011). Independent travel: Colonialism, liberalism and the self. *Critical Sociology*, *37*(4), 465–482.

Lozanski, K. (2014). Desire for danger, aversion to harm: Violence in travel to 'Other' places. In H. Andrews (Ed.), *Tourism and violence* (pp. 33–47). New York: Routledge.

MacCannell, D. (1976). *The tourist: A new theory of the leisure class*. New York: Schocken Books.

McClintock, A. (1995). *Imperial leather: Race, gender, and sexuality in the colonial contest*. New York: Routledge.

Rivers-Moore, M. (2007). No artificial ingredients? Gender, race and nation in Costa Rica's international tourism campaign. *Journal of Latin American Cultural Studies*, *16*(3), 341–357.

Rutherford, S. (2011). *Governing the wild: Ecotours of power*. Minneapolis, MN: University of Minnesota.

Said, E. (1978). *Orientalism*. New York: Vintage.

Saldanha, A. (2007). *Psychedelic white: Goa trance and the viscosity of race*. Minneapolis, MN: University of Minnesota Press.

Seshadri-Crooks, K. (2002). *Desiring whiteness: A Lacanian analysis of race*. New York: Routledge.

Slotkin, R. (1973). *Regeneration through violence: The mythology of the American frontier, 1600–1860*. Norman, OK: University of Oklahoma Press.

Thorpe, J. (2012). *Temagami's tangled wild: Race, gender, and the making of Canadian nature*. Vancouver: UBC Press.

Urry, J. (1990). *The tourist gaze*. London: SAGE.
Werry, M. (2011). *The tourist state: Performing leisure, liberalism, and race in New Zealand*. Minneapolis, MN: University of Minnesota Press.
Wood, R. E. (1998). Touristic ethnicity: A brief itinerary. *Ethnic and Racial Studies*, *21*(2), 218–241.
Zhihong, B. (2007). Ethnic identities under the tourist gaze. *Asian Ethnicity*, *8*(3), 245–259.

4 Rock climbing and the "good life"

Cultivating an ethics of lifestyle mobilities

Jillian M. Rickly

Introduction

The moral turn in tourism studies strives to make the ethical implications of travel more personal for researchers and tourists alike (MacCannell, 2011, 2012; Caton, 2012, 2015; Freudendal-Pedersen, 2014; Mostafanezhad & Hannam, 2014). In a time of increasingly mobile, yet globally connected societies, an ethical lens works to bridge studies of the politics of mobility (Cresswell, 2010) with research concerned with social and personal responsibility (see Caton, 2012, 2015; Freudendal-Pedersen, 2013; Mostafanezhad & Hannam, 2014; Grimwood, Yudina, Muldoon, & Qui, 2015). Studies of ethics are about the responsibility we take, or do not take, in our everyday lives and therefore how responsibility extends to our travel choices (Fennell, 2000; MacCannell, 2011; Caton, 2012; Freudendal-Pedersen, 2014). However, critical investigations of ethics have only more recently garnered attention in tourism studies, which Caton (2012) remarks is particularly pertinent given that tourism studies operate on loaded moral territory, speaking to both light-hearted pleasure and heavy social consequences (see also MacCannell, 2011; Mostafanezhad & Hannam, 2014).

More broadly, MacCannell (2011) observes that there are new moral imperatives thriving in contemporary society that command us to "Enjoy!" These imperatives are being substituted for ethical choice in both our everyday lives and our tourism experiences. Because tourism foregrounds notions of desire, freedom, habit, repetition, and character, it is fertile ground for a discussion of ethics (MacCannell, 2011, 2012). Expanding upon this, it will be argued that lifestyle mobilities offer a means to further explore these ideas, as this form of mobility ventures beyond the definitional boundaries of tourism and leisure to make travel a way of life. Everyday behaviours and habits are significant indicators of ethics, as they are indicative of how personal understandings of right and wrong rest within, or contest, broader social moral imperatives (see also Cooke, this volume). Lifestyle mobilities break down the dichotomies of home/away and work/leisure, fostering social relations that produce distinct notions of personal and shared responsibility that are inherently mobile such that one's tourism ethics may also be one's everyday behaviours and habits.

This chapter examines lifestyle rock climbing, a particular type of lifestyle mobility in which rock climbers pursue the sport full-time. In so doing, these travelling rock climbers give up more sedentary residences, living instead in mobile abodes (van, RV, car, or even a backpack). As a result of the natural setting required to practice the sport, these climbers often find themselves in isolated campgrounds far from urban areas. Lifestyle climbers are not professional climbers, and most are not sponsored by gear companies. Rather, they self-fund their travels, finding temporary work in the places they moor or maintaining internet-based employment along the way. Although rock climbing is the primary factor informing their travel behaviour and lifestyle choice, examining the ethical dimensions of lifestyle mobility suggests that individuals' sense of self, social responsibility, and morality are also motivating factors. So while the research that informs this paper did not directly ask participants about their ethics, interviewees often framed their lifestyle choice and motivation for travel and rock climbing in terms of "freedom", "choice", "responsibility", "trust", "fun", and even "sacrifice".

This chapter follows a similar delineation of ethics and morals used by Mostafanezhad and Hannam (2014) – "Ethics tends to refer to individual behaviour or codes of behaviour for a social group (professional ethics, family ethics, etc.) while morality refers more broadly to beliefs regarding how things ought to be across the range of human experience" (p. 3). Pursuing this ethical line of questioning extends a politics of mobility (Cresswell, 2010; Rickly, 2016) to further address social relations that are both contested and fostered through collective mobile practice by asking whether lifestyle climbing, as a particular form of nature-based mobile lifestyle practice, functions as means or an end to individuals' decision-making regarding lifestyle choice and further inquires as to the broader social trends that motivate this choice, as well as result from it. When lifestyle climbers take up hypermobile lifestyles that prioritize rock climbing, are they in pursuit of a "good life" that necessitates lifestyle change, or is this the pursuit of pleasure at the expense of responsibility? What role does the spatiality of this sport – indoor versus outdoor climbing – play in the performances of ethics, responsibility, and conformity?

Lifestyle mobilities and ethics

Mobilities is a uniquely appropriate framework from which to analyze tourism and leisure practices, as it accounts for the multiplicitous ways that such pursuits blur these definitional boundaries (see Sheller & Urry, 2006; Hannam, 2009; Cohen et al., 2015; Duncan, Cohen, & Thulemark, 2015; Rickly, Hannam, & Mostafanezhad, 2016). Lifestyle mobilities are sustained, ongoing process of semi-permanent moves with varying durations, which are integrated into everyday practices (Cohen et al., 2015; Duncan et al., 2015). Whereas lifestyle travel finds individuals working to save money in order to return to traveling, lifestyle mobilities exhibit stronger leisure components that are incorporated into continuous travel patterns (see Boon, 2006; Filho, 2010; Rickly, 2016). Yet, lifestyle mobilities are also similar to, while distinct from, seasonal migration (see Thorpe, 2012) and lifestyle migration (Benson & O'Reilly, 2009; Benson, 2011). A mobilities perspective maintains the relationality of these modalities, rather than categorically isolating them.

Developing a politics of mobility, Cresswell (2010) outlines six facets that drive and/or hinder mobility: motive force, speed, rhythm, route, experience, and friction. Others have added to these, including "turbulence" (Cresswell & Martin, 2012) and "remove" (Vannini, 2011). While these facets are useful analytic tools for deconstructing mobilities, they do not fully account for the community dynamics of lifestyle mobilities, which also include cultural processes, power relations, and ethical considerations (Rickly, 2016). Indeed, considering a politics of lifestyle mobilities necessitates attention to what Urry (2002) terms "co-presence", which is relational to "nearness *and* farness, proximity *and* distance, solidity *and* imagination" (p. 266).

The performance of lifestyle mobilities is enacted both collectively and individually, as a mobile lifestyle necessitates both spatial proximity to and distance from others of a similar lifestyle choice (see also Vannini, 2011). While proximity fosters the development of social bonds, spatial distance is a factor of the lifestyle and community that is accepted as part of what it means to be hypermobile. Although community is a primary sense of belonging (Cohen, 1985), lifestyle mobilities communities are comprised of individuals following their own travel itineraries. Because lifestyle sport subcultures are "fundamentally about 'doing it', about taking part" and participating in the appropriated subcultural spaces (Wheaton, 2004, p. 4) (oftentimes within "natural" and/or outdoor spaces), those who pursue lifestyle sport mobilities do not need continuous proximity to have a sense of community and belonging (see also Wheaton, 2004; Boon, 2006; Duncan, 2008; Filho, 2010; Thorpe, 2012, 2014; Rickly-Boyd, 2012; Rickly, 2017). Their travel patterns are informed by similar leisure pursuits making them more likely to encounter one another again and again over the course of months and years. Social networks develop from these encounters so that as one arrives to an area s/he will likely have relationships or share mutual connections that facilitate inclusion.

Lifestyle is understood as a distinctive and recognizable mode of living (Sobel, 1981), and as such, is a central concept of lifestyle mobilities. Further defined, Stebbins (1997) notes that lifestyle is "organized around a set of coherent interests or social conditions or both, that is explained and justified by a set of related values, attitudes, and orientations and that, under certain conditions, becomes the basis for a separate, common social identity" (p. 350). Lifestyle is about performances of personal, internal understandings of the self as well as external, social identities. As Anderson and Erskine (2014) state, "lifestyle travel is not the active pursuit of mobility for its own sake (i.e. simply to keep moving from one random place to another), rather it is to realize identity challenge and transformation" (p. 131). Thus, Freudenhal-Pedersen (2013) suggests that, for many, mobility becomes the way to the "good life", or the means through which components of everyday life are fitted together.

In lifestyle mobilities, everyday life is made mobile. In the di-differentiation of home/away and work/leisure, distinctions between everyday life and touristic practices are also blurred suggesting that different ethical ways of being cannot be neatly segregated to home or tourism. In this way, the ethics of lifestyle mobilities is distinct from studies of tourism ethics in which touristic behaviour can be compared to everyday practices (cf. Cooke, this volume). So, while tourist practices are inspired by pursuits of pleasure, are lifestyle mobilities also pursuits of pleasure or are these about the "good life"? Pleasure, according to Aristotle is experienced in the pursuit of "the good" but may also result from unethical choices.

Importantly, lifestyle mobility is a choice that stems from privilege, as a change in lifestyle that prioritizes leisure and travel is a choice, similar to lifestyle migration (Benson & O'Reilly, 2009; Benson, 2011) and lifestyle travel (Cohen, 2010a, 2010b, 2011). Examining ethics in lifestyle mobilities hinges on the simultaneous negotiation of individuals' ethics in relation to broader social morals. Cultivating an ethics of lifestyle mobilities means attending to the sources of motivation, internal and/or external, as well as actions and social relations that result from it. One's lifestyle and mobility choices have implications for the individual in society and for fellow citizens. Ethics, thus, applies to all scales of life. Following the work of pragmatist Richard Rorty, Caton (2012) asserts that we must acknowledge the various subject positions that accompany all life's pursuits: "a full and happy life will almost inevitably involve both deeply private projects that may have no meanings to anyone else and rich public engagements that produce a sense of connection with one's fellows" (p. 1918). Similarly, Bauman (1995) discusses two scales of morality: conformity and responsibility. In conformity, individuals act within broader social conventions and institutional rules, while with responsibility the individual acts in relation to a personal commitment. In both cases, Rorty's subject positions and Bauman's relations of morality, ethics is negotiated across social scales. Thus, individuals' enactment of ethics is highly circumstantial, contextual, and informed by their own needs and relations to others involved.

Research design

The rock climbing community is divided into myriad and sometimes overlapping subcultures (see Kiewa, 2002; Cailly, 2006; Taylor, 2010). Indeed, the particular style of climbing, defined in relation to specific features of the natural environment, is central to rock many climbing identities, for examples aid, traditional, sport, bouldering, and ice climbers all engage distinct aspects of vertical natures. Lifestyle climbers, while not defined by one style of climbing instead, exhibit their dedication to the sport by maintaining minimalist, hypermobile lifestyles that prioritize climbing. Importantly, these climbers are not professionals and do not earn an income from their climbing. Yet, in giving up their sedentary residences, they travel between climbing destinations and take up temporary and/or internet-based employment along the way. While lifestyle rock climbing is a global phenomenon, most can be found in North America, with many also travelling international circuits. Lifestyle climbers are a distinct form of lifestyle mobility and, at the same time, as a subculture of the rock climbing community, there are palpable rifts and conflicts among lifestyle climbers as to the performance of this identity (see Rickly-Boyd, 2012, 2013; Rickly, 2017; Rickly & Vidon, 2017).

By their very nature, hypermobile communities are constantly in movement. Individuals travel a variety of circuits and pathways, thus making them rather difficult to study (see D'Andrea, 2006; Merriman, 2014). Therefore, this research employed a mixed-method, multi-scale approach to data collection, working from online forums to fieldwork. For on-site, qualitative investigation, one popular destination – Red River Gorge, Kentucky, USA, during its peak climbing season – was the focus of observation, interviews, and surveys. I lived in the Red August through November of 2011 observing and interacting with lifestyle climbers as they arrived for the season, moored for a few weeks to months, then departed for their next destination. Time in this community resulted in a total of 21 interviews with lifestyle climbers – six females and 15 males. The age of participants ranged from 22 to 56 years, with time spent pursuing lifestyle climbing ranging from six months to 17 years. These lifestyle climbers, as reflected in the rock climbing population in general, were predominantly white (see Erickson, 2005). All but two of the interviewees were Americans, with the exception of one Canadian and one person from France. Two respondents self-identified as gay and lesbian, respectively.

Data collection and discourse analysis also extended to social media, including the popular climbing website, Rockclimbing.com, and the local climbing website, Redriverclimbing.com, as well as climbing media (magazines, films, guidebooks, and other websites). In an age of increasing globalization, social media can foster communities that span vast distances, so while climbers do meet and perform group identities on the ground, in specific locations, websites' forums may facilitate community development and maintenance. As a result, Altheide, Coyle, and DeVriese (2008) suggest "an ethnographic perspective can be brought to bear on symbolic communication in other than 'physical spaces'" (p. 135; see also Hine, 2008).

An ethics of lifestyle climbing

For lifestyle rock climbers, the primary motivation for taking up a hypermobile lifestyle is a desire to rock climb full time. The sport thus becomes the center of their lifestyle, community, and mobility decisions. Yet, when pressed further about the lifestyles they leave behind in choosing to pursue rock climbing full time, these same individuals offer more specific social and personal contexts for this lifestyle decision. Indeed, the actual practice of rock climbing becomes a structural element upon which they can focus in order to facilitate greater change in the way they live their lives. They frequently discuss feeling alienated in their previous lifestyles and appreciative of the strong sense of community that accompanies lifestyle climbing (see Rickly-Boyd, 2012, 2013). Their framing of the decisions to take up lifestyle climbing in terms of freedom, choice, responsibility, self, trust, fun, and even sacrifice raises questions as to the ethics of their motivations and the resulting social structures that come from collective practices of lifestyle rock climbing, particularly as this pursuit is distinctly associated with outdoor climbing (as opposed to indoor "gym" climbing).

In taking responsibility for their own happiness and fulfilment, these same individuals contest normative ideals about social responsibility. That does not necessarily make their lifestyle mobility pursuit unethical, but rather encourages further interrogation of the motivations for lifestyle climbing and the social relations that result. As will be argued, while demonstrating aspects of the kind of happiness Aristotle theorizes in his *Ethics*, lifestyle climbers also challenge some of the good citizenship practices posited in his *Politics*. In other words, lifestyle climbers described senses of community that produce more deeply felt feelings of belonging and subcultural responsibility. Their citizenship practices are more insular and pragmatic within the rock climbing community. As such, attending to scale is crucial to understanding their ethics. While a responsibility to the self is foregrounded, and conformity to broader social conventions is resisted, within the rock climbing community ethics and morality are openly displayed and continually (re)negotiated.

The pursuit of pleasure

Ethics informs our sense of responsibility. Tourism, MacCannell (2011) notes, serves as an example *par excellence* of one's ethics – "The tourist embodies every modality of classical discourse on ethics: desire, freedom of choice, habit, repetition, character, and ultimate ideas about what is good, or what defines the good life" (p. 47). A question of tourist ethics, however, must extend beyond obligations and rules of conduct to the purpose and source of these rules (see Fennell, 2000). Indeed, in investigating the rules of tourism, MacCannell (2011) uncovers a new social voice of conscience: "Enjoy! [. . .] Fun in life is no longer thought to be supplementary, the result of unusual good fortune or reward for good work" (p. 51). Rather, he posits, society tells us we must seek out fun, pleasure, and enjoyment as evidence of social capital. This has become a new moral imperative. While questions of the ethics of sightseeing are important to understanding touristic motivation, expanding a similar social imperative of enjoyment to lifestyle mobilities suggests considerable ethical implications when leisure pursuits become everyday practice.

This new social and moral imperative to enjoy is a motivating force for many lifestyle climbers. While a passion for rock climbing was inspired by leisure practice, as the following quote suggests, climbing is rarely the sole reason for making such a drastic lifestyle change. This climber wrote on an online forum over the course of several months chronicling her decision process to pursue, and her preparations for, rock climbing full time. In this post, she summarized her motivation:

> I'm so looking forward to a simpler life. I'm only 26, but I feel 40. There is so much that I need to leave behind right now, so that I can focus on me. It's my

> time to be selfish, and I will relish this selfish period for as long as I can. [. . .] I feel so fortunate to have had this "awakening" at a young age . . . I can only imagine the basketcase [sic] I would be if I kept being miserable for 10 more years. I need to get to know myself, cause [sic] I've nearly forgotten who I am. I have been groomed into a corporate lemming, and nearly lost sight of what is TRULY important to me.
>
> (RC T8P32)[1]

In this excerpt, this climber hints at several aspects of ethical discourse – freedom of choice, habit, and character. Indeed, rock climbing is rationalized as both a means and an end to living the "good life". Yet, she is torn between the social pressure of career, success, and responsibility and the desire for a "simpler" and "awakened" life. But underlying this discourse is also the new social moral imperative to have as much fun as possible and to enjoy one's life. Indeed, she expressly fears not having enough fun and interprets this as a personal responsibility to "be selfish" and foreground her own pleasure. Lifestyle climbing offers a means to do this. It prioritizes one's leisure and travel desires, but the focus on rock climbing offers structure as well. Climbing becomes the central point around which lifestyle climbers can organize their new way of life and accompanying self-reflection.

According to Aristotle's (2000) *Politics*, leisure is an essential part of life. Yet, a focus on leisure in the pursuit of happiness, he argues, "would be the end of life" (p. 302), as there would be nothing left to pursue, nothing to encourage good action. This is taken up more in his *Ethics* and his description of self-indulgence, which he suggests is actually the pursuit of pleasure rather than happiness. To what extent is this lifestyle climber, and others like her, pursuing pleasure rather than happiness? Are they motivated to accumulate experiences as a form of social currency in response to the command, "Enjoy!"? These questions are not intended to pass a "right/wrong" judgment (see Freudendal-Pedersen, 2014), but to open up a dialogue on such issues. Such lifestyle pursuits are indicative of changing social behaviours and senses of responsibility to the self and to society. Thus, it is appropriate to further interrogate the motivations behind such changes, the sources of these motivations, and the social relations they produce.

The following climber offers a case in point, as he emphasizes the lifestyle component of lifestyle rock climbing and the personal responsibility it necessitates.

Climber: This is like, even if I wasn't a climber, this is my preferred lifestyle choice.

Interviewer: So rock climbing had nothing to do with this?

Climber: It definitely did. I like, you know, cozy little spaces like my van. I like to have all my stuff right there; I like the simplicity of it. I always felt like I missed my generation by a couple hundred years. So I can emulate that lifestyle in this van a little bit, with no running water, no electricity, well, limited electricity, cooking, I can see my propane going down, I can see my water going down.

> It's not like a non-renewable resource. I can, like, tell that I need to get some water. I feel like I'm more in touch with it, instead of just turning the faucet on or flicking the light on and getting a bill at the end of the month. Like, how much I use, how much I waste. I like the mobility and the freedom. And, umm . . . I don't do well with stress and with commitment, so it's nice to be able to like change locations when I need to. (Male, late 20's, lifestyle climbing for seven years)

In taking up a mobile lifestyle dedicated to climbing, this climber is minimizing his social responsibilities as well as limiting the resources at his disposal. While both he and the above climber speak about the desire for a simplified life, his is framed by notions of "freedom". He does not comment on the desire for fun or existential searching, rather freedom to be mobile and freedom from commitments to economic and financial institutions. So while he does not assert an ethical dimension to his decision to choose this lifestyle, he nevertheless frames his motivation in the virtues of moderation and temperance. In other words, he prioritizes responsibility morality over conformity morality (Bauman, 1995). This lifestyle, which requires mooring in natural environments in close proximity to climbing areas, not only necessitates such a mindset but offers the structure for which to organize one's life around these virtues.

Selfishness or social protest?

While we can identify the social imperative to have fun being taken up with this lifestyle choice, these individuals are also frequently criticized for their selfishness, both within the broader rock climbing community and from outside of it. Indeed, many leisure and hobbyist climbers criticize lifestyle climbers, or "dirtbags", as they are known within the community (see Rickly-Boyd, 2012, 2013), for fostering a negative image of all rock climbers. And while some lifestyle climbers will admit to certain elements of selfishness, many also return the criticism suggesting the more profound ethical problems lie with social ideals that are constraining to the individual, unrealistic, or unsustainable (socially, economically, and/or ecologically). These climbers challenge such social norms:

> What are we all supposed to be producing? Units of consumption or widgets to fuel the economy? Anyone can go get a job and "contribute to society"; it takes a real man/woman to embrace the ideals of freedom and sacrifice the comforts of financial gain.
>
> (RC T2P16)

> They think we're wasting our time. But, again, if you look at it from our point of view, I think it's highly pathetic to see people in traffic for two hours going into the city, working for the man, pushing the wheel, and then coming home to credit card debit, house debit, car debit, the kids crying, family problems,

> crack cocaine on the fucking street [. . .] I think it's a value that we just don't seem to understand. I don't get it, I don't know how I could work every day, 50–60 hours a week, two-weeks vacation in the summer and two-weeks in the winter and then at the end of my life I can't do anything. Might as well just do it now. That's how I see it.
>
> (Male, mid-30's, lifestyle climbing for 12 years)

If ethics is about the responsibility we take, or do not take, in our everyday lives, these climbers are quick to question, figuratively and rhetorically, the social norms that assert one's responsibility and contribution to society. Both climbers above suggest this lifestyle mobility is a rejection of consumerism as an unethical social condition. While the first climber frames her/his pursuit of the climbing "good life" as an embracing of freedom and a sacrifice of comfort that comes with consumerism, the second climber is more specific about the effects of debt burdens on quality of life. In other words, both suggest that a "good life" is much less achievable when operating within the social norms of consumerism.

Thus, we can ask further ethical question of lifestyle mobilities, inspired by lifestyle climbing. If lifestyle climbers pursue rock climbing full-time as a counterforce to consumerism, are they taking responsibility for their lives or just temporarily avoiding responsibility? What are the social relations that result from individuals collectively performing lifestyle climbing; do individuals maintain autonomy or do they forge alternative social responsibilities? In attending to social scales, from the personal to social, ethics continues to be a productive vein to mine for lifestyle mobilities.

Responsibility and trust

While most lifestyle climbers travel solo along individualized circuits of destinations, which are influenced by seasonality and regional preferences, circuits sometimes overlap so that climbers find themselves together in campgrounds and at crags. Global telecommunications may facilitate coordinated movements; nevertheless, most do not synchronize their arrivals and departures. As a result, individuals oftentimes find themselves amongst climbers they have never met. So while climbing may inspire their individualistic and solo travels, they depend on encountering one another at climbing destinations. Climbing is most often, and arguably most safely, performed with a partner – someone who acts as a belayer. Climbers trade off the responsibility of acting as the safety in control of the rope. Arriving at a new destination, lifestyle climbers mingle, exchanging travel stories and names of potential mutual friends. In getting to know one another, which can happen over a few hours to a couple of days, they quickly build a rapport that precipitates the shared responsibility of one another's safety while climbing. In other words, they both understand that in order to climb, they must be able to trust one another to be safe. So while lifestyle climbers leave behind many normative social responsibilities, their lifestyle mobility inspires other responsibilities and conformities. The following conversation among three lifestyle climbers illustrates the ways in which these everyday habits of safety and practices of trust cultivate a sense of community that remains at odds with social norms while also fostering shared social responsibility.

Dave: It is a vacation, really. I mean, I've had almost no responsibilities since I came down here, other than taking care of myself.

James: I feel like it isn't [a vacation], when you consider the amount of effort. The amount of work that gets put into climbing harder while you're at this location is like work. It's the same dedication, the same level of motivation to get it done.

Dave: I agree with you on that.

Leah: I'm really curious about what you just said, where you're like, "well, I have no real responsibilities when I'm here". But don't you think about having somebody else's life in your hands when you're belaying everyday? We don't even think about that as a responsibility sometimes, but wouldn't you say that's maybe more meaningful than, like, writing numbers into your computer?

Dave: No, you're right. . . [interrupted]

Leah: But why do you think that, like, culturally or as a society it's so easy to forget about a responsibility that is that kind of major and life changing, versus, like, "oh, my responsibility of getting up and being at a place at 7:00 every morning"?

Dave: No, it's a good point. I didn't think about the responsibility of belaying.

James: It influences the community a lot too. [. . .] And, I feel like having your life in someone else's hands so often, having that in the air, just builds a great, strong community.

Dave: Yeah, there's a lot of trust here.

By using socially normative rhetoric that readily distinguishes work/leisure, the conversation begins by equating lifestyle climbing to a vacation. Importantly, this comment is made by a novice lifestyle climber (Dave) who has been following this pursuit for about six months, which suggests his assessments of responsibility and freedom are more greatly informed by social norms. The juxtaposition of strict daily work schedules from his previous life make the daily freedoms of choice and leisure time on the road feel like a "vacation." The others in this conversation have been lifestyle climbing for two (James) and seven (Leah) years. Their everyday lives are much further removed from their previous work-a-day lifestyles, and as such, they are now habitually immersed in the ways in which responsibility and trust are enacted in this more insulated and isolated community. Habits and actions of trust are part of the everyday exchanges of lifestyle climbers, because in order to rock climb full time, each individual needs a partner at the rock face (Figure 4.1). That partner must offer care and attention so as to assure safety, because as Leah notes, engaging in the vertical natures of climbing and being a climbing partner means having that person's life in your hands. This is a more grievous responsibility than most face on a daily basis. Thus, at

Figure 4.1 Climbing and belaying: practices of trust and responsibility.

Photo by the author.

the heart of this mobile lifestyle community is trust, so that each is able to pursue one's leisure interest. This suggests that for the lifestyle climber community, personal pursuits are nested within broader social values; in fact, they necessitate a community-level ethic with rock climbing specific conformity morality. In terms of Bauman's (1995) morality framework, personal responsibility morality is integrated into the institutional conformity morality of the lifestyle climber subculture.

The sense of trust that the climbers in the above conversation describe is a core element of lifestyle climbing. However, the social practices surrounding performances of trust have changed as the climbing community has grown. This has resulted in changes in the way social responsibility, conformity, safety, and trust are communicated. For example, the following climber describes the mentorship-based community he was initiated into a decade ago, but which has faded in recent years with repercussions for safety, as well as community belonging.

> I definitely came from a climbing scenario where it was more mentorship based. There was the stewards of climbing, there was the folks who were interested in taking the new climber under their wings, showing the ropes, everybody's safe, and it all works out well and this knowledge trickles down. That's just not the case now. And nobody's really to blame. There's just not enough time to educate the masses. It's just not going to happen. So you have people, when you see folks doing things unsafe the community tends to turn their eyes and leave as opposed to approaching that person and helping. A big part of that is climbers are more and more entitled too, they have more information at their fingertips, they can learn in the gym, they learn in a book, they can YouTube how to belay with a gri-gri 5000 or whatever. They feel like they know how to do it, and so most of the climbers I feel like I approach come off as a little more defensive than they used to be.
>
> (Male, late 20's, lifestyle climbing for ten years)

While this climber waxes a bit nostalgic, the community structure he describes had clear mechanisms of entry and inclusion. The mentorship-based community through which he learned to climb speaks to conformity morality (Bauman, 1995). It was a system that established one's responsibility to the climbing community as part of an integration process. As a result, conformity morality was aligned with responsibility morality in that safety practices were institutionalized as collective morals.

While safety and trust remain crucial to the performance of lifestyle climbing, many of the internal mechanisms for communicating technique and monitoring safety are diminishing. This climber correlates these changes with the growth in popularity and numbers of climbers, as well as the greater availability of online resources. In other words, as the climbing community has grown considerably in the last two decades the institutionalization of community ethics is not being communicated in the same manner, which exemplifies growing perceptions of the distinctions between indoor (gym) climbing and outdoor climbing in practice and culture (see also Rickly & Vidon, 2017). Noble (2014) further elaborates on this dilemma in an article for *Climbing* magazine, advocating for climbing gyms to take more responsibility in "training" new climbers, as this is now where most are introduced to the sport before venturing outdoors. The above climber, while noting gyms as part of the challenge of maintaining traditions of ethics and safety, also notes that the wide availability of climbing information online means that a new climber no longer feels the need to be mentored. Most of the basic information about climbing is easily accessible.

Thus, he describes a lack of communication in both respects. Veteran climbers, he notes, are becoming less inclined to intervene with safety concerns and novice climbers are interpreted as more defensive when they attempt to do so. The effects of this, however, would require a longitudinal study to more fully assess the effects of (a lack of) mentorship on safety. However, it is worth noting that within the climbing community, it is common for each generation to be criticized by those that preceded them (see Taylor, 2010). Nevertheless, the ethical implications of this climber's observation are worth considering, as it suggests within this community that already privileges personal responsibility over social responsibility, the specific points where conformity morality have been emphasized are being challenged and potentially eroding. The particular ways that conformity morality, in terms of safety and trust, as well as mentorship and communication of etiquette, has been institutionalized amongst lifestyle climbers has contributed to what Aristotle described as effective politics. In other words, personal and social agendas have coincided with overlapping goals, as ends and means. This potential breakdown of mentorship and communication of safety, that many veterans increasingly "turn their eyes and leave" when they see potential danger rather than offer assistance, can have repercussions for the continuation of shared social responsibility and practices of trust that established an ethical relationship and shared morals amongst lifestyle climbers.

Conclusion

Taking up a hypermobile lifestyle informed by the pursuit of rock climbing foregrounds one's own pleasure by prioritizing personal leisure interests. Further, the performance of lifestyle climbing removes, to varying degrees, citizens from interaction with the state (economic, political, and/or financial institutions), which is counter to Aristotle's good citizenship practices. However, the social relations that are produced within the subcultural community of lifestyle climbers bring together individual and collective agendas, which Aristotle would deem effective politics. Moreover, the collective performance of lifestyle climbing produces shared responsibility and trust, which integrates a subcultural conformity morality into individual's responsibility morality (Bauman, 1995).

Is this lifestyle mobility a means or an end to the "good life"? Does this lifestyle pursuit offer a way to re-focus one's life, challenge social norms, and establish fewer but more meaningful social relationships? Does lifestyle climbing prioritize the individual's personal wants and desires, cut family and social responsibilities and provide spatial distance from the pressures of career, work, school, or other social institutions? Indeed, it does all of these things. But the extent to which each individual engages in this lifestyle mobility as a means or end is contextual and varied. Nevertheless, these are important questions to ask of our research subjects and of ourselves. Despite the variety of responses such lines of questioning produce, they facilitate conversations of "ought" rather than "is", of ethics rather than truth (Caton, 2012). What's more, as Freudendal-Pedersen (2014) suggests, when turning an ethical lens on our mobile subjects, we need to attend to *their* experience and *their* reasoning for *their* lives, no matter how we may attempt to rationalize their motives.

This area of inquiry has been gaining ground in tourism mobilities research, specifically. In MacCannell's (2011) investigation of the ethics of sightseeing, he finds that new moral imperatives to have fun are being substituted for ethical choice, and further argues that, "[e]thical tourists take responsibility for understanding their own pleasure and what, if any, 'good' it serves" (p. 53). In a similar vein, Caton (2012) advocates for a "moral turn" in tourism studies by stating that tourism must be recognized as a space that awkwardly houses both the individual's pursuit of pleasure as well as issues of social justice (see also Mostafanezhad & Hannam, 2014). Lifestyle mobilities, then, is a logical extension of this ethical lens to a situation in which travel behaviour becomes a way of life, fostering new communities and social relations which produce distinct notions of personal and social responsibility while on the move. In other words, for those that practice lifestyle mobilities, one's tourism ethics and desires are often also one's everyday behaviours and habits.

Note

1 Refers to quote from online forum discussion threads. References to individual's comments are cited in terms of the tread number and post number; in this case, RC T8P32 represents post number 32 within conversation three eight of Rockclimbing.com forum.1

References

Altheide, D., Coyle, M., & DeVriese, K. (2008). Emergent qualitative document analysis. In S. N. Hesse-Biber & P. Leavy (Eds.), *Handbook of emergent methods* (pp. 127–151). New York: The Guilford Press.

Anderson, J., & Erskine, K. (2014). Tropophilia: A study of people, place and lifestyle travel. *Mobilities*, *9*(1), 130–145.

Aristotle. (2000). *Politics*. Mineola, NY: Dover Publications, Inc.

Bauman, Z. (1995). *Life in fragments: Essays in postmodern morality*. Oxford: Blackwell Publishers.

Benson, M. (2011). The movement beyond (lifestyle) migration: Mobile practices and the constitution of a better way of life. *Mobilities*, *6*(1), 221–235.

Benson, M., & O'Reilly, K. (2009). Lifestyle migration: Escaping to the good life. In M. Benson & K. O'Reilly (Eds.), *Lifestyle migration: Expectations, aspirations and experiences* (pp. 1–14). Burlington: Ashgate.

Boon, B. (2006). When leisure and work are allies: The case of skiers and tourist resort hotels. *Career Development International*, *11*(3), 594–608.

Cailly, L. (2006). Climbing sites as counter-sites? Essay on neo-community forms and territorialisation processes at work in the practice of rock climbing. *Journal of Alpine Research*, *94*(3), 35–44.

Caton, K. (2012). Taking the moral turn in tourism studies. *Annals of Tourism Research*, *39*(4), 1906–1928.

Caton, K. (2015). Growing on the go? Moral development and tourism. *Annals of Leisure Research*, *18*(1), 1–8.

Cohen, A. P. (1985). *The symbolic construction of community*. London: Elias Horwood.

Cohen, S. A. (2010a). Chasing a myth? Searching for 'self' through lifestyle travel. *Tourist Studies*, *10*(2), 117–133.

Cohen, S. A. (2010b). Personal identity (de)formation among lifestyle travellers: A double-edged sword. *Leisure Studies*, *29*(3), 289–301.
Cohen, S. A. (2011). Lifestyle travellers: Backpacking as a way of life. *Annals of Tourism Research*, *38*(4), 1535–1555.
Cohen, S. A., Duncan, T., & Thulemark, M. (2015). Lifestyle mobilities: The crossroads of travel, leisure and migration. *Mobilities*, *10*(1), 155–172.
Cresswell, T. (2010). Towards a politics of mobility. *Environment and Planning D: Society and Space*, *28*(1), 17–31.
Cresswell, T., & Martin, C. (2012). On turbulence: Entanglements of disorder and order on a Devon beach. *Tijdschrift voor economische en sociale geografie*, *105*(5), 516–529.
D'Andrea, A. (2006). Neo-Nomadism: A theory of post-identitarian mobility in the global age. *Mobilities*, *1*(1), 95–120.
Duncan, T. (2008). The internationalisation of tourism labour market: Working and playing in a ski resort. In C. M. Hall & T. Coles (Eds.), *International business and tourism* (pp. 183–197). London: Routledge.
Duncan, T., Cohen, S. A., & Thulemark, M. (Eds.). (2015). *Lifestyle mobilities: The crossroads of travel, leisure and migration*. Aldershot, Hampshire: Ashgate.
Erickson, B. (2005). Style matters: Explorations of bodies, whiteness, and identity in rock climbing. *Sociology of Sport Journal*, *22*(2), 373–396.
Fennell, D. A. (2000). Tourism and applied ethics. *Tourism Recreation Research*, *25*(1), 59–69.
Filho, S. C. (2010). Rafting ruides: Leisure, work and lifestyle. *Annals of Leisure Research*, *13*(2), 282–297.
Freudendal-Pedersen, M. (2013). Ethics and responsibilities. In P. Adey, D. Bissell, K. Hannam, P. Merriman, & M. Sheller (Eds.), *The Routledge handbook of mobilities* (pp. 143–253). Oxon: Routledge.
Freudendal-Pedersen, M. (2014). Searching for ethics and responsibility in everyday life mobilities: The example of cycling in Copenhagen. *Sociologica*, *8*(1), 1–24.
Grimwood, B. S. R., Yudina, O., Muldoon, M., & Qui, J. (2015). Responsibility in tourism: A discursive analysis. *Annals of Tourism Research*, *50*(1), 22–38.
Hannam, K. (2009). The end of tourism? Nomadology and the mobilities paradigm. In J. Tribe (Ed.), *Philosophical issues in tourism* (pp. 101–113). Bristol: Channel View Publications.
Hine, C. (2008). Internet research as emergent practice. In S. N. Hesse-Biber & P. Leavy (Eds.), *Handbook of emergent methods* (pp. 525–541). New York: The Guilford Press.
Kiewa, J. (2002). Traditional climbing: Metaphor of resistance or metanarrative of oppression? *Leisure Studies*, *21*(1), 134–161.
MacCannell, D. (2011). *The ethics of sightseeing*. Berkeley, CA: University of California Press.
MacCannell, D. (2012). On the ethical stake in tourism research. *Tourism Geographies*, *14*(1), 183–194.
Merriman, P. (2014). Rethinking mobile methods. *Mobilities*, *9*(1), 167–187.
Mostafanezhad, M., & Hannam, K. (Eds.). (2014). *Moral encounters in tourism*. Honolulu, HI: Ashgate Press.
Noble, C. (2014). The mentorship gap: What climbing gyms can't teach you. *Climbing*. Cruz Bay Publishing, Inc.
Rickly, J. M. (2016). Lifestyle mobilities: A politics of lifestyle rock climbing. *Mobilities*, *11*(2), 243–263.

Rickly, J. M. (2017). "I'm a Red River local": Rock climbing mobilities and community hospitalities. *Tourist Studies*, *17*(1), 54–74.

Rickly, J. M., Hannam, K., & Mostafanezhad, M. (Eds.). (2016). *Tourism and leisure mobilities: Politics, work, and play*. New York: Routledge.

Rickly, J. M., & Vidon, E. S. (2017). Contesting authentic practice and ethical authority in adventure tourism. *Journal of Sustainable Tourism*, *25*(10), 1418–1433. http://dx.doi.org/10.1080/09669582.2017.1284856

Rickly-Boyd, J. M. (2012). Lifestyle climbers: Towards existential authenticity. *Journal of Sport & Tourism*, *17*(2), 85–104.

Rickly-Boyd, J. M. (2013). 'Dirtbags': Mobility, community and rock climbing as performative of identity. In T. Duncan, S. A. Cohen, & M. Thulemark (Eds.), *Lifestyle mobilities: Intersections of travel, leisure and migration* (pp. 51–64). Aldershot, Hampshire: Ashgate Publishers.

Sheller, M., & Urry, J. (2006). The new mobilities paradigm. *Environment and Planning A*, *38*(2), 207–226.

Sobel, M. E. (1981). *Lifestyle and social structure: Concepts, definitions, analyses*. New York: Academic Press.

Stebbins, R. A. (1997). Lifestyle as a generic concept in ethnographic research. *Quality & Quantity*, *31*(3), 347–360.

Taylor, J. E. (2010). *Pilgrims of the vertical: Yosemite rock climbers & nature at risk*. Cambridge, MA: Harvard University Press.

Thorpe, H. (2012). Transnational mobilities in snowboarding culture: Travel, tourism and lifestyle migration. *Mobilities*, *7*(2), 317–345.

Thorpe, H. (2014). *Transnational mobilities in action sport cultures*. Houndmills: Palgrave Macmillan.

Urry, J. (2002). Mobility and proximity. *Sociology*, *36*(2), 255–274.

Vannini, P. (2011). Constellations of ferry (im)mobility: Islandness as the performance and politics of insulation and isolation. *Cultural Geographies*, *18*(2), 249–271.

Wheaton, B. (2004). Introduction: Mapping the lifestyle sport-scape. In B. Wheaton (Ed.), *Understanding lifestyle sports: Consumption, identity and difference* (pp. 1–28). London: Routledge.

5 Dogs will be destroyed

Moral agency, the nonhuman animal, and the tourist

Arianne Reis and Eric J. Shelton

Introduction

In this chapter, we explore how nonhuman animals are represented by humans, particularly tourists, depending on how they fit within narratives that have been constructed to contain them. We do so through a first-person account of, and reflection about, an experience that triggered the initially rudimentary, though for some rather obvious, realization that contradictions in our relationships with nonhuman animals offer a useful platform to initiate philosophical discussions about constructions of meaning and worldmaking in mundane as well as "extraordinary" (or touristic) spaces. The choice of a reflective account to explore this particular experience and these contradictions is based on a trajectory that has taken both authors from the "first moment" of research to a "fifth moment" (Denzin & Lincoln, 2005), where the boundaries between researchers and subjects, as well as their worldmaking (Hollinshead, 2009), are understood as blurred, and engagement with research becomes embodied (Ali, 2012). It is also based on the acknowledgement that our research experiences and actions have impacts on our thinking, formulations, and development of critically founded narratives. In this sense, "e share Richardson's (2004) position that writing is more than "a mode of 'telling' about the social world. . . [w]riting is also a way of 'knowing' – a method of discovery and analysis" (p. 473). With this framework in mind, we build our arguments and discussions as a "writing story" (Richardson, 1995; Reis, 2011) weaved through a narrative journaled by Arianne some years ago after first encountering what she thought was a curious, if not intriguing, sign at a significant tourist location in the city of Dunedin, New Zealand. The sign read: "Dogs will be destroyed."

A reflective account of a moral trajectory

Arriving in Aotearoa/New Zealand from Brazil, I quickly learned the significance (or lack thereof) of some animals within the country's cultural landscape. Coming as I did from a country that alone is almost the area of a whole continent, and that possesses one of the largest biodiversity hot spots on the planet, I found many New Zealanders' relationships with certain species of animals a complete surprise. Brazil does not have a particularly positive record of nature preservation; between 2003 and 2014, the number of animals on the endangered species list increased by 75%, reaching 1173 species (ICMBio, 2016). Due to its physical size, its bioregional diversity, the alarming number of endangered species found there, and many other contingencies, Brazil's focus on fauna preservation today seems to be, at least to the lay audience, more general rather than specific – although, obviously, there are specific species that are targeted by specific environmental organizations.

In Aotearoa/New Zealand, the scenario is quite different. Land mammals were introduced to the island state only upon the arrival of humans (King, 1990). Following these introductions, relationships between human and nonhumans evolved to a point where currently nonhuman animals and plants tend to be placed in one of two categories: (1) those that qualify as endemic, that is, those which are either "native" species or self-introduced, and therefore likely to be eligible for protection, and (2) all the rest, labelled as "introduced" species (see Franklin, this volume, for a discussion of "feral" species in Australia). This binary reflects ways in which certain ideas of nature (Reis & Shelton, 2011) have become associated with, and foundational to, Aotearoa/New Zealand cultural narratives (Shelton & Tucker, 2008) and *nativist* discourses that afford native and endemic species certain rights that are not shared by species deemed to have been introduced (Warren, 2007).

Due to the vulnerability of native birds as prey for introduced rodents and larger mammals, specifically mustelids, the Department of Conservation (DOC), the governmental organization responsible for nature conservation in New Zealand, implements strict policies for native fauna protection throughout the nation. However, a few species, due to their endangered status and, often, their charisma, receive significantly more attention from the media, sponsoring businesses, environmental NGOs, the general public, and, consequently, government agencies like DOC. The yellow-eyed penguin (*Megadyptes antipodes*) is one such species. This bird has been the sole focus of an NGO, the Yellow-eyed Penguin Trust, and plays a central role in ecotourism on the southern coast of South Island.

In an attempt to protect penguins, a sign at a popular tourist destination and wildlife refuge in the Otago region of New Zealand warns visitors that their "dogs will be destroyed" if caught in the area where penguins, particularly yellow-eyed penguins, but also little penguins (*Eudyptula minor*), are to be found, and where they often breed. Although I now know that the word "destroyed" is often used in the English language when referring to unwanted animals, at that moment, the term caught my attention. In my first language of Portuguese, a word with parallel meaning would never be used in reference to nonhuman animals; for me, it represents the objectification of nonhuman animals as "things" that can simply be destroyed.

It is important to note that this experience came to me as a shock long before I became involved with the animal studies field. I was aware at that moment, however, that language, especially metaphor, plays an important part in the construction of meanings, which then influence social behaviour, and that if the word "destroyed" is acceptable to be used in relation to an animal, any animal for that matter, then it certainly implies a view that animals are as disposable as any other thing. A document is destroyed; a person is killed, murdered, or executed. What struck me at that moment was that when nonhuman animals, and in this particular case dogs, are unwanted, they can easily be cast as things to be destroyed. A hunter once told me, when commenting on rabbit shooting, "I'm just getting rid of that bug, that annoying little creature that's frustrating me" (Reis, 2014, p. 300). If we were to take the word "creature" seriously and ascribe to it moral and ethical considerations, we would never add "just" to our description of it. The endemic-native/introduced binary (Warren, 2007) always is in danger of promoting the view that we should destroy "that annoying little creature" simply for the fact of its being there.

Two points are worth raising here – points that are worthy of debate and for which there are no clear answers. The first is that yellow-eyed penguins often are represented as "charismatic" fauna and therefore attract tourists' interest and, consequently, revenue for the tourism industry and for conservation. Hence, there are issues far beyond their endangered status at play in their protection. In fact, some authors argue that charismatic fauna tend to attract more funding for their protection than do other less "interesting" animals (Leader-Williams & Dublin, 2000). The appropriateness of yellow-eyed penguin protection is not in question here; we certainly value their protection. But what is to be done if their protection comes at the expense of other living creatures, much like the dogs referred to in our illustration? If preservation/conservation involves the claim that every species of animal, and every individual of every species, should have their place, then we are confronted with the ethical difficulties that emerge in attempting to achieve both of these often mutually exclusive goals. We are also left to question how and why we choose certain behaviours and use certain language to deal with nonhuman creatures unwanted in a particular location.

The second, and arguably more complicated, point is that dogs are particularly popular human-companion animals in New Zealand, a country where bird life too is highly regarded, due to many bird species' endemic and native status. Cats, although also extremely popular, are more understandably regarded as problematic predators, due to the widespread recognition that they hunt many species of native birds. Dogs, in contrast, are less often viewed in such light. As in almost every Western country, dogs in New Zealand receive significant care and attention in their everyday experiences. However, dogs are also predators of penguins, as well as kiwi, and hence receive dual and contradictory treatment from local government and the general public. On one hand, dogs are a beloved companion of humans; on the other, they can be cast as unwanted things that can simply be destroyed.

The production of protection

The production of protection for endemic/native flora and fauna is situated within a politics of conservation, preservation, and restoration in Aotearoa/New Zealand.

This politics is not always obvious. When the Conservation Management Strategy for the Subantarctic Islands was approved in 1998:

> an island categorisation system was developed; visitor impacts (including tourists) were closely controlled on a precautionary basis; the status of *Olearia lyalli* as a naturally occurring species rather than a weed was established; and the eradication of pigs and cats was explicitly stated as an objective
>
> (Roberts, 2006, n/p).

The classification status of *Olearia lyalli* is particularly interesting. This species of tree daisy comprises the dominant cover of the Snares Islands and is now colonising the northern part of the Auckland group, displacing the existing Southern rata *Metrosideros umbellata*. The decision to treat *Olearia lyalli*'s colonisation as a natural process was the end result of political lobbying by individuals and groups with different opinions on how the situation should be formulated and managed. Clearly, species may have their protected/unprotected status established and changed through political processes. Engaging with this question, therefore, situates the yellow-eyed penguin also within political ecology (see Shelton, Tucker, & Zhang, 2017).

One aspect of the production of protection that has been receiving increasing attention over the last thirty years has been that of its ethics, in particular the nature of proper ethical relationships between human animals and all the rest of the nonhuman world. It is worth noting that, in general, two approaches are available in environmental ethics discourse: either (1) a particular approach to ethics may be identified, for example Kantian ethics, and its application to environmental protection explored, or (2) environmental issues may be identified and the ethical positions involved in possible responses to them discussed and adopted. Jamieson (2008) offers an analysis situated in the latter approach and, having described the ethical tensions inherent both in economically deterministic and ideas-based conceptions of environmental protection, is adamant that conservation efforts may be expended ethically without such analytic tensions having been resolved: "we do what we can, when we can" (Jamieson, 2008, p. 24). This approach to conservation ethics is clearly and openly political. For example, some birds are carried on a storm to a remote island that they begin to colonize. At issue is not just that a species from another island is colonizing, but how it got there. If it arrived through its own efforts, then is it important whether or not it was a native bird or an introduced one expanding its range? Several species of bird in New Zealand are self-introduced from Australia and, when they establish themselves, qualify as native in current conservationist ideals held by agencies such as DOC, environmental NGOs, and ecology scientists.

Jamieson's (2008) approach to the relationship between philosophy, specifically ethics, and environmental problems is that "environmental goods involve morally relevant values, and that environmental problems involve moral failings of some sort" (p. 24). He then continues to argue that "environmental problems challenge our ethical and value systems" (p. 24) and that "our thinking about the environment will improve by thinking about it in this way, and our moral and political conceptions will themselves become more sophisticated as a result of their confrontations with real environmental problems" (Jamieson, 2008, p. 25). Jamieson's ethical approach, which acknowledges the interface between ethics and politics, does away with the traditional mutually exclusive ethics/politics binary and is capable of creating negotiated moral space both for the dog and the penguin. This moral space is the result of the ongoing debate between ethics and politics as they are argued in any specific environmental situation. Aotearoa/New Zealand has an unusual environmental narrative that, since the landing of the first human animals, has included the dog.[1] James Cook's arrival in 1769 saw the beginning of a long process of Europeans transforming the already modified ecosystem to be more useful for their purposes and pleasing to the Romantic eye. This ongoing process of mixing endemic, native, and introduced flora and fauna into modified and unmodified habitat and landform, often is referred to as the production of hybrid nature (Fall, 2005; Robbins, 2004). This hybrid nature, through rendering the endemic/native/introduced argument redundant, is moral space where human animals, through environmental practice, again construct nature to suit their own purposes no less than do those who are wedded to the moral-high-ground claim of the concepts of nativism. Ultimately, for example, the hybrid nature lobby may logically claim there is no environmental reason to create national parks other than for recreational purposes, while the nativist lobby, equally logically, may lobby for ever increasing numbers of protected areas to preserve habitat for species favoured by their criteria. This is an ethical and political debate that produces moral space, while also accommodating day-to-day practice.

The problematics of language

The problematics of labelling species as endemic/native/exotic/introduced, with some being labelled as "pest species" as a descriptor for what are better described as "individual animals and animal species unwanted by particular people in a particular location at a particular time", have long been discussed (Warren, 2007). Potts (2009) described the role of language in producing pest status for the brushtail possum (*Trichosurus vulpecula*), a species demonized (through figurative language) in Aotearoa/New Zealand and protected (also through figurative language) in Australia. Changes in language also may lead to changes in the legal status of a species; for example, in Aotearoa/New Zealand, the stoat (*Mustela ermina*) was moved from being a farmed resource to a prohibited pest species. Such a change in status – from being a resource farmed for profit to being a pest on which money is spent in order to achieve their eradication – often is embedded within some form of narrative of nature. Individual people perform specific narratives of nature/environment and in these embodied roles inescapably engage, either explicitly or implicitly, with some system of philosophy of nature. These systems may include an ethics of environment, however muddled, involving their relationships with landforms, flora, and fauna (the last of which can include other human animals present). Grimwood (2011) engages with such ethics of environment when he envisions enhanced individual responsibility within the multiple natures of recreational canoe travel as constituting moral space in its consideration and practice.

Another important aspect of language that has been deliberately challenged in this text is the use of the terms "human animal" and "nonhuman animal" rather than "human" and "non-human animals," let alone "humans" and "animals." This semantic nicety does very little to alter the human – other species binary, nor does it alter the fact that presumably only humans, through language, construct the world this way. However, it does indicate an acknowledgement that, although irrevocably separate from human animals, other animals are part of the moral and ethical world we have constructed.[2]

Those nonhuman animals who best qualify as charismatic fauna are those who most appeal to humans, in part because human values can most easily be imposed upon them. For example, in Africa, the class of charismatic fauna seems often limited to the "big five" on the Serengeti. The inclusion/exclusion rules for being charismatic vary from tourism product to tourism product and are not based on membership of any particular ecosystem array. Invertebrates are crucial to ecosystems but are unlikely to be frequently featured as the basis of a tourism product.[3]

There are obvious complexities associated with popular rhetoric and the philosophies of nature related to these conflicting positions held by dogs in the narrative presented above. The use of the word destroyed demonstrates the dual character that dogs, and some other nonhuman animals, possess in our society: a creature that we need and want to gaze at, or even interact with, versus a simple object that can be easily disposed of. In this sense, nonhuman animals, in general, never reach the status of subjects in human animal society. Jamal, Everett, and Dann (2003), particularly with respect to natural area destinations, identify "the performative and ideological nature of language (and) how subjects are 'interpellated' by language . . . discursively produced as a subject through the performative speech-act . . . The 'subject' is enacted through language ([and] hence should be thought of as a linguistic category)" (p. 158–159). Certain individual nonhuman animals are chosen to act as the embodiment of such a subject position. The status of subject is constructed by the human animal and then granted to, or imposed upon, the individual nonhuman animal based on the kinds of interaction the two are to engage in. *Free Willy*, for example, was a campaign where many thousands of human animals granted the status of subject to one whale, a nonhuman animal, situating it then within human moral space. Statements like "I love my dog, she understands everything I say" resonate here, as subject status is granted by the human animal to the nonhuman animal. Each species, however, of which these individuals are constitutive, seems to be forever stuck in a position of some sort of objectification, being stuck as an incomplete subject, where human animals attach to them the meanings that are convenient to the human animals at any particular time. Using an academic postcolonial term, they are always the "other," who we try to understand only so we can benefit from the knowledge gained. It is an instrumental perspective that guides the standard human interaction with all other animals of this planet. Pet dogs satisfy some of our emotional needs, while our taking good care of them serves almost as their reward. That same dog, however, if caught killing a penguin, then would qualify for destruction, as he would be interfering with another aim of ours, that is, protecting a species for which we human animals are, in fact, the cause of its endangered status through habitat loss and the introduction of the dog in the first place. The dog and penguin both have rights, and rights-based ethical systems are problematic. Subjecthood incorporates both a conceptual repertoire and a location for human and (some) nonhuman animals

> within the structure of rights for those that use that repertoire. Once having taken up a particular position as one's own, a person inevitably sees the world from the vantage point of that position and in terms of the particular images, metaphors, storylines and concepts which are made relevant within the particular discursive practice in which they are positioned.
>
> (Davies & Harre, 1999, p. 46)

In the case of Arianne's encounter with the "dogs will be destroyed" sign, it seems that, upon entering a particular touristic world, for example that of nature-based tourism, dogs become "out of place." The dog as a nonhuman animal finds itself loved when in its domestic setting, and vilified when it attacks and kills the charismatic fauna that form the raw material for a nature-based tourism product. In fact, we contend that dogs are being moved, through language and practice, between two distinct positions in moral space, and that in being so moved, their status is changed from creatures worthy of care to predators of protected species. The first, familiar space is the moral space where dogs are well established and regarded as companions and as part of the family. This privileged position may be revoked if, for example, the dog attacks and seriously injures a family member, in which case, it is put down. Allowing for such exceptions, it is, in most instances, the urban space where dogs are bred to be owned and taken care of. A second, less familiar space is the wild space, where dogs are viewed as alien and treated as invasive, feral, and predatory. When certain contingencies are operating, these two socially constructed nonhuman animal subject positions may be embodied in the same individual dog, depending upon which behavioural repertoire it is performing. When moved within moral space, say, pet to predator, the descriptive language associated with each subject position needs to be modified and adapted in order to determine the dog's new social status. Therefore, language that often is used to refer to pests, vermin, and invasive species is then employed to refer to dogs when they are performing a subject position where they now are considered alien. The objectification of the nonhuman animal is clear in such a space, not only through this specific use of language, but also through the practices derived from such language. If subsequently moved back to a moral space where dogs are accepted, provisionally, "as they are," they may receive compassionate treatment; NGOs are available, dedicated to their care, and, if their suffering is deemed to be excessive, they are "put down." Again, language here performs an important role in the objectification of the nonhuman animal. For human animals, euthanasia is the word to be employed, and it is a highly contested practice. In order to be applied to dogs, the language is adapted again, but now works to reflect a more compassionate response from human animals. There, the practice is a common one and is regarded as being "humane." The nature tourist, insightfully or in ignorance, engages in worldmaking while enmeshed in these linguistic complexities.

Moving on through language: the Aotearoa/ New Zealand nature-tourist space

In 2016, the New Zealand government committed itself to an aspirational vision of making the entire country predator-free by 2050 (Department of Conservation, 2017). Such a plan fits well with the kind of nature-based tourism product this country is best known for (Shelton & Tucker, 2008). Alongside any move toward predator-free status, and its inherent intensive species management approach to conservation, conceptually there has been a marked paradigm shift from the notion that there is a self-regulating, long term "balance of nature" to the idea of the "flux of nature," where ecosystem arrays are forever changing and, consequently, there is no possibility of stasis, currently or anytime in the future. This is a "move that is now virtually complete" (Callicott, 2008, p. 571). However, moving toward predator-free status still is better suited to a balance of nature paradigm since such status is at least in part intended to reproduce older, allegedly stable, regional ecosystems. Morton (2007) goes as far as to claim nature itself is "a transcendental term in a material mask" (p. 1), but, nevertheless, the idea of a material Nature retains its strong position as a contextual space within which to situate actions labelled preservation, environmental protection, and conservation (Soper, 1995, 2011). Different and competing ideas of nature, such as those described by Reis and Shelton (2011), produce different and competing notions of care, and how contestations are inscribed/interpreted and possibly negotiated through different and competing languages/discourses, including that of tourism.

Tourists' production and consumption of such space may be situated within various notions of nature (Reis & Shelton, 2011), one of which is moral space, understanding morality to be the "capacity for considering how things should be" (Caton, 2012, p. 1907). This understanding involves the notion of "the good" (Parker, 2007). Behind every element of nature-tourist performance are the key "goods" the performers live by, shaping their acts of moral deliberation and choice.

Within tourism, one specific good is authenticity. Jamal and Hill (2002) pointed out that "[w]hen it comes to the tourist's experience, the search for authenticity is an . . . ethical/moral and spiritual quest" (p. 101). Engaging in performances of tourism that promote conservation is such an ethical/moral quest. As part of their "last chance" (Lemelin, Stewart, & Dawson, 2012) touristic worldmaking, ecotourists demand to see particular endangered species, in this case, penguins. This demand is intended to encourage conservation of these species and hence affects the ways other animals are morally positioned with respect to the protected species. In this case, dogs are the other species and are positioned as predators, instead of as, for example, working dogs or pets.

The nature-based tourist may perform conservation by invoking a particular notion of worldmaking where "the declarative and clearly pungently political force of tourism . . . is deployed in worldmaking fashion in concert with . . . other . . . narrative-issuing mediating forces in and across society" (Hollinshead, 2009, p. 140). One such narrative-issuing mediating force is the print and other media produced by the tourism industry and offering tourists a popular (mis) understanding of nature. We claim, through our narrative of the "dogs will be destroyed sign," that nonhuman animals, thus produced and considered by world-making tourists as anthropomorphic moral actors, may be subjected to an imposed spatial and temporal moral trajectory. This moral trajectory means nonhuman animals may fall in and out of favour, according to the intentions of the very tourists who have brought them into narrative existence. By this we mean that of all the nonhuman animals available, only those that fit within a useful narrative are given attention. This morality gestures to Mostafanezhad and Hannam's (2014) insight that "morality is embedded in histories and landscapes of power and uneven social relations" (p. 1). This situation characterizes postcolonial relationships between tourists, making their worlds, and the nonhuman animals who are forced to inhabit these gazed-upon touristic worlds. Charismatic fauna, especially those whose existence is under threat, are attributed the moral high ground, while unwanted pests are allocated to narratives that focus on a worsening environmental situation (Shelton & Tucker, 2008) and are of dubious worth as moral agents.

The flux of nature paradigm, with its notion of nature as dynamic and never fixed, is able to incorporate the notion also of hybrid nature, where endemic, native, and introduced species all are attributed intrinsic and extrinsic value, either deliberately or through everyday practice. This allocation of value allows for acts of management of nature to be both moral and practical, whereas a balance of nature paradigm makes intervention and management within a strictly nativist perspective problematic. Tourists may hold either paradigm or may hold views that are inconsistent and theoretically incoherent (Reis, 2012). One such widely held, but unfounded, belief is that the balance of nature is maintained by the evolutionary processes associated with Charles Darwin's ideas on the "survival of the fittest." Darwin never actually proposed such a process, but this "fake truth" has entered the lexicon and must be taken into account when estimating tourists' assumed knowledge. However incorrect, these ill-informed beliefs constitute moral space that allows for the tourists' well-meaning performances of what they consider to be the good.

Part of tourists' worldmaking involves the production of such moral space, through which moral trajectories, that is, the good in time and space, may be imposed on nonhuman animals. That "the dodo became extinct because it couldn't adapt" is an example of such an imposition [countered by Fuller (2002)]. For the human animal (a generalist), adaptation is a moral process, worthy of praise, while the dodo (a specialist) is judged harshly for allowing itself to become extinct. Our intention here is to draw attention to the complexity of the various environments nonhuman animals inhabit. Charismatic fauna help exemplify this complexity; even if iconic-single-species-focused conservation is the least effective form of whole-of-ecosystem conservation, this is unlikely to change the moral trajectory, of say, effort involved in reintroduction to the no longer available wild.

The Aotearoa/New Zealand government's current aspirational conservation goal of making the country predator-free by 2050 may usefully be considered as a more sophisticated version of a previous New Zealand project to eradicate *hydatids*, a parasite passed from untreated dogs to sheep. Signs to the effect that, if found on farmland, "dogs will be destroyed" were common, and this warning was intended to protect the national sheep flock of over 70 million at its peak in 1982. Rhetoric around the relationship between livestock, the destruction of dogs, and profitable agricultural practice is central to the New Zealand story of nationhood. The current predator-free plan also may be considered to be a series of species-specific or more general uneven social relationships involving human animals and nonhuman animals. We claim the predator-free by 2050 campaign provides a focus and structure for the production and delivery of conservation ideology and effort in a way similar to the "dogs will be destroyed" threat of a previous era, but now reformulated within a tourist economy.

Conclusion

In summary, what that sign "dogs will be destroyed" reveals is a dramatic inconsistency, not only in our treatment of nonhuman animals, even of individuals of the same species, but, more importantly, an inconsistency in the philosophies of selfhood and subject position underpinning the pet/predator/charismatic raw material for nature-based tourism narrative. In all three categories, there is an instrumental and utilitarian ethics governing the appropriate use of, say, dogs. However, in one instance, there is an acknowledgement of rights, welfare, interests, and sentience, providing for an interest-based moral treatment. As a predator of charismatic fauna or, more appropriately, of a valued tourism product, the dog loses its status of being worthy of moral consideration, although retaining mandated ethical consideration. This moral/ethical overlap highlights the fact that these ethical tensions have not been, and are unlikely ever to be, solved.

It is important also to note that this tension is in part created by the fact that penguins too have interests, and that their interests are ignored by the predatory instincts of dogs, alien to the penguin environment. Therefore, in order to guarantee the penguins' interests are met, humans act, through legislation, regulation, and practice, to extinguish the dogs' interests, since the penguins are classified as endangered and are therefore to be protected. Also, as noted, often the penguins are regarded as charismatic fauna and form the basis for ecotourism. This extinguishing of one species' interests, by human animals, in order to privilege the interests of another species of animals, is central to conservation efforts in Aotearoa/New Zealand. Human animals' introduction of previously absent species into existing ecosystems has created situations that now are irreversible. Human animals have adopted the position of being arbiters and managers of nonhuman animals' interests, but this management always is moderated by human animals' own interests.

To return to earlier aspects of our discussion, language is central to the construction of meanings of the material world and the values of human animal society. Our use of complex language is one of the reasons why some academics differentiate our society from other animals' societies. Therefore, the interpretations that can be drawn from our use of language are significant, as they not only help in the construction of meanings but also influence, and can often dictate, behaviours. To inform dog owners that their dogs can be destroyed if not "well behaved" does not contribute positively to the construction of a society that is predicated upon an understanding that all living things are integral elements of the same, shared planet. Nature-based tourists' engagement in ethical and moral worldmaking should involve critical engagement with the various interests of the nonhuman animals encountered.

Notes

1 Prior to the arrival of human animals, New Zealand had been isolated from the other constituent parts of the supercontinent of Gondwana for long enough to have evolved as a landmass dominated by birds. Mammals were limited to bats and marine mammals. Maori, the first settlers, brought with them both Kiore (*Rattus exulans*) and a companion dog, Kuri (*Canis familiaris*).

2 Here we wish to draw the reader's attention to the fact that we are aware of the philosophical debate that deals with the question of what constitutes a human being and what constitutes an "animal" or a "beast." However, this debate is beyond the scope of this chapter and is not a theme we will pursue here. A seminal reference for this discussion is Tim Ingold's (1988) edited book *What Is an Animal?*

3 For examples of exceptions to this rule, see the work of Lemelin on insects and tourism/leisure (Lemelin, 2007, 2009, 2013a, 2013b).

References

Ali, N. (2012). Researcher reflexivity in tourism studies research: Dynamical dances with emotions. In I. Ateljavic, N. Morgan, & A. Pritchard (Eds.), *The critical turn in tourism studies: Creating and academy of hope* (pp. 13–26). London: Routledge.

Callicott, J. (2008). The implications of the 'shifting paradigm' in ecology for paradigm shifts in the philosophy of conservation. In M. P. Nelson & J. Callicott (Eds.), *The wilderness debate rages on: Continuing the great new wilderness debate* (pp. 571–600). Athens, GA: University of Georgia Press.

Caton, K. (2012). Taking the moral turn in tourism studies. *Annals of Tourism Research, 39*(4), 1906–1928.

Davies, B., & Harre, R. (1999). Positioning the discursive production of selves. *Journal for the Theory of Social Behaviour, 20*(1), 43–63.

Denzin, N. K., & Lincoln, Y. (Eds.). (2005). *The Sage handbook of qualitative research* (3rd ed.) Thousand Oaks, CA: SAGE.

Department of Conservation. (2017). *Predator free 2020.* Retrieved from www.doc.govt.nz/predator-free-2050.

Fall, J. (2005). *Drawing the line: Nature, hybridity and politics in transboundary spaces.* Aldershot: Ashgate.

Fuller, E. (2002). *Dodo: From extinction to icon.* London: Harper Collins.

Grimwood, B. S. (2011). “Thinking outside the gunnels”: Considering natures and the moral terrains of recreational canoe travel. *Leisure/Loisir*, *35*(1), 49–69.

Hollinshead, K. (2009). The ‘worldmaking’ prodigy of tourism: The reach and power of tourism in the dynamics of change and transformation. *Tourism Analysis*, *14*, 537–555.

Ingold, T. (Ed.). (1988). *What is an animal?* London: Unwin Hyman.

Instituto Chico Mendes de Conservação da Biodiversidade (ICMBio). (2016). *Brazil red book of threatened species of fauna*. Brasília: ICMBio.

Jamal, T., Everett, J., & Dann, G. M. (2003). Ecological rationalization and performative resistance in natural area destinations. *Tourist Studies*, *3*(2), 143–169.

Jamal, T., & Hill, S. (2002). (Post)touristic spaces of (in)authenticity? In D. Graham (Ed.), *The tourist as a metaphor of the social world* (pp. 77–107). New York: CABI Pub.

Jamieson, D. (2008). *Ethics and the environment*. Cambridge: Cambridge University Press.

King, C. M. (Ed.). (1990). *The handbook of New Zealand mammals*. Oxford: Oxford University Press.

Leader-Williams, N., & Dublin, A. T. (2000). Charismatic megafauna as ‘flagship species’. In A. Entwistle & N. Dunstone (Eds.), *Priorities for the conservation of mammalian diversity: Has the panda had its day?* (pp. 53–84). Cambridge: Cambridge University Press.

Lemelin, R. H. (2007). Finding beauty in the dragon: The role of dragonflies in recreation and tourism. *Journal of Ecotourism*, *6*(2), 139–145.

Lemelin, R. H. (2009). Goodwill hunting: Dragon hunters, dragonflies and leisure. *Current Issues in Tourism*, *12*(5–6), 553–571.

Lemelin, R. H. (2013a). To bee or not to bee: Whether ‘tis nobler to revere or to revile those six-legged creatures during one’s leisure. *Leisure Studies*, *32*(2), 153–171.

Lemelin, R. H. (Ed.). (2013b). *The management of insects in recreation and tourism*. Cambridge: Cambridge University Press.

Lemelin, R. H., Stewart, E., & Dawson, J. (2012). An introduction to last chance tourism. In R. H. Lemelin, J. Dawson, & E. Stewart (Eds.), *Last chance tourism: Adapting tourism opportunities in a changing world* (pp. 3–9). London: Routledge.

Morton, T. (2007). *Ecology without nature: Rethinking environmental aesthetics*. Cambridge, MA: Harvard University Press.

Mostafanezhad, M., & Hannam, K. (2014). Introduction to moral encounters in tourism. In M. Mostafanezhad & K. Hannam (Eds.), *Moral encounters in tourism* (pp. 1–16). London: Routledge.

Parker, D. (2007). *The self in moral space: Life narrative and the good*. Ithaca, NY: Cornell University Press.

Potts, A. (2009). Kiwis against possums: A critical analysis of anti-possum rhetoric in Aotearoa New Zealand. *Society and Animals*, *17*, 1–20.

Reis, A. C. (2011). Bringing my creative self to the fore: Accounts of a reflexive research endeavour. *Creative Approaches to Research*, *4*(1), 2–18.

Reis, A. C. (2012). Experiences of commodified nature: Performances and narratives of tourists on Stewart Island, New Zealand. *Tourist Studies*, *12*(3), 304–323.

Reis, A. C. (2014). Hunting the exotic: Practices, discourses, and narratives of hunting in New Zealand. *Society & Animals*, *22*, 289–308.

Reis, A. C., & Shelton, E. (2011). The nature of tourism studies. *Tourism Analysis*, *16*(3), 375–384.

Richardson, L. (1995). Writing-stories: Co-authoring ‘The Sea Monster’, a writing-story. *Qualitative Inquiry*, *1*(2), 189–203.

Richardson, L. (2004). Writing: A method of inquiry. In S. N. Hesse-Biber & P. Leavy (Eds.), *Approaches to qualitative research: A reader on theory and practice* (pp. 473–495). Oxford: Oxford University Press.

Robbins, P. (2004). Comparing invasive networks: Cultural and political biographies of invasive species. *Geographical Review*, *94*(2), 139–156.

Roberts, A. (2006). *Present management of the Auckland Islands National Nature Reserve by the Department of Conservation*. Paper presented at the Royal Society of New Zealand Subantarctic Symposium, Wellington, New Zealand.

Shelton, E. J., & Tucker, H. (2008). Managed to be wild: Species recovery, island restoration and nature-based tourism in New Zealand. *Tourism Review International*, *11*, 205–212.

Shelton, E., Tucker, H., & Zhang, J. (2017). A political ecology of the yellow-eyed penguin in southern New Zealand: A conceptual and theoretical approach. In I. Borges de Lima & R. Green (Eds.), *Wildlife tourism, environmental learning and ethical encounters* (pp. 21–32). Geoheritage, Geoparks and Geotourism (Conservation and Management Series). New York: Springer.

Soper, K. (1995). *What is nature?* Oxford: Blackwell Publishers.

Soper, K. (2011). Tim Morton: The ecological thought. *Radical Philosophy*, *165*, 55.Warren, C. (2007). Perspectives on the 'alien' versus 'native' species debate: A critique of concepts, language and practice. *Progress in Human Geography*, *31*(4), 427–446.

6 Vegetarian ecofeminism in tourism

Emerging tourism practices by institutional entrepreneurs

Giovanna Bertella

Introduction

Ecofeminism is often described as a value system resulting from a critical analysis of our position in the world in relation to other humans, animals, and nature (Gaard, 1993; Adams & Gruen, 2014). At the core of ecofeminism is the call for the end of any kind of oppression and the exposure of the frequently implicit forces upon which oppressive behaviours rely. Within tourism contexts, ecofeminism can offer important alternatives to traditional approaches of environmentalism and animal ethics (Yudina & Fennell, 2013). More specifically, vegetarian ecofeminism can be adopted to approach the study of food-related tourism business activities.

This chapter reports on a case study of tourism entrepreneurs who are vegetarian and whose practices seemingly align with the main tenets of ecofeminism. Vegetarian food experiences viewed as alternative to mainstream food experiences have been previously studied adopting an ecofeminist perspective (Bertella, 2018). Similarly, vegetarian food practices initiated by entrepreneurs can be viewed as alternative business practices and can be studied adopting the ecofeminism perspective. Based on this idea and adopting central concepts from the institutional entrepreneurship literature, this chapter aims to investigate how tenets of ecofeminism are being put into practice by tourism entrepreneurs, and how these entrepreneurs contribute to the emergence of new practices as the first level of institutional change. The case study concerns two rural tourism organizations in Italy, one private and one community owned. The focus of the empirical investigation is placed on (1) the institutional fields where the organizations operate, (2) the entrepreneurs' perspectives on the central tenets of ecofeminism in relation to nature and animals, and (3) the entrepreneurs' capacities in terms of introducing change in the tourism sector.

The chapter begins by presenting the main tenets of ecofeminism, with special focus on vegetarian ecofeminism. Such tenets are discussed in relation to the tourism business context using central concepts of the institutional entrepreneurship literature – more specifically, the concepts of institution, institutional field, institutional change, practice, proto-institution, and institutional entrepreneur. The method applied to investigate the case study is then described, followed by the main findings and the conclusion.

Theoretical background

Ecofeminism

In her essay "Feminism and Ecology: Making Connections," Karen Warren (1987) argued that the connections between the oppression of women and the oppression of nature are often ignored. Warren was among the early ecofeminists who argued that environmental theories tend to overlook dominant underlying hierarchical dualisms according to which nature is viewed as subaltern to culture and instrumental to human needs (Birkeland, 1993; Gaard, 1993; Adams & Gruen, 2014). For example, Birkeland (1993) reviews several environmental theories, such as eco-Marxist theory and Deep Ecology, and argues that although useful in the analysis of specific aspects of environmental problems, these theories are embedded in a patriarchal construction of reality and lack an integration of individual and institutional impediments to change.

Similarly, ecofeminism challenges animal ethics positions of utilitarianism and animal rights (Gruen, 2011, 2015). Although each of these positions shares a concern about the limited moral relevance recognized and practiced towards animals by humans, ecofeminism has a distinctive approach that, conceptually, locates humans together with other animals and, methodologically, does not privilege the use of rationality and abstraction at the expense of emotions and a contextual perspective. Ecofeminism highlights the importance of all animals in their individuality, as well as the emotional relationships among animals and between humans and animals. On this basis, ecofeminists, in particular those ecofeminists following the so-called "care tradition," highlight the moral responsibility that we humans have towards each animal, recognizing its differences from and similarities to us and other animals (Donovan & Adams, 2007). These ecofeminists argue for the importance of conceptualizing our relations with animals using our emotional moral capacities, described often in terms of compassion (Curtin, 2014; Gruen, 2015).

Vegetarian ecofeminists

Some ecofeminists advocate vegetarianism as a moral choice of compassion. Vegetarian ecofeminism emerges from criticism of ecofeminism itself (Gaard, 2002). Vegetarian ecofeminists argue that there are numerous animal-related conceptualizations and activities that are in clear conflict with the main philosophical foundations of ecofeminism (Gaard, 2002; Adams, 1993). An example of this is the representation and use of women's and animals' bodies and body parts as consumable and disposable in today's society, an aspect broadly discussed in relation to society's structures of oppression by Carol Adams (1990) in her book *The Sexual Politics of Meat: A Feminist-Vegetarian Critical Theory*.

Vegetarian ecofeminists argue that the discrimination against animals based on their belonging to other species – referred to as speciesism – is akin to various forms of oppression towards some human groups, such as women (Young, 1990; Gruen, 1996; Hawkins, 1998). In contrast to other ecofeminists who tend to overlook this aspect, vegetarian ecofeminists engage in the debate about the use of animals by humans. According to their view, animal oppression is widespread in our society, often as part of tradition and as a consequence of the industrial production system. This is particularly evident in those cases where animals are used as food. Here, animals are exploited and positioned as an "object" violently enacted upon.

Some ecofeminists recognize that animal-derived food activities are influenced by several factors, and thus warrant a contextual approach to vegetarianism. Although not justifying oppressive behaviours, contextual factors are taken into account in order to understand animal-derived food production and consumption and to propose feasible alternatives (Curtin, 1991; Twine, 2014). For example, Curtin (1991) notes that emergency and geographical circumstances can make vegetarianism difficult. The same can be said for specific social and cultural environments where meat-eating is the dominant norm.

Eating animals and tourism practices by vegetarian entrepreneurs

Eating animals and the rejection of eating animals can be studied using the institutional theory framework (Scott, 2007). An institution is a set of formal rules, informal agreements, and assumptions that are shared within an organization or community (Bruton, Ahlstrom, & Li, 2010). Eating animals can be viewed as an institution that is the result of cultural-cognitive and normative forces – those that point to the legitimacy and opportunity of conforming to assumptions that are taken for granted. These assumptions concern the view of animals as being the objects of legitimate oppression in relation to the use of their bodies, which can provide food (nutrition, symbolic value, entertainment) for humans.

Within the institutional theory framework, entrepreneurship scholars focus on how actors can change institutions. In this context, the concept of "institutional entrepreneurs" is used to indicate "actors who leverage resources to create new or transform existing institutions" (Battilana, Leca, & Boxenbaum, 2009, p. 68). Three levels of institutionalization are identified: practices, standards, and policies (Pacheco, York, Dean, & Sarasvathy, 2010). Practices are the first level towards institutional change and can be described as not formalized and explicitly regulated behaviours that are performed by a more or less limited group of people. Standards and policies reflect deeper levels of institutionalization, with standards being often explicit sets of rules, and policies being characterized by formally and officially approved rules. The idea of institutional change is that practices are performed and can become normalized and developed into standards and policies, and, ultimately, into new institutions.

Bava, Jaeger, and Park (2008) note that food practices are repetitive behaviours based on internalized ideas that are implicitly shared among the members of a group and perceived as legitimate and meaningful by those who perform them. Eating animals in particular is rooted in our society and supported by complex mechanisms of self-identity and belonging, which turn it into an institutionalized practice of oppression (Loughnan, Brock, & Haslam, 2014; Cudworth, 2015).

Eating animal is also regulated by standards and policies, like those concerning slaughtering methods and animal agriculture. Accordingly, the eating of animals qualifies as an institution.

Ethical vegetarian entrepreneurs

In the last two decades, the number of vegetarians in several Western countries has increased considerably, with important consequences on food-related activities, including consumption acts, such as shopping and dining out (Rivera & Shani, 2013). Motivations for being vegetarian can be health-related, ethics-driven, or both. In the ethics case, motivations are often linked to a moral standpoint that rejects animal oppression and values concern for the natural environment or social justice issues (Ruby, 2012). Ethical vegetarianism thus represents an alternative lifestyle movement centred on the rejection of the dominant perspective of ethics (Haenfler, Johnson, & Jones, 2012).

It can be assumed that some of the people who work in tourism and hospitality are ethical vegetarians, adhering more or less explicitly to the main tenets of vegetarian ecofeminism. In this case, the type of business they develop, their strategies, and their daily activities may be affected by their lifestyle. These tourism operators can be seen as institutional entrepreneurs who follow and promote their lifestyle – that is, change agents within institutions who mobilize resources to transform those institutions in ways that align with their own values or interests (Di Maggio, 1988; Pacheco et al., 2010). Applying this definition, vegetarian tourism entrepreneurs are entrepreneurs who develop their businesses on the basis of beliefs and values that are alternatives to the dominant ones concerning eating animals. This can be explained by their need for coherence in relation to their beliefs, their desire to promote such beliefs, and their interest in exploiting a business opportunity targeting a growing market segment.

The institutional entrepreneurship literature identifies entrepreneurs' capacities as relevant factors in the emergence of new practices and institutions (Battilana et al., 2009). Crucial among these are the creativity and the business-related skills required to gain access to the necessary resources for the implementation of innovations. Here, the communication of an entrepreneur's vision and ideas are particularly important in contributing to and gaining broader acceptance. For example, entrepreneurs aligned with vegetarian ecofeminism can frame their ideas by referring to the moral dimension of eating animals and highlight the rational and emotional aspects of making such food choices. Social capital is also recognized as an important factor, together with the contextual position of the entrepreneurs in terms of legitimacy and authority (Battilana et al., 2009).

Vegetarian tourism practices

Although their motivation can be personal, vegetarian entrepreneurs initiate and participate in the implementation of changes to existing institutions, promoting new beliefs and values (Battilana et al., 2009; Bruton et al., 2010). In this context, the emergence of vegetarian tourism practices can be analyzed by adopting the concept of the "institutional field" (Battilana et al., 2009). This is understood as "a set of organizations that constitute a recognized area of life, are characterized by structured network relations, and share a set of institutions" (Lawrence & Phillips, 2004, p. 690). In the case of food and tourism, the specific institutional field is relative to all those organizations that are recognized as legitimate and relevant actors in food-related practices, and their relations. This includes, for example, restaurants, specialized shops, and food producers. The shared set of institutions among such organizations is based on the assumption presented above about the subordinate status of animals in comparison to humans.

The literature identifies the following factors as relevant to institutional field dynamics: the degree of heterogeneity and institutionalization, the presence of "institutional defenders," and the social position that the entrepreneurs as change agents have in the specific field (Levy & Scully, 2007; Battilana et al., 2009). The case of ethical vegetarian entrepreneurs can be particularly challenging with regard to these elements, as in many places, eating animals is a widespread and deeply rooted phenomenon, and, although there has been a recent increase, vegetarians are still a minority of the population in Western countries.

Eventually, the practices of vegetarian entrepreneurs may initiate a process that leads to the emergence of proto-institutions, understood here as institutions-in-the-making, which are "narrowly diffused and only weakly entrenched, but that have the potential to become widely institutionalized" (Lawrence, Hardy, & Phillips, 2002, p. 283). Change towards a new institution can emerge through the collaboration of the organizations performing such practices, and also in a more distributed and uncoordinated way (Battilana et al., 2009; Rao, Morrill, & Zald, 2000). So, for example, in the context of vegetarian tourism practices, this can lead to a network of collaborating organizations, including the tourism and food sectors, as well as other sectors offering products and services potentially related to vegetarianism, and also non-profit organizations concerned about animals and environmental issues.

Method

In order to explore how tourism practices emerge in line with vegetarian ecofeminism, an empirical investigation was conducted in the form of a case study. The aims were to uncover the following:

1. The relevant institutional field related to food practices: degree of heterogeneity and institutionalization, the presence of institutional defenders;
2. entrepreneurs' perspectives on the central tenets of ecofeminism in relation to nature and animals;
3. entrepreneurs as potential change agents: their capacities in terms of creativity, business-related skills, and communication strategies, and their social capital and position in the food-related institutional field.

Italy was chosen as a relevant context due to the importance of its gastronomy in a tourism context. The case selection processes aimed to find extreme cases, meaning that the food practices developed by the entrepreneurs had to be innovative and unique in relation to the traditional food practices of the local context (Flyvbjerg, 2006).

The empirical research was organized in three phases. The first phase involved an online search concerning companies that might be relevant to the study due to their location and their characteristics. The focus was on the local gastronomy and its use in the tourism context. This phase ended with the selection of two companies offering vegetarian/vegan food to their guests and located respectively in the Parma province and in the Alpine area. The chosen geographical areas were investigated through online search of information concerning local gastronomy, culture, tourism, and economy.

The Parma area is known as the Italian Food Valley, characterized by the presence of several important food-related actors, such as Barilla, and famous for two local internationally known animal-derived food products (Parmigiano cheese and Parma ham). The selected case is Borgo di Tara, an *agriturismo* – that is, a farm that engages in agricultural and hospitality activities that are regulated by the Italian national and regional laws. It was established in 2013 by a couple originally from Milano. It is located in the Borgotaro municipality (approximately 7000 inhabitants in an area of 152 km^2), where it is the only vegan *agriturismo*.

The Italian Alpine area is famous for its gastronomic heritage based on animal-derived food (dairy and speck). The local hospitality sector is characterized by a traditional typology of restaurants, including the *malga* – that is, a hut usually owned by the local community, which uses it for the seasonal droving of livestock in the summer, for the production of dairy products, and also as a restaurant for tourists. An Internet search revealed the existence of one vegetarian *malga* in the Italian Alps: M. S. Pietro. This *malga*, managed by an entrepreneur, is located in the province of Bolzano in the region of Trentino Alto Adige, in the municipality of Nova Ponente (approximately 3,900 inhabitants in an area of 112 km^2).

The second phase of the research involved a first contact with the three entrepreneurs by mail, followed by semi-structured interviews using Skype. During these interviews, questions about the origin of the *agriturismo* and the *malga* were asked in order to gain some background information and to uncover the main drivers behind the entrepreneurs' choice of offering vegetarian/vegan food to their customers. These interviews were recorded and transcribed with the permission of the respondents.

In the third phase, the researcher visited the *agriturismo* and the *malga*. During these visits, several informal conversational-style interviews were held with the couple owning and managing Borgo di Tara, and with the manager of M. S. Pietro and his fiancé. Several topics related to vegetarianism/veganism and tourism entrepreneurship were discussed. These included the challenges that the entrepreneurs had to face in the past and are still facing, and their perception in relation to possible conflicts caused by their vegetarian/vegan choice with customers, competitors, and more generally, the local communities. Questions were asked to clarify issues that had emerged during initial Skype interviews. These included questions about entrepreneurs' engagement in activities concerning animal welfare and environmentalism. Some of these conversations were spontaneous and quite long, touching several aspects concerning the entrepreneurs' and also the researcher's perspective on animal ethics. This allowed the establishment of a respectful and trustful relationship with the respondents.

Findings

The food institutional fields relative to Borgo di Tara and M. S. Pietro

The areas where the investigated tourism facilities are located are both characterized by quite a diffuse presence of organizations that can be related to animal-derived food production and consumption. Some of these organizations play a central role in the local economy, history, and cultural heritage. An example is the consortia of Parma ham. The web pages of these organizations show that they tend to profile themselves by referring to the high quality of their products and their adherence to local traditions. Such organizations can be seen as institutional defenders of food practices, based on the view of animals as sources of nutrition, enjoyment, and cultural meaning for humans. Slow Food is among these organizations. Within the Slow Food system of the regions where both Borgo di Tara and M. S. Pietro are located, there is a prevalence of animal-derived foods.

Local animal-derived foods are broadly used in the tourist context of both areas. The ability to taste these products and join gastronomic tours, including visits to production facilities and museums, is described with both text and pictures.

Although the animal-derived foods are numerous in the gastronomic area of Parma, the food institutional field relative to Borgo di Tara presents some signs of heterogeneity. An example is Verdiano, the vegetarian version of Parmigiano cheese. The official tourist information office website of Parma and the marketing plan of the Parma municipality do not identify vegetarians and vegans as particularly interesting target groups. Despite this, a few vegetarian and vegan food-related businesses have recently started in the Parma province. Finally, the *Parma Etica Festival* is an event that is arranged yearly and promotes vegetarianism as a lifestyle based on respect for animals, nature and sustainability.

The situation in the Alpine area where M. S. Pietro is located is different: the institutional food field seems to be more homogeneous, with very few cases of food-related practices that are alternatives to the dominant view.

The entrepreneur perspective of nature and animals

None of the interviewed entrepreneurs were familiar with the concept of ecofeminism, but the data suggests that many of their beliefs can be related to this ethical position. The Borgo di Tara website shows that choices concerning a vegan profile are related to ethical motivations. The vegan business profile is specifically defined as a philosophy and lifestyle choice. The idea to enter the hospitality sector was described as follows: "We love the idea of welcoming our guests, giving them the chance to know, live and appreciate the anti-speciesist culture and the alternative ethical choice in agriculture." The ethical motivation behind the business was confirmed when the first contact was made via mail, during the interview, and in conservations during the visit. The couple mentioned the concept of anti-speciesism several times and commented on the numerous forms of discrimination and oppression that take place in today's society, concerning not only animals, but also some groups of people belonging to various minorities. In this regard, one of the entrepreneurs of Borgo di Tara said:

> the mechanisms behind the exploitation of animals in the food industry . . . are very similar to the systematic discrimination of minorities among people: they, animals or for example immigrants, are pictured as 'the others,' sometimes enemies, sometimes almost as ghosts. The immigrants seem not to have names and faces . . . they are 'the immigrants.' Similarly, meat is just meat and not part of an animal who wanted to live.

As shown by this interview extract, the entrepreneurs' vegan choice is part of a broader issue that is not limited to food choices. Considerations about nature were also made in relation to the choice of using eco-friendly methods.

Similar is the position of the *malga* manager, as his choice of local, biological, and fair trade products confirm. The ethical motivation behind this choice is described in the *malga* website in the following words:

> Since 2013, M. S. Pietro has had a vegetarian-vegan menu. The consumption of a large amount of meat can be criticized from an ecological point of view and is against the principle of honouring and respecting all the living beings of the universe. Let's have a clean conscience when we sit at the table!

The natural environment plays a central role in the *malga* manager's perspective, according to which nature has value in itself, as well as benefits for humans in helping us find serenity. This is evident in the slogan of the M. S. Pietro: "nature heals." The *malga* offers activities with the aim of teaching children living in urban environments to be physically active, to discover nature, to learn to cope with various challenges, and to cooperate. His understanding of nature also seems to be in line with ecofeminism in relation to the recognized role of emotions:

> For me it's important that we know nature through our body, our brain and our heart. Emotions are important and the modern school system tends to ignore this . . . children are taught to think and to 'stay in their brain.' They lack a direct experience with nature . . . they are very far from all the emotions you can get from being out in the nature, being part of it.

With regard to the animals, as well as not seeing them as food resources, all the entrepreneurs commented on the importance of recognizing their dignity.

Domestic animals, such as the dogs living at Borgo di Tara, are given care in the form of sustenance, medical treatment when necessary, and freedom of movement, on the condition of their safety and that of others. Caring behaviours were observed between the entrepreneurs and their domestic animals, including dogs, cats, and horses, during the visits. The *malga* manager referred to animals as fellow living beings with which we humans share the planet. He stated clearly that he rejected the view of animals as resources. He commented on the habit of having pets in a way that also shows a recognition of the animal's dignity: "I'm not a big fan of having pets. It's not easy to give an animal, a dog for example, a good life . . . I mean a life that is good for the dog, not for you, the owner!"

Wild animals, such as the deer, were mentioned in relation to the curiosity and wonder that casual encounters can provoke. The wolves living close to the *agriturismo* were described in relation to their possible co-existence with humans. This is in opposition to the perspective of the vast majority of local people, who are in favour of hunting down the wolf species.

Entrepreneurs as change agents

The processes through which the entrepreneurs are introducing vegetarian/vegan food practices are described by the entrepreneurs in similar terms. A critical element noted in all the interviews was the strong motivation of the entrepreneurs in relation to finding a job that is in line with their beliefs and can contribute to societal change. For instance, the *malga* manager commented:

> I feel that I have to try to contribute with something positive in the direction of a social change . . . also to feel better with myself! It's a matter of justice and honesty and it makes me feel a sort of inner peace.

In addition to motivation, the quote also shows the importance of "having a thick skin" and being confident. These are particularly important aspects in relation to the challenges of developing an alternative tourism product. Some challenges can be related to the usual challenges of small businesses run by people who are new to a sector. Other challenges are related to the innovative and provocative message underlying both businesses. In both cases, the entrepreneurs have chosen to adopt typically traditional rural formulas (*agriturismo* and *malga*) and innovate them. The entrepreneurs seemed to be particularly aware of the importance of the context in which they operate. Although not sharing the same view of many members of the local community, the Borgo di Tara entrepreneurs emphasized that they do not try to force their opinion on others. This was also the case for M. S. Pietro, where the manager is a vegan but adopts a vegetarian profile for the *malga*. He explained that a *malga* is, by definition, linked to dairy production, and the decision to exclude such products from the menu would lead to a community decision to find another manager. He also explained that it took six years to achieve a vegetarian menu, due to his first partners and the alleged expectations of tourists. In relation to this, he explained:

> I have done a lot of 'lobbying' . . . the community started understanding my way of working and in this way I have gained their trust. They saw that I work in a responsible way . . . I explain to them my ideas about meat and also dairy production and, to a certain degree, we agree in many aspects . . . the personal relationships I have developed with the members of the community who decide about the management of the *malga* are positive and this helps a lot.

The entrepreneurs embraced a strategy of informational guiding in communication with customers. This was noted in all the interviews, where the respondents highlighted the importance of avoiding conflicts and establishing constructive dialogues.

In terms of social capital, the two cases are different. The *malga* manager belongs to the local community: he has a direct and personal relationship with the rest of the community and a broad network of friends and acquaintances. In Borgo di Tara, the entrepreneurs are outsiders. Although lacking a broad local social network, they have numerous contacts with vegans as a consequence of fifteen years as members of a national animalist movement. This contributes to increasing their confidence and also legitimizing their business, at least in the eyes of those customers and locals who tend to be positive about veganism.

From their point of view, the entrepreneurs view themselves as the bearers of an important message concerning a new way of living and doing business in tourism. This was very clearly stated by one of the entrepreneurs from Borgo di Tara: "It might sound arrogant but we feel like a sort of cultural avant-garde!" This entrepreneur feels that this is recognized by a growing number of people. Many tourists ask advice about practical aspects of the vegan lifestyle. This is explained by the entrepreneurs as a consequence of their being vegan for more than ten years and the perception customers might have of them as "experts."

The *malga* manager still seems to strive to gain acceptance from customers. This is due to the broad variety of tourists that the *malga* hosts, due to its proximity to a famous sanctuary and several outdoor activity opportunities. It is not unusual for tourists to comment negatively or ironically on the vegetarian menu, for example. In this regard, the entrepreneur reflected as follows:

> There will be always the tourist who is disappointed and sometimes also the tourist who makes inappropriate comments on vegetarianism . . . I work in the way that I consider the most responsible . . . I can tolerate some resistance, scepticism and, even if I really don't like it, sometimes rudeness from people.

The data thus suggest that the investigated entrepreneurs have quite a marginal position in their specific food institutional fields. In both cases, the interviews reveal that the entrepreneurs are aware of belonging to a minority, as they all reported that many members of the local communities have labelled them "the weird ones."

Conclusion

Adopting an institutional entrepreneurship perspective, this study has investigated the emergence of tourism practices that are in line with vegetarian ecofeminism. Viewing eating animals as the dominant institution, emerging alternative practices are here understood as the first level towards institutional change (Pacheco et al., 2010). Such change challenges society's rooted assumption about the subaltern position of animals in relation to humans (Loughman, Brock, & Haslam, 2014; Cudworth, 2015). This can be interpreted as a new form of morality according to which tourism businesses can develop on the basis of the moral rejection of using animals as resources to be exploited in a consumptive way, and as a way to promote values of inter-species compassion as advocated by vegetarian ecofeminists (Curtin, 2014; Gruen, 2015).

The focus has been on entrepreneurs who, driven mainly by ethical motivations, develop innovative products within the hospitality sector. Several aspects concerning the investigated entrepreneurs can be related to the main tenets of vegetarian ecofeminism, and, in this sense, these entrepreneurs can be viewed as change agents (Gaard, 2002; Levy & Scully, 2007). These entrepreneurs can be described by their belief in the inner value of each individual animal and of nature, and the related rejection of any kind of oppression based on the supposed superiority of humans. These elements are explained and practiced using both rationality and emotions, with explicit attempts to give both domestic and wild animals, as well as nature in general, the respect that, according to the entrepreneurs, they deserve.

The findings suggest several critically important factors in the emergence of these practices. One is the dialogue-based approach that the entrepreneurs take in their relationships with the local community and customers. This is in line with those ecofeminists arguing for a contextual vegetarianism, and with the idea that institutional change depends heavily on the characteristics of the related field, in particular its homogeneity, the presence of "defenders," and the change agents' position (Curtin, 1991; Lawrence et al., 2002; Lawrence & Phillips, 2004; Battilana et al., 2009). The findings show that all the entrepreneurs had long reflected on the local context, their position in it, and the perceptions that local people tended to have of their businesses and of the vegetarian lifestyle. As a consequence of such reflections, they had adopted a careful and dialogue-oriented approach. The investigated cases confirm what is suggested by the institutional entrepreneurship literature concerning the critically important factors of the entrepreneurs' strong motivation, their self-confidence, and, to a certain extent, their social capital (Battilana et al., 2009). With regard to the last of these, the two empirical cases studied differ from each other, as the entrepreneurs differ in terms of being locals or outsiders, as do the contexts with regard to their degree of homogeneity.

Based on these findings, the tourism practices investigated can be described as in their infancy, on their way to developing into proto-institutions (Lawrence et al., 2002). Such development would presumably continue, through mostly informal relationships with local and non-local groups of people and individuals sharing the same view on the main tenets of ecofeminism.

This study contributes to the understanding of the emergence of new ways of doing business in tourism in accordance to non-anthropocentric ethics. The reported cases highlight the way vegetarian ecofeminism is put into practice by entrepreneurs who act as change agents in relation to the institution of using animals for food. According to such entrepreneurs, doing business in tourism is not only about making money and offering opportunities for memorable experiences to their guests; it is also about being consistent with their inner beliefs concerning the positions of humans in relation to animals and nature, and, ultimately, about contributing to societal change.

References

Adams, C. (1990). *The Sexual politics of meat. A feminist-vegetarian critical theory*. New York: Bloomsbury Academic.

Adams, C. (1993). The feminist traffic in animals. In G. Gaard (Ed.), *Ecofeminism: Women, animals, nature* (pp. 195–218). Philadelphia, PA: Temple University Press.

Adams, C., & Gruen, L. (2014). *Ecofeminism: Feminist intersections with other animals and the earth*. New York: Bloomsbury.

Battilana, J., Leca, B., & Boxenbaum, E. (2009). How actors change institutions: Towards a theory of institutional entrepreneurship. *The Academy of Management Annals*, *3*(1), 65–107.

Bava, C. M., Jaeger, S. R., & Park, J. (2008). Constraints upon food provisioning practices in 'busy' women's lives: Trade-offs which demand convenience. *Appetite*, *50*, 486–498.

Bertella, G. (2018). Animals off the menu: How animals enter the vegan food experience. In C. Kline (Ed.), *Animals, food and tourism*. Oxford: Routledge.

Birkeland, J. (1993). Ecofeminism: Linking theory and practice. In G. Gaard (Ed.), *Ecofeminism: Women, animals, nature* (pp. 13–59). Philadelphia, PA: Temple University Press.

Bruton, G. D., Ahlstrom, D., & Li, H.-L. (2010). Institutional theory and entrepreneurship: Where are we now and where do we need to move in the future? *Entrepreneurship Theory and Practice*, *34*(3), 421–440.

Cudworth, E. (2015). Killing animals: Sociology, species relations and institutionalized violence. *The Sociological Review*, *63*, 1–18.

Curtin, D. (1991). Toward an ecological ethic of care. *Hypatia*, *6*(1), 60–74.

Curtin, D. (2014). Compassion and being human. In C. Adams & L. Gruen (Eds.), *Ecofeminism: Feminist intersections with other animals & the earth* (pp. 39–58). New York: Bloomsbury.

Di Maggio, P. (1988). Interest and agency in institutional theory. In L. Zucker (Ed.), *Institutional patterns and culture* (pp. 3–22). Cambridge, MA: Ballinger Publishing Company.

Donovan, J., & Adams, C. J. (2007). *The feminist care tradition in animal ethics*. New York: Columbia University Press.

Flyvbjerg, B. (2006). Five misunderstandings about case-study research. *Qualitative Inquiry*, *12*(2), 219–245.

Gaard, G. (1993). *Ecofeminism: Women, animals, nature*. Philadelphia, PA: Temple University Press.
Gaard, G. (2002). Vegetarian ecofeminism: A review essay. *Frontiers: A Journal of Women Studies*, *23*(3), 117–146.
Gruen, L. (1996). On the oppression of women and animals. *Environmental Ethics*, *18*(4), 441–444.
Gruen, L. (2011). *Ethics and animals: An introduction*. Cambridge: Cambridge University Press.
Gruen, L. (2015). *Entangled empathy: An alternative ethic for our relationships with animals*. Brooklyn, NY: Lantern Books.
Haenfler, R., Johnson, B., & Jones, E. (2012). Lifestyle movements: Exploring the intersection of lifestyle and social movements. *Social Movement Studies*, *11*(1), 1–20.
Hawkins, R., Z. (1998). Ecofeminism and nonhumans: Continuity, difference, dualism, and domination. *Hypatia*, *13*(1), 158–197.
Lawrence, T. B., Hardy, C., & Phillips, N. (2002). Institutional effects of interorganizational collaboration: The emergence of proto-institutions. *Academy of Management Journal*, *45*(1), 281–290.
Lawrence, T., B., & Phillips, N. (2004). From Moby Dick to Free Willy: Macro-cultural discourse and institutional entrepreneurship in emerging institutional fields. *Organization*, *11*(5), 689–711.
Levy, D., & Scully, M. (2007). The institutional entrepreneur as modern prince: The strategic face of power in contested fields. *Organization Studies*, *28*(7), 971–991.
Loughnan, S., Brock, B., & Haslam, N. (2014). The psychology of eating animals. *Current Directions in Psychological Science*, *23*(2), 104–108.
Pacheco, D. F., York, G. G., Dean, T. J., & Sarasvathy, S. D. (2010). The coevolution of institutional entrepreneurship: A tale of two theories. *Journal of Management*, *36*, 974–1010.
Rao, H., Morrill, C., & Zald, M. N. (2000). Power plays: How social movements and collective action create new organizational forms. *Research in Organizational Behaviour*, *22*, 237–281.
Rivera, M., & Shani, A. (2013). Attitudes and orientation toward vegetarian food in the restaurant industry. *International Journal of Contemporary Hospitality Management*, *25*(7), 1049–1065.
Ruby, M. B. (2012). Vegetarianism: A blossoming field of study. *Appetite*, *58*, 141–150.
Scott, W. R. (2007). *Institutions and organizations: Ideas and interests*. Thousand Oaks, CA: SAGE Publications.
Twine, R. (2014). Ecofeminism and veganism: Revisiting the question of universalism. In C. Adams & L. Gruen (Eds.), *Ecofeminism: Feminist intersections with other animals and the earth* (pp. 191–208). New York: Bloomsbury.
Warren, K. (1987). Feminism and ecology: Making connections. *Environmental Ethics*, *9*(1), 3–20.
Young, I. M. (1990). *Justice and the politics of difference*. Princeton, NY: Princeton University Press.
Yudina, O., & Fennell, D. (2013). Ecofeminism in the tourism context: A discussion of the use of other-than-human animals as food in tourism. *Tourism Recreation Research*, *38*(1), 55–69.

7 Between awareness and activism

Navigating the ethical terrain of eating animals

Carol Kline and R. Cody Rusher

Introduction

Like many vital matters of today, the moral issue of eating animals calls for both individual and societal consideration. Eating animals is firmly embedded in most cultures, economic systems, and religions, as well as in many family traditions; it exists along a continuum of animal welfare and across a spectrum of contexts. Industrialized animal production has been the subject of criticism due to associated environmental hazards and documented violations of animal welfare. Serious deliberation of industrialized animal production brings to light weighty issues such as animal pain and sentience; antibiotic overuse and resistance; ineffective processing of excrement, methane, and other wastes; corn production and land use; the well-being of farm and slaughterhouse workers; and meat-heavy diets leading to cardiovascular disease.

The ethics of eating animals has been considered, examined, and criticized from a number of perspectives including philosophical, spiritual, economic, anthropological, psychological, political, and feminist approaches. All of these studies fall within a larger body of work that examines relationships between human and non-human animals. Animal protein occupies a large portion of most restaurant menus, culinary tourism development has a wide swath of dedicated literature, and food and beverage are an ever-growing dimension of destination marketing. Nevertheless, tourism and hospitality scholars have been late to address the critical and moral issue of eating animals.

The hospitality and tourism industry is dependent on food quality and variety for creating an overall positive experience for customers and is equally as vulnerable to the whims of consumers. However, many stakeholders in the industry have only recently elevated the ethical and moral issue of sustainable food production to a serious issue for consideration, rather than treating it as merely a social fad. Within the Millennial generation, there holds promise of addressing some of the ethical and moral dilemmas created by eating animals, as this population group has demonstrated an ethic of care both socially and environmentally (Sheahan, 2005). Relative to travel, Millennials have exhibited a desire for helping others through volunteer tourism, a positive outlook toward diversity, and an urge to experience authentic local cultures (Moscardo & Benckendorff, 2010).

Compounded with the sheer size of this generation, it seems prudent to understand more about how they view the critical moral issue of eating meat and eating meat within the context of tourism.

Despite the entrenched nature of eating animals, many individuals have the economic and social power to choose if and how to engage with this practice. Those who choose a vegetarian or vegan lifestyle do so for a variety of reasons: health, environmental, economic, and animal-welfare related. Those who have considered "going veg" but have not, often cite one of several reasons: meat tastes good, vegetarianism is expensive, it is unclear what is "allowed" in a vegetarian diet, or vegetarianism is a futile gesture because one person's actions do not have an effect on larger food systems (Cooney, 2010). This chapter explores these perceptions surrounding eating meat by embedding the domain of Perceived Consumer Effectiveness within a series of interviews with college students. We explore three research questions: *How do Millennials view the eating of animals within the current context of issues surrounding the production of animal protein? To what extent are these issues changed through travel? To what extent does Perceived Consumer Effectiveness contribute to Millennials' decisions about eating meat?* Contextual scenarios embedded within hospitality and tourism related to family tradition, culture, social pressure, economic constraints, animal welfare, and environmental conservation are navigated through the use of vignettes.

Millennials: hope for the future

The term "Millennials" generally refers to people born between the early 1980s and the early 2000s, a cohort of individuals who are between the ages of roughly 15 and 35 as of 2017. This massive generation, composed of an estimated 80 million individuals, is said to routinely question traditional values and lifestyles. Although known as the most technologically proficient group of individuals in history, relatively little research has centred on Millennials' beliefs and ethical viewpoints (Philips, 2014).

Millennials are commonly regarded as confident, assertive, and opinionated when it comes to making decisions, especially in terms of trends, fashion, and lifestyle (Pew Research Center, 2010). Additionally, Millennials are often characterized by their social, cultural, and environmental mindfulness (Sheahan, 2005); their concerns for the environment are at least in part the product of the values passed on to them from their Baby Boomer parents (Benckendoff, Moscardo, & Murphy, 2012). However, rather than accepting conventional norms, Millennials largely prefer to seek out practices that make more sense to them. Consequently, they have played a key role in the evolution of food culture in recent years. For example, The Hartman Group (2011) found that nearly 12% of Millennials are committed to vegetarianism, as opposed to some 4% of Generation X members and only 1% of Baby Boomers. This growing trend of embracing plant-based diets symbolizes an important shift in the way Millennials are thinking about food.

As such, Millennials have the potential to cause an unquestionable disruption in the agricultural industry because they are navigating the ethical and environmental terrain associated with eating animals differently than generations before them. One contributing explanation for this trend may be Millennials' aforementioned technological fluency, especially when combined with the widespread availability of media dedicated to the economic, social, and environmental aspects of sustainability. Whereas previous generations primarily obtained knowledge from direct observations and experiences, word of mouth, and formal education, Millennials have grown up with the ability to learn continuously and efficiently by accessing copious amounts of online information. As such, an array of potentially eye-opening materials is both easily accessible and readily available to Millennials, such as documentaries addressing the environmental issues associated with animal agriculture, reports of gruesome discoveries investigators have made in factory farms, and graphic videos where animals are transported and slaughtered through brutal means. Although the Millennial generation is a diverse group, these individuals are unified by their familiarity with and dependence upon the Internet. This connectivity influences the development of Millennial values and beliefs and, in turn, consumption behaviours (Riggs, 2016). Regarded as the most powerful population of consumers in the global marketplace, this generation is a critical niche for consumer research (Farris, Chong, & Danning, 2002).

Millennials surpassed Baby Boomers to become the largest generation within the U.S. population, allowing them the power to significantly shape market activity (Pew Research Center, 2010). Fuller (2013) estimated the spending power of the Millennial market to be $200 billion. Despite their ability to influence the market, their perspective on environmentally oriented behaviours remains relatively poorly understood today (Heo & Muralidharan, 2017). Within this study, we sought to learn more about how Millennials view eating meat, particularly within the context of the myriad environmental, social, economic, and moral issues that accompany the meat industry. We further wished to understand how their perceived ability to influence the market shaped their perceptions and behaviours regarding eating meat, particularly within the context of travel. Therefore, the study employs the concept of Perceived Consumer Effectiveness as the underlying framework for this inquiry.

Perceived Consumer Effectiveness

Ethical consumers are increasingly aware of the ethical repercussions associated with their purchasing decisions, and they adjust their behaviours accordingly (Harrison, 2005). These consumers are partially motivated by the notion of Perceived Consumer Effectiveness (PCE), a term first introduced by Kinnear, Taylor, and Ahmed (1974), who outlined the concept as "a measure of the extent to which a respondent believes that an individual consumer can be effective" (p. 21). Seminal work by Ellen, Wiener, and Cobb-Walgren (1991) found that consumers with more environmental knowledge were more likely to perceive their individual efforts as valuable contributions towards solving environmental problems than those with less environmental knowledge. A later perspective defined PCE as "the extent to which the consumer believes that his/her personal efforts can contribute to the solution of the problem" (Vermeir & Verbeke, 2006, p. 175). These researchers provide a framework which suggests that PCE has the potential to predict environmentally oriented behaviour. In the current study, we look to PCE for help in understanding how individuals make eating decisions while travelling.

Of particular interest to us is the relationship between Millennial travellers' attitudes towards meat and their subsequent consumption patterns. Perhaps due to generational identifiers such as their aforementioned technological fluency, Millennials have developed unique perspectives on meat consumption in contrast to previous cohorts (Namugayi, 2014). The Food Marketing Institute found in their 2017 study *The Power of Meat* that, compared to other generations, Millennials were more interested in on-pack information and environmentally friendly packaging when shopping for meat. Additionally, the importance of sustainability and living a healthy lifestyle has been ingrained into the minds of Millennials from a young age (Palmer, 2017). It seems logical that an awareness of environmental issues in combination with a health-conscious upbringing would translate into conscious decision-making when it comes to food. However, none of the respondents in a survey of Millennials by Namugayi (2014) outwardly acknowledged the associations between their food choices and sustainable action. This disconnect warrants further investigation as to how Millennials process their decision making in situations where their actions can have considerable positive or negative impacts. PCE, which reminds us that awareness of these ethical issues may not translate into activism, is a starting point for our investigation.

In 1997, Mainieri, Barnett, Oskamp, Unipan, and Valdero suggested that there is an attitude-behaviour gap when it comes to just how far consumers are willing to go in order to help the environment. Across six categories of "everyday" products such as laundry detergent and paper products, they found that only 14%–30% of consumers had purchased a particular brand because of the environmental impact they believed it would have. Vermeir and Verbeke (2006) identified a similar gap concerning the purchasing of sustainable food products. Iurkevych, Gustin, Blecher, and Reiboldt (2014) found that within college students, PCE had an effect on their intention to dine at green restaurants. However, as global tourism exports continue to grow annually, there is a lack of investigation into the link between PCE and eating animal products, especially within the context of travel (Vanhonacker & Verbeke, 2009). As our society becomes increasingly mindful of topics such as animal welfare, support for small and local farms, social justice in agriculture, and environmental sustainability, PCE may provide insight into individual decision-making. When considering Millennials, PCE has the potential to serve as an investigative tool for examining the alignment of their ethical beliefs with their actual consumption behaviours. The current study is warranted by the implied presence of an attitude-behaviour gap, the deficiency of literature dedicated to the Millennial generation and their beliefs and behaviours concerning eating meat, and the lack of research surrounding the potential relationships between PCE, animal consumption, and travel.

Methods

Vignette-based interviews were chosen as the method for this study because vignettes, or short stories, can be used to prompt informants' beliefs and convictions about real-life scenarios that might pertain to sensitive topics (Atzmüller & Steiner, 2010). By using a third-person approach in discussing a topic, vignettes allow the interview participant to "distance" themselves from the subject. This is an effective and gentle approach when the research topic may be contentious and nuanced (Aguinis & Bradley, 2014). Lee and Scott (2015) employed this method in their study examining racism and black travel patterns in tourism. Their research consisted of in-depth vignette-based interviews with 13 middle-class African-Americans and yielded five striking themes regarding their topic. Additionally, vignettes allow researchers to extract an individual's reaction to a situation without having to personally expose them to that condition. Altschuler (2014) used a vignette approach in his travel research investigating identity affirming and disaffirming tourist experiences. He measured the reactions of approximately 60 Chinese and 60 American individuals to the same travel-based vignettes and found significant differences between their emotional reactions. It would have been extremely costly and ethically problematic (if possible at all) to create the same scenarios in real life.

Wason, Polonsky, and Hyman (2002) proffer a number of benefits to this type of research design including providing greater realism by introducing complex and seemingly realistic situations; supplying standardized prompts to participants which enhance internal validity, measurement reliability, and ease of replication; reducing social desirability bias; and enhancing respondent involvement. Using vignettes instead of direct questioning can reduce feelings of discomfort and self-editing by the informant, leading to richer insight into feelings, intentions, attitudes, and behaviours within complex situations (Aguinis & Bradley, 2014; Wason, Polonsky, & Hyman, 2002).

Vignette design

While vignettes can be presented in multiple formats [e.g., written, images, or video (Aguinis & Bradley, 2014)], the vignettes in this study were written. Participants were provided with multiple vignettes, thus allowing for comparison and helping to ground responses contextually (Aguinis & Bradley, 2014). We used a within-subjects design, wherein each informant received the same vignettes (Atzmüller & Steiner, 2010). In creating the vignettes, we provided detailed scenarios to enhance the air of realism (Wason, Polonsky, & Hyman, 2002).

Each vignette (see Textbox) was created with the overarching research questions in mind: *How do Millennials view the eating of animals within the current context of issues surrounding the production of animal protein? To what extent are these issues changed through travel? To what extent does Perceived Consumer Effectiveness contribute to Millennials' decisions about eating meat?* The protocol used for the interviews was shared with participants ahead of time and used as a guide during each interview session. After reminding the participant of the purpose of the study, we asked them to read the vignettes one at a time.

Following each vignette, we asked participants a series of open-ended questions regarding their reaction to and perspective on the story:

1. What are your immediate thoughts after reading this story?
2. How do you feel about what happened in the story?
3. Please describe in your own words what (character 1) is thinking or feeling. What about (character 2)?
4. Have you or someone you know experienced anything similar/related to this story?
5. Do you identify with any of the characters in the story?

Textbox 7.1

Vignette 1. Priyank's family is visiting him in the United States for the first time since he moved from India to begin college. Although Priyank eats some meat, his parents have not eaten meat or any other animal products for as long as he can remember. While out to lunch, Priyank orders a vegan veggie burger for each of his parents. After their meal, Priyank's father asks the waitress what their vegan veggie burgers are made of. When the waitress mentions honey as one of the ingredients, Priyank's parents are furious that he ordered the burgers for them and that the restaurant mislabeled their item as vegan when honey is produced by bees.

Vignette 2. Chris and Sidney were so excited about the cruise they were about to take! Not only were they going to get to see several parts of Alaska, the whole entire food service catered to vegans. Chris knew that cruises were highly criticized in the environmental community for the negative impacts they have on oceans, but he also felt good about the positive effect he has by eating a plant-based diet. Because beef production is one of the largest contributors to methane production, by not eating meat, he felt better about his personal "footprint."

Vignette 3. Within the last eight months, Brittany, Deja, and Covell have experienced extraordinary success with their start-up tech venture. So much, in fact, that they were invited to Beijing to close a deal with an important buyer of their company's product. On the evening that they were to sign the contract, they met at an upscale restaurant to have a celebratory meal. Their local host and soon-to-be business partner ordered dinner for the table, and a few minutes later, Brittany, Deja, and Covell realized they were being served pangolin, an endangered mammal that is served on special occasions to honor guests. The fact that the pangolin is on a critically endangered global watch list is the very reason it is chosen to demonstrate how very special the guest is. Brittany and Covell had no clue what was happening, but Deja had learned about this practice as she was preparing for the trip. She whispered to Brittany and Covell to fill them in, and all three were stunned about how to respond.

Data collection and analysis

The sampling frame for interview participants included graduate and undergraduate students at a regional public university in North Carolina. Both researchers work at the university; therefore, the sampling frame was convenient. The university was also chosen based upon several unique and important characteristics related to this exploratory study. In particular, the university, which has around 16,000 undergraduate and 1,600 graduate students (most of whom are Millennials), has a reputation for its leadership in sustainability.

Participants were solicited from the departments of psychology, sociology, management, marketing, recreation management, physics, public administration, and sustainable development. A solicitation email was sent to one professor in each of these departments, who in turn distributed it to their classes. Interested students then directly contacted the researchers to schedule an interview. Ten interviews occurred in January and February 2017; a total of eight women and two men were interviewed, all of whom were in their early 20's. A set of eight vignettes were used, including three that were developed specifically whereby the vignette characters might be influenced by feelings of "effectiveness" as a consumer, or PCE. The interviews, which lasted between 25 and 40 minutes, were audio recorded and later transcribed by a third party. Each researcher conducted five interviews.

Interview transcripts were analysed using inductive conventional content analysis in a four-step process (Kodish & Gittelsohn, 2011). First, the two researchers met to discuss general perceptions of the informants, the vignettes, and the process that were revealed from the text; these perceptions were recorded as possible themes for the next step. The second step involved each researcher coding the transcriptions from the other's interviews, highlighting content related to PCE and the aforementioned thematic perceptions. Next, the primary researcher coded transcription text into emergent concepts, which further clarified the themes; the secondary researcher weighed in on the findings as they were developed, questioning early drafts of the chapter narrative and adding coded data and interpretation where needed. This data analysis spiral continued with and between both researchers until no additional data could be extracted from the transcripts. The researchers met one last time to discuss the final themes, and findings were not confirmed until agreement was reached on all matters. This type of analysis is useful in exploratory studies such as this one because it can result in conceptual development or model building (Kodish & Gittelsohn, 2011). Findings are outlined below by theme after a general discussion of the vignette approach. Participants are referred to under pseudonyms.

Findings

Overall, the use of a vignette interview design was effective. Each story resonated with the informants differently depending on their consumption of meat, family and background, travel experiences, awareness of issues surrounding meat production, and social relationships. The conversational style of data collection and its focus on issues about a third party (the vignette's characters) seemed to elicit candid and top-of-mind reactions as well as reflective action on participants' behalf.

One reason for the variety of responses was the different levels at which informants could identify with the characters or relate to the situation in the story. When identification level was higher, participant responses were likely to be based on their own experiences as opposed to relying solely upon the fictional content of the vignette. Generally speaking, informants seemed to easily switch back and forth between their own experiences and those of the characters in the vignettes throughout the interview.

Our first research question related to how Millennials view the eating of animals within the current context of issues surrounding the production of animal protein. Commonalities emerged as informants reflected upon their own experiences and how they felt characters in the vignettes should act, their justifications or reasoning behind these reflections, and their worldview that shapes their actions and reasoning. The second research question asked to what extent their perception of these issues changed within the context of travel, and the third used the lens of PCE to explain participants' responses. Themes addressing the first two questions reflected the concept of "an animal continuum," the desire to be culturally appropriate, and the expressed need of "finding balance." Lastly, we noted varying levels of PCE among participants, as well as indications of whether PCE influences their consumption behaviour.

The culturally laden animal continuum

Participant comments reflected the notion of an animal "continuum," wherein it is acceptable to eat certain animals but not others. Informants further suggested that the acceptability of consuming some animals but not others is culturally relative. This particularly came to light within the vignette of the Beijing business deal, where the idea of eating a pangolin was acknowledged as a cultural phenomenon by several informants, regardless of the animal's status as an endangered species. For example, Anna noted,

> [The Chinese] are saying '[This] animal is endangered but we respect you so much that we want to serve it to you, and we want you to enjoy it.' It's that limited resource that they're offering. I think for the people from America, where it's not as culturally accepted to do something like that, it could be a bit of culture shock.

Another informant, Felicia, mentioned one of her American peers had eaten dog while on a study abroad trip to China, but that he said would never do that again. Additionally, two informants (Danielle and Isabelle) assumed that Priyank's family's veganism was culturally inspired because they lived in India. Isabelle noted,

> I don't think there's anything wrong with [eating honey] because it's not like we're actually hurting the animal getting the honey, it's what they do

> naturally. I don't see anything wrong with it. I can see where they come from just because of their culture. I understand all the cultures are so different. Other than that, I don't see any problem.

These responses suggest that not all animals are regarded equally in terms of how humans "use" them, reflecting a continuum of animals which are acceptable to eat and which are not; reactions seemed to be much stronger regarding consumption of animal protein versus a by-product such as honey. This notion has been supported in popular and academic literature (Cooney, 2010; Joy, 2011). Additionally, participants felt that this continuum would differ according to culture and held an overall flexible position on eating meat while traveling in light of this. Conflicting motivations and attitudes can emerge during times of travel, as these experiences often expose tourists to cultural differences, including differing animal continuums, notions of the exotic or the "other," eating habits, and the desire to fit in or be "culturally appropriate." The dissention between the desire to be culturally sensitive and one's individual sense of morals or values warrants further investigation within the rich context of travel and tourism.

Rationalization, bargaining, and finding balance

The vegan cruise vignette sparked discussions about value prioritization, bargaining, and empowerment. Informants seemed to be more aware of the potential environmental impacts of beef production than those of cruises. This highlights the lack of mainstream attention ethical tourism has received, which likely translates into a lack of action. However, opinions diverged beyond this point of agreement. Some informants felt that Chris was "rationalizing" taking the cruise whereas others agreed with his premise. As Bradley put it,

> Rationalization, as we've learned it in our classes, is the way you're saying that what I'm doing is valid because it either neutralizes this other effect or it benefits me to the point where the negative effect is ignorable.

Claire identified with Chris and admitted,

> Yeah, I've definitely had a couple of instances where I know I'm doing something not technically right but not technically wrong, and having an internal conflict, and trying to convince myself that I'm doing something relatively more right than more wrong.

Kathryn felt Chris was justified because:

> The fact that the cruise that he chose to go [on] was vegan. I mean he's already going on a cruise. If you're getting on a cruise and you're worried about your footprint, I mean, that's probably the least footprint creating cruise you can go on.

She elaborated,

> I would say there's a balance . . . you can't just be sitting in your room all the time to not create a footprint. I know there are airplane companies where you can donate money to offset their carbon footprint. So it's a way to justify or like make you feel better for it . . . I'm sure like cruises will start doing that . . . Because I know going on a cruise, there was a lot of meat provided . . . Just thinking about, also, the waste that they have because some are like all you can eat. So obviously, they're not going to keep a bunch of meat out all day, every day. You have to throw that out. Repeat. Just thinking about how much food to feed a thousand people on the boat is going to be a big footprint. I think, for him, he's doing the best that he can do.

While Kathryn brought up the issue of waste on cruises, particularly related to meat, she also mentioned the possibility of carbon offset programs being used to compensate for otherwise damaging travel behaviour. Danielle addressed the issue of rationalization in this way:

> [Chris] definitely is making a good choice by not contributing to the one part of it, [so] I guess he has the right to feel better about it, but he's just justifying bad behaviour with another good behaviour, which is something a lot of people do.

As such, there was consensus among the informants that a limit exists as to what and how much anyone (including themselves) will sacrifice for a greater cause. Therefore, the data raised some important questions: When presented with a plethora of environmental woes, how do individuals decide where they want to contribute? Furthermore, how does one decide what they are and are not willing to give up? Do those who are more aware of environmental issues (like Chris) engage in "bargaining" conversations with themselves to "balance out" the known negative effects of an action? Are the coping strategies for this cognitive dissonance the same when it comes to eating animals? Does rationalization or bargaining increase to compensate for unique or exceptional circumstances when one is travelling internationally? These questions could not be explored within this study because of interview time limits and other research priorities; however, they stand as ready priorities for future inquiry, particularly in relation to how much people believe that their individual action can make a difference (PCE).

The vignette that centred on eating pangolin generated the most internal conflict among informants, as well as the strongest opinions. Reactions to this vignette primarily focused on three aspects of the story: the cultural practice of eating pangolin, the endangered status of the pangolin, and the impending business deal that might be negated if the characters were to refuse the offering. While we have discussed the "cultural aspect" of eating pangolin, here we contrast the other two issues. In general, our participants expressed a distaste towards the proposition of eating an endangered animal, but varied in whether or not they would have indulged in the meal if they were to find themselves in this situation.

Jessica explained:

> This is a company type dinner for the success of their start-up venture, so they're wanting to make sure that this goes smoothly. It doesn't say that any of them are vegetarians, but at the same time they are stunned about the fact that this in an endangered critter they're about to eat. For the sake of social etiquette, they might do it because of business relations and not wanting to seem rude or offensive. That's a toughie to be in. Yeah, they are probably [thinking about] that ethical dilemma of 'this thing's in danger. I'm eating this. I'm contributing to the end this species that's on its way out.'

The same participant admitted that she would eat the pangolin "to be polite, probably. I'd feel bad about it, but at the same time I want to remain a successful business person." This respondent understood the ethical concern, but was not willing to sacrifice her job status in order to act, possibly because she did not believe that her actions would have a meaningful impact in the grand scheme of things. If this is a commonly shared mind-set across the Millennial generation, then their aforementioned power over the market will likely not be utilized to disrupt patterns and norms. Without higher levels of PCE, Millennial empowerment and concern may never translate into large-scale action.

Kathryn admitted that she would probably eat the pangolin, but might seek atonement afterwards.

> That's a hard thing because, like I said before, [if] *everyone* eats 'a special thing' only one time, [it] continues to support [the system]. If people are buying it, then they keep trafficking that animal . . . Yeah, because it's part of the culture. If they say no, it's disrespectful. They may not have that business deal anymore if they decide not to eat that food. Maybe, if anything – after that trip, find out more about it and support the issue. Contribute money or something to the people who are against trafficking and trying to catch [traffickers]. Really, that is going to be a bigger impact than deciding not to just eat it once. I know that's what I would do.

Acceptance of others' consumption choices

In most cases, participants believed that it was not difficult to find vegetarian food options while traveling, but suggested that it was harder to follow a vegan diet. Many Millennials within the United States, particularly those who have the financial means to attend university, have grown up in a context where food options are diverse and bountiful. Additionally, their technological proficiency allows them to readily locate options using mobile applications, even when travelling. Therefore, having to find vegetarian/vegan food options or having a vegetarian/vegan friend was not considered to be out of the ordinary or terribly burdensome.

Related to this, participants appeared relatively accepting of others' food views and felt that individuals have the right to make their own decisions about consumption behaviour. Even though some disclosed that they could never foresee themselves becoming vegetarian or vegan, they did not seem critical of the motivations behind others' decisions to do so. In general, they did not perceive vegetarians and vegans as high-maintenance or preachy. This could have been a reflection of social desirability bias, given that the purpose of the study was to explore Millennial perceptions of eating animals, or a reflection of the university's culture where the research took place, as environmental stewardship is a core value of the school. However, there was one exception: when discussing the vegan cruise vignette, Isabelle stated "The whole boat catered vegan food? That just seems really weird." When asked why, she elaborated,

> Because when you think about it, especially over here, there are so many people that eat mainly meat, compared to vegetables . . . A lot of people eat more meat than they do sides. Potatoes, or a salad, or something like that. It's not what we consider our main course.

Even this respondent did not necessarily seem intolerant of vegetarian ideals, just surprised by the existence of tourism options which cater to specific needs.

While a general acceptance of other opinions may seem laudable at the surface level, it could also signify an ethical complacency or a lack of critical, moral thinking. The notion that "everyone's opinion is okay" could relegate ethics to an individual's whim and dispel any need to subscribe to a larger moral code. It could erode or confound higher ideals or constructs, such as the belief in environmental sustainability as a necessity or the sentience of non-human animals. The current study did not explore where one's moral boundaries lie in terms of accepting other people's choices of consumption; however, such a pursuit would be valuable in a future study. To elaborate on this point, the acceptance of other individual's right to make his/her own decisions about consumption may be embedded in a worldview shaped by neoliberal capitalism. If this ideology operates below the surface of people's ethical code and subsequently influences their behaviours, what hope do animals have?

Consumer effectiveness

Relating directly to this study's underlying framework of PCE and the final research question, participants expressed contrasting views on whether or not their individual actions can make a difference. For example, Jenna and Howard both seemed to display a high level of PCE. When Jenna was asked to elaborate on why she chose to become vegetarian, she noted that "I think I save a handful of animals a year. I don't know if it's true but just the idea of it is totally rewarding to me." In reference to the pangolin, Howard suggested that:

> when you say, 'No, thank you,' then maybe other people at a restaurant will see it. Then they'll tell their friends. Just the power of one thing, that butterfly

> effect. If everyone thinks that someone else should be doing it, then it's division of responsibility. They're like, 'Oh, well, someone else can stand up for this.' If one person decides that it's not OK, then maybe they can tell their friends about it. Maybe that friend who goes to the restaurant and refuse [pangolin] and it becomes something like a normal thing. Maybe restaurants will even order less of it, or not have that food option at all.

Participants commonly felt that Priyank's parents were denied the opportunity to be "effective" consumers because of the restaurant's mislabelling. Emily stated "I would not be mad at the person who ordered it for me that was trying, but I am concerned with the corporation trying to label it as something that it's not." Additionally, Kathryn commented,

> It's not really [Priyank's] fault, in the sense that . . . the restaurant didn't label that there's honey in it . . . maybe suggest the restaurant say also, well our veggie burgers contain honey. It's important to be transparent with your customers.

Emily, who is vegan, acknowledged that it is difficult to yield "consumer effectiveness" when others are cooking for you:

> Even with, sometimes, how people sauté their vegetables. If they do that in butter instead of oil and it just gets to a point of, you don't want to be so nit-picky, like, 'Tell me your whole process of how you cook this.' I've definitely even experienced that just with my friends, making me food. Also, the majority of veggie patties that they sell in the frozen section of grocery stores are not vegan at all. They have egg and milk in them and I've definitely eaten those then afterwards been like, 'Why did I assume this? Why didn't I look at the label closer?'

Even though she was strongly motivated to be vegan and demonstrated high PCE, she acknowledged these difficulties. This suggests that high levels of PCE alone are not always enough to translate into action and opens up the door for future research on possible covariates or moderating and mediating variables.

Conclusions

PCE, or the belief that one's consumption behaviour could "make a difference," was a motivator for reducing meat consumption for some of Millennials in this study. However, even when participants deemed an action to be detrimental to their health, the community, the environment, or non-human animals, they were sometimes still inclined to do so regardless. Common justifications for consuming animal protein included the following:

- The animal is already dead so not eating it won't "save" the animal;
- Meat eating is a prevalent societal norm;
- Some animals are meant for eating (while others are not);

- I don't want to be offensive to the host culture (different from my own);
- I may never have the chance to eat this again;
- It's all a trade-off; we can't do everything (in the name of sustainability).

And in the case of eggs, dairy, or honey, *it's not like you're killing the animal; you are just using their by-products.*

Our findings agree with previous studies on consumption behaviour, in that an individual's attitudes and values may not translate into aligned action (Joy, 2011; Namugayi, 2014; Vanhonacker & Verbeke, 2009; Vermeir & Verbeke, 2006). However, some of the informants in this small sample struggled on a daily basis to "walk the talk" of their values. This was often prompted by underlying beliefs regarding meat's contribution to environmental degradation and lack of animal welfare and, to a lesser extent, questioning the need to eat large quantities of meat as a source of protein.

The informants in our sample were knowledgeable about general environmental issues, including factory farming. They had adopted a worldview that cultural differences and individual choices were to be tolerated and consequently applied this worldview to each vignette. They believed that sustainability was a balancing act, and acknowledged that it is difficult to do the right thing every time and, thus, have decided not to feel bad about compromises they make in that regard. Whereas morals and priorities might typically precede a high PCE, we observed a sense of PCE compromised by other values. All of the informants found reasons not to "flex" their consumer effectiveness in certain situations; clearly, this stance aligns with relativism in ethics and warrants further investigation among the soon-to-be dominant millennial market.

Therefore, we suggest two key research directions emerging from this study: PCE's role in decision-making relative to eating animals and the influence of travel on animal products consumption behaviour. Within these, a host of subtopics might be explored such as the animal continuum, the boundaries of accepting the right for everyone to make their own consumption choice, the limits of cultural tolerance, consuming the exotic, and rationalization or finding balance.

PCE's role in decision-making

Because the actions one can take to better the environment, community, animals, and others are limited, there exists a finite "space" where one's values and priorities lie. For some, this space may include going to church, being kind to neighbours, and fostering community. Others may prefer donating to charity or curtailing their consumption behaviour. Based on the findings of the current study, one's level of PCE is interwoven in this decision-making space. Further research is warranted in order to better understand how people make choices about what they are and are not willing to sacrifice to benefit the greater good; we are interested in this decision-making process relative to eating animals, relative to different contexts (various culturally laden scenarios; at home vs. travelling; within different meal situations, e.g., a business dinner vs. a holiday meal with family); and across varying generations.

Effects of travel on eating behaviour

Regarding tourism, several research directions unfolded. Traveling can alter your habits out of necessity or curiosity. Several informants spoke of modifying their diet while overseas for matters of convenience or for the purpose of experiencing something new; some acknowledged that these changes were temporary while others became more permanent adjustments. In terms of which animals are eaten, what some deemed "exotic" bordered on horrifying for others. However, the emerging sentiments of *I feel bad about it, but I'll try it just this once* and *I don't want to offend the host culture* generally pervaded. Future research should investigate the human desire to experience new things regardless of cognitive dissonance and under what circumstances it is tolerable for individuals to sacrifice their own morals for someone else's cultural norms. Is travel being used as a justification for doing something you do not believe in? Or, are people more tolerant/respectful when travelling? Finally, do actions differ according to one's purpose for traveling, e.g., a business trip versus a family vacation?

The current findings are certainly limited within the context of the study's sampling frame. However, many of these sentiments ring familiar with previous consumption, marketing, and tourism literature. Beyond consumer market implications, our study is situated within the larger realms of sustainability, moral reasoning, and ethics. While it is admirable for us to be tolerant of other's individual preferences and cultural differences, we ought not lose sight of the fact that our individual decisions can have catastrophic consequences for society as a greater whole. Through both informal and formal educational efforts, marketing messages, social pressure, and expanded civic consciousness, the world has made some significant moral strides, although additional challenges certainly lie ahead. Perhaps the vast array of technology which has become increasingly central to our lives, and has played a role in the dissemination of information regarding factory farming and its effect on a sustainable future, could also serve as a tool to help reconcile our multiple values that may seemingly conflict. This new research direction within the realm of tourism studies is ripe for additional qualitative and quantitative investigations. Through further research efforts, we can continue to unravel the complexities that underlie people's reasoning and decision-making processes when it comes to navigating the ethical terrain of eating animals.

References

Aguinis, H., & Bradley, K. J. (2014). Best practice recommendations for designing and implementing experimental vignette methodology studies. *Organizational Research Methods*, *17*(4), 351–371.

Altschuler, B. (2014). *Emotional responses to identity affirming touristic vignettes in middle class Chinese and American individuals*. Unpublished dissertation, The University of Utah, Salt Lake City.

Atzmüller, C., & Steiner, P. M. (2010). Experimental vignette studies in survey research. *Methodology*, *6*, 128–138.

Benckendoff, P., Moscardo, G., & Murphy, L. (2012). Environmental attitudes of Generation Y students: Foundations for sustainability education in tourism. *Journal of Teaching in Travel & Tourism, 12*(1), 44–69.

Cooney, N. (2010). *Change of heart: What psychology can teach us about spreading social change*. Brooklyn: Lantern Books.

Ellen, P. S., Wiener, J. L., & Cobb-Walgren, C. (1991). The role of perceived consumer effectiveness in motivating environmentally conscious behaviour's. *Journal of Public Policy & Marketing, 10*(2), 102–117.

Farris, R., Chong, F., & Danning, D. (2002). Generation Y: Purchasing power and implications for marketing. *Academy of Marketing Studies Journal, 6*(2), 89–101.

Food Marketing Institute and North American Meat Institute. (2017). *The power of meat: An in-depth look at meat and poultry through the shoppers' eyes*. Prepared for the Annual Meat Conference, Food Marketing Institute, Arlington, Virginia. Retrieved from www.meatconference.com/sites/default/files/books/Power_of_meat_2017.pdf.

Fuller, B. (2013). *Baby-Boomer marketers are misreading millennials' media behaviour*. Retrieved May 25, 2017, from http://adage.com/article/guest-columnists/marketers-losing-money-misreading-millennials/241407/.

Harrison, R., Newholm, T., & Shaw, D. (2005). *The ethical consumer*. London: SAGE.

(The) Hartman Group, Inc. (2011). *Culture of millennials 2011*. Retrieved June 21, 2017, from http://store.hartman-group.com/content/Millennials-2011-overview.pdf.

Heo, J., & Muralidharan, S. (2017). What triggers young Millennials to purchase eco-friendly products? The interrelationships among knowledge, perceived consumer effectiveness, and environmental concern. *Journal of Marketing Communications*, 1–17. doi:10.1080/13527266.2017.1303623.

Iurkevych, O., Gustin, L., Blecher, L., & Reiboldt, W. (2014). College students' attitudes, perceived consumer effectiveness and intention to dine at a green restaurant. *International Journal of Science Commerce and Humanities, 2*(1), 61–73.

Joy, M. (2011). *Why we love dogs, eat pigs, and wear cows: An introduction to carnism*. Newburyport, MA: Conari Press.

Kinnear, T., Taylor, J., & Ahmed, S. (1974). Ecologically concerned consumers: Who are they? *Journal of Marketing, 38*(2), 20–24.

Kodish, S., & Gittelsohn, J. (2011). Building credible and clear findings; Systematic data analysis in qualitative health research. *Site and Life, 25*(2), 52–56.

Lee, K. J., & Scott, D. (2015). Racial discrimination and African Americans' travel behavior: The utility of habitus and vignette technique. *Journal of Travel Research, 56*(3), 381–392. doi:10.1177/0047287516643184.

Mainieri, T., Barnett, E. G., Oskamp, S., Unipan, J. B., & Valdero, T. R. (1997). Green buying: The influence of environmental concern on consumer behavior. *The Journal of Social Psychology, 137*(2), 189–204.

Moscardo, G., & Benckendorff, P. (2010). Mythbusting: Gen Y and travel. In P. Benckendorff, G. Moscardo, & D. Pendergast (Eds.), *Tourism and generation Y* (pp. 16–26). Cambridge, MA: CABI.

Namugayi, D. (2014). *Social and cultural drivers of meat consumption among Mexican-American millennials in Tempe, AZ*. Unpublished doctoral dissertation, Arizona State University, Tempe, AZ.

Palmer, S. (2017). *Ask the EN experts: February 2017. Young vegetarians on the rise*. Retrieved May 25, 2017, from www.environmentalnutrition.com/issues/40_2/asken/Ask-EN-February-2017_153068-1.html.

Pew Research Center. (2010). *Millennials: A portrait of generation next*. Retrieved June 6, 2013, from http://pewsocialtrends.org/pubs/751/millennials-confident-connected-open-to-change.
Philips, M. (2014, June 30–July 6). The 23 year-olds will save America. *Bloomberg Business Week*, 15–16.
Riggs, B. (2016). What will change as Millennials age? *Convenience Store News*, *52*(9), 68–70.
Sheahan, P. (2005). *Generation Y: Thriving and surviving with generation Y at work*. Prahan: Hardie Grant Books.
Vanhonacker, F., & Verbeke, W. (2009). Buying higher welfare poultry products? Profiling Flemish consumers who do and do not. *Poultry Science*, *88*(12), 2702–2711.
Vermeir, I., & Verbeke, W. (2006). Sustainable food consumption: Exploring the consumer "attitude – behavioral intention" gap. *Journal of Agricultural and Environmental Ethics*, *19*(2), 169–194.
Wason, K. D., Polonsky, M. J., & Hyman, M. R. (2002). Designing vignette studies in marketing. *Australasian Marketing Journal*, *10*(3), 41–58.

8 Tourist desires and animal rights and welfare within tourism

A question of obligations

Neil Carr

Introduction

This conceptual chapter highlights the relation between current animal rights and welfare debates and tourist desires relating to animals and their interaction with them in the holiday environment. These debates are grounded in discussions surrounding whether animals are sentient beings – a highly contested and emotive issue with far reaching implications. The chapter is based on the notion that animals are sentient beings, while recognising that the level and nature of sentience differs across and within species. Within this context, the chapter debates the sustainability of current animal-human interactions within tourism and the associated implications for the tourism industry, society in general, and animal welfare.

A human-centric animal typology

"Some we love, some we hate, some we eat"; so goes the title of Herzog's (2010) book, and it seems a fitting way to begin discussing the relationship between tourists and animals. Into the first category we can place those animals identified as "flagship, charismatic, iconic, emblematic, marquee and poster species" (Small, 2011, p. 232). Such adjectives coalesce around the panda, emblem of the World Wildlife Fund and perhaps the most iconic of poster species. Whether pandas really are charismatic is irrelevant in this context, as it is the human-centric view that is dominant. In this way, the panda is charismatic only because humans have interpreted it as being so; it is only iconic because of the human construction of the panda as cute, cuddly, lovely. Such constructions are utilised and reinforced by the presentation of the panda by everything from the World Wildlife Fund to DreamWorks Animation's *Kung Fu Panda*.

The panda is, of course, not the only animal humans love. Rather, this love tends to be most easily expanded to encompass mammals (Small, 2012; Moss & Esson, 2010), particularly larger ones (Sommer, 2008; Ward, Mosberger, & Kistler, 1998), and ones that make a connection (real or imagined) with us (Bitgood, Patterson, & Benefield, 1988). In this sense, the domesticated dog becomes iconic given the ease with which it engages with humans and, indeed, its apparent yearning for such engagement.

In contrast, there are the animals we hate. These tend to include those that slither, scuttle, and creep. They incorporate the reptiles and invertebrates (Cushing & Markwell, 2011). One suggestion to explain why we hate these animals is not because of what they do but because of how different they are to us (Moss & Esson, 2010; Small, 2012). This hatred, which has a large dollop of fear at its root, is fed upon and reinforced by popular conceptualisations of these animals. The snake, Nagini, in the *Harry Potter* series is a wonderful example of this. She is an animal to be both hated and feared, so the storyline goes.

Then there are the animals we eat. If we adopt a purely Western-centric and beige, conservative, and mundane gaze then defining these appears easy enough: cow, chicken, pig, sheep. However, if I open up the well-known cookery book *Joy of Cooking*, which, while first produced in 1931, was given to my wife and me by her brother in the early years of this century, a much more complex picture begins to emerge. Here I can discover how to cook squirrel, rabbit, hare, opossum, bear, raccoon, muskrat, deer, elk, and moose. I can also, of course, add goose and duck to the list. If we branch out further we can find dog is a meat that has been eaten in virtually all parts of the world (including Western nations) and continues to be consumed in many places (Carr, 2014). Beyond that, we can include giraffe, cat, elephant, horse, whale, turtle, shark, and just about every type of fish from the most mundane (perhaps cod) to the most exotic (pufferfish, perhaps). We can also, of course, include snakes, spiders, rats, and cockroaches by considering even broader cultural food practices. In short, once we begin to move beyond the banal foods we find in the typical Western supermarket, there is virtually no limit to the meats which humans have and do consume.

It is through looking at the variety of animals that humans eat that we can begin to understand that it is far from easy to categorise animals into three discrete groups: love, hate, eat. Rather, different societies and cultures at different times have a role to play in such categorisations, as do personal experiences and preferences (both of which are not fixed but temporally specific). Furthermore, as noted in Carr (2014), with specific reference to the dog, it is possible for a single species to be loved and eaten within the same society at the same time by differentiating between breeds (Reis and Shelton, in this volume, also suggest that dogs might well be hated in certain places). In other words, species can and do exist across these categories rather than being confined to anyone, even within a specific time and place.

It is, I think, also pertinent to add a fourth category to Herzog's list: animals that may be defined as the "invisible." They are the ones we do not hate, love, or eat. Rather, they are the ones we simply do not think about but instead live in ignorance (blissfully or determinedly) of. Through this ignorance, these animals can be classified as the ones we simply do not care about. These are the mundane animals, "the little brown jobs," to borrow Gerald Durrell's term (Durrell Wildlife Conservation Trust, 2015), ones that are chronically difficult to get the general public to engage with because their physical appearance renders them unappealing. The endangered Meller's duck is an example of Durrell's little brown jobs, given that its appearance, to the casual eye, is little different from the common mallard.

Tourism and animals

The tourism experience has arguably always been linked with animals. In the most banal sense, just as in their everyday lives, people (aside from vegans and vegetarians) on holiday eat meat. While eating meat on holiday may largely be identified as passive rather than active engagement with animals, where humans are simply after sustenance, it can also be identified as active from another point of view. Here I am thinking of the active searching for the exotic meal available in the holiday experience, the desire to consume the "other." Moving beyond food, the seeking out of animals in the holiday experience has a long history. The zoo is arguably one of the oldest tourism experiences to offer the opportunity to gaze upon and interact with animals, especially for the masses who have traditionally been unable to afford the luxury of excursions into the "wild" to witness exotic animals in their natural environments. Indeed, Benbow (2004) has noted the existence of zoos as long ago as 4,500 years.

While excursions to see wild animals may have traditionally been the preserve of a minority, this has begun to change (Curtin, 2010, 2005). Today, as well as people being able to wander off on their own in search of wild animals, a plethora of tourism operators exist to act as expert guides. Through these operators, it is possible to see a diverse range of animals, including polar bears, black bears, sharks, dolphins, orca, whales, gorillas, albatross, penguins, lions, tigers, rhino, and otters. A quick look at the Internet will provide numerous example of tourism operators offering wildlife experiences around the world. The result is that the wild animal tourism experience has become a mass tourism phenomenon.

Excursions into the wild or to the zoo are focused around the opportunity and the desire to see, and to be seen by others to see, animals that may be defined as exotic, distinctly different from the mundane. Yet today, tourism experiences that provide access to mundane animals are also widespread. Many farms have partially, or even wholly, remodelled themselves as tourist attractions, where people can come to see common farm animals. Here there is the opportunity to pet a sheep, feed a chicken, or even milk a cow. To some this may sound banal: I have chickens and ducks wandering around my garden, and I pass sheep and horses on my walks around the village I live in. Yet others who live in sanitised urban areas may feel disconnected from such animals (Carr, 2015). This disconnect arguably transforms these animals from banal features of domestic life into exotic others.

As tourists, we can even take on holiday with us the banal animal. Many types of tourist accommodation now present themselves as dog friendly, and it is not uncommon for some to be willing to temporarily house other pets. Alternatively, we may leave our pets behind while we go on holiday, not in a sterile cage, but at a pet hotel, designed to pander to human guilt by offering the family pet a holiday experience of its own (Carr, 2014). Within the tourism experience we can also engage with the banal animal. For example, visitors to Whistler, Canada, who have not been able to take their dog or cat with them and are missing its company, are welcomed at the local animal rescue centre for a dose of pet therapy.

Animal rights and welfare

Whether animals have rights and welfare needs is a question that can only be addressed by first examining whether they are objects or, instead, sentient beings, with active agency, capable of feeling, experiencing, and reacting to the world around them, and of thinking. This is not the same as wondering if non-human animals are the "same" as humans. The answer to that is that they are clearly not, and to think otherwise is to belittle them. Rather, we need to wonder if sentience is a multi-hued phenomenon rather than a case of all or nothing.

The dominant position of the twentieth century was that most animals are not capable of conscious thought, are not self-aware, are not able to experience pleasure or pain other than as an autonomic survival mechanism, and as a result are not quantifiable as sentient beings capable of active agency (Thio, 1983; Thomas, 2000; Masson, 1997). All of these terms have arguably been used interchangeably within the literature on animals (both human and non-human). Furthermore, the same terms have often been used for very different purposes – namely, in animal welfare and rights debates, on both sides of the issue. Consequently, the concept of sentience is a contested one.

For the purpose of this chapter, sentience is seen as encompassing conscious thought, self-awareness, active agency, and the experience of feelings (including pain and pleasure) as more than just survival mechanisms. Boakes (1992, in McConnell, 2005) exemplified the dominant view of the twentieth century when stating that "[a]ttributing conscious thought to animals should be strenuously avoided in any serious attempt to understand their behavior, since it is untestable, empty, obstructionist and based on a false dichotomy" (p. 271). As a direct result of this view, while humans have been self-defined as sentient and therefore deserving of inherent rights and welfare needs, animals have been constructed as deserving of none of these (MacFarland & Hediger, 2009). This view of animals is closely associated with the concept of anthropocentrism, wherein all natural objects are seen to exist for the benefit of human beings, and any consideration of their treatment is given "not for their sake but for their potential to make life better for human beings" (McLean & Yoder, 2005, p. 135).

This traditional view of animals as lacking sentience is the foundation upon which laws regarding animals have been built. Such laws have identified animals as objects or property of humans (Rudy, 2011; Bekoff, 2007; Sanders, 1999). In the eyes of these laws, animals are positioned as entities little different from inanimate possessions. From here, it is a simple step to argue that inanimate possessions have no need of welfare considerations or inalienable rights, and that, therefore, neither do animals (Francione, 2004).

The dominant notion of animals as unthinking and unfeeling automatons is now, however, highly contested. We now recognise that an ever-increasing range of animals are capable of a range of complex emotions (Duncan, 2006). This shift is neatly exemplified by Bradshaw's (2011) recognition that "dogs share our capacity to feel joy, love, anger, fear and anxiety. They also experience pain, hunger, thirst and sexual attraction" (p. 210). The view that animals are self-aware, sentient beings is increasingly widespread (Low, 2012; Emel & Urbanik, 2010; Lehman, 1997; Bostock, 1993; Warkentin, 2010). At the forefront of this shift in thinking about animals, Jane Goodale (2007) has evocatively stated that "[t]here was increasingly compelling evidence that we are not alone in the universe, not the only creatures with minds capable of solving problems, capable of love and hate, joy and sorrow, fear and despair" (p. xii). This new position regarding animals may be likened to a biocentric orientation, which "gives moral standing to all living things" (McLean & Yoder, 2005, p. 136).

Based on the shift in thinking about the sentience of animals, Bekoff (2007), amongst others, has suggested that "ethical values tell us that animals should not be viewed as property, as resources, or as disposable machines that exist for human consumption, treated like bicycles or backpacks" (p. 18). Recognising that the law is a moral and ethical construct, Bekoff's statement reads as a call for not just a change in how we perceive and treat animals, but also for how the law defines them. Such a shift has begun, with laws now in existence around the world ostensibly designed to protect and ensure the wellbeing of a diverse range of animals in a variety of settings. Our shifting views regarding the sentience of animals is the ground upon which the five freedoms for animals [i.e., freedom from hunger and thirst; freedom from discomfort; freedom from pain, injury, and disease; freedom to express normal behaviour; freedom from fear and distress (Royal Society for the Prevention of Cruelty to Animals, 2012)] have been constructed. Finally, the shift in thinking about animal sentience has been both driven by and the foundation for calls for recognition of the rights and welfare needs of animals.

It is at this point that we must differentiate between animal rights and animal welfare. The most extreme animal rights protagonists would claim that humans should not make use of animals in any way whatsoever, to the point of dismissing the notion of animals as pets of humans (Fennell, 2012). Tom Regan (1985) is arguably the founding father of such a position. In questioning the anthropocentric position, Regan has stated: "[t]he fundamental wrong is the system that allows us to view animals as our resources, here for us – to be eaten, or surgically manipulated, or exploited for sport or money" (p. 14). Animal welfarists make no such claim about the need to disassociate animals and humans completely, recognising the lives of all animals and humans are, to varying degrees, intertwined (Carr, 2014). Yet animal welfarists should not be identified as claiming animals have no rights. Rather, they would state that animals have rights that exist within the context of their relations to humans and that such rights are meaningless without welfare concerns.

Is this then the end of the story? Are we now on the right path to recognising animal rights and welfare needs? Arguably not. Rudy (2011) would suggest this is because "humans still hold all the power" (p. 9). Accordingly, it is necessary to go beyond mere recognition of rights and welfare needs and to recognise that with power comes the responsibility to utilise that power responsibly to ensure the needs of animals are met. In this way, the core issue is not power but responsibility, or the responsible use of power. Part of this requires listening and responding to the other, rather than simply imposing rights and welfare needs on them. In this way, it is our responsibility to bend our ethical and moral positions to meet with animals as conscious beings, rather than simply impose our beliefs and positions on them. Within this context, it is important to realise that there are inherent differences (including differing levels and types of sentience) between different types of animals (including humans). In this way, I agree with Singer's (2004) view that the concept of equality extends beyond treating different animals in exactly the same way or giving them all the same rights. The important point is not equal treatment but equal consideration, which can lead to different rights and recognition of different welfare needs for different animals. Following this logic, recognition of animal rights and welfare needs is not, in itself, sufficient. Rather, these rights and needs must be recognised from the perspective of animals and applied for the benefit of animals rather than for the benefit of the human conscience.

There is also the need to recognise the importance of the concept of "obligations" in this context (Broom, 2006). Humans are normally in a position of power in relation to animals. Yet to say humans hold all the power is to miss the point that if an animal is sentient and, therefore, an active agent, then it will hold some measure of power, however little (Carr, 2014). Our twin obligations are to ensure we understand the welfare needs of animals from the perspective of animals and to ensure we utilise our power to meet our obligations to ensure those needs are met. This position is not a utilitarian one, as it is more than simply about balancing good and bad.

Tourist desires and animal obligations

Clearly, within the tourism experience, not all animals are given equal consideration. Some are venerated and positioned as "must see" attractions – the great apes are a good example (Carr, 2016a). One way for tourists to see these animals is to visit them in their natural landscape. Such tours are, of course, expensive and, as such, out of reach for many people. Tourists can also view these animals by visiting the myriad zoos around the world. In the case of Durrell Wildlife Park in the UK, the primary animal attractions are the gorillas and orangutans (Carr, 2016b). In the case of zoos, like Durrell Wildlife Park, an emotive debate continues to rage surrounding whether they should exist or be closed as symbols of all that is wrong with how humans have traditionally viewed and treated animals (see Carr & Cohen, 2011). Those advocating for closure see zoos as places that people go to in order to be entertained by animals (Jamieson, 1985). Animals are little more than objects whose roles are to titillate bored humans. This links zoos to the anthropocentric view of animals noted by McLean and Yoder (2005) and sets them against animal rights proponents such as Regan (1985). Closure advocates also point to the conditions in which wild animals are kept in zoos: enclosed in spaces smaller than those they would experience in their native habitat and often given relatively little space to hide from the gaze of visitors, which forces them to always be on display. Finally, closure advocates point to the all-pervasive control humans exert over animals within zoos. These animals eat, sleep, procreate, and often die according to the rules of humans. This is arguably exemplified by the decision of Copenhagen zoo in 2014 to kill Marius the giraffe. The zoo stated that this decision was made to prevent inbreeding. After being put down, Marius's remains were dissected in public and his flesh fed to the zoo's lions (Eriksen, 2014). Viewed from a particular lens, this was a case of humans controlling the life, and death, of an animal and then objectifying the animal in death by undertaking the dissection in public. Cohen and Fennell (2016) provide a detailed discussion of Marius and his treatment, dealing with the often-competing issues of species conservation and individual welfare.

From the perspective of recognising our obligations to animals as sentient beings, there is a lot of value in what those who wish to see zoos close have to say. There are many zoos around the world where animals exist in extremely poor spaces that are detrimental to their mental and physical wellbeing. Such spaces hark back to the earliest zoos that were clearly created with attention only to the benefits for humans and were based on a view of animals as nothing more than curious animated objects. However, if we are concerned with our obligations to animals rather than our desires to assuage our own conscience (something that can arguably be construed as an objectification of animals in its own right, as it gives primacy to human feelings over our obligations to animals), then we need to recognise a more nuanced reality that surrounds zoos. As noted by Carr and Cohen (2011), there are well-run zoos that are not merely sites of animal objectification for human entertainment, but are also engaged in conservation efforts that include educating the general public of the importance of such work. In addition, we must move beyond an animal welfarist position that merely quantifies welfare through a human-centric, scientific perspective [see Fennell (2013) for a discussion of this type of approach] and towards adopting one that truly identifies animals as active agents, sentient beings capable of assessing their own welfare. This speaks to the work of Haraway (2008) and Warkentin (2010), amongst others, which talks about the need to engage with animals to learn about them, from them. In turn, this position arguably flows into (and out of) an ecofeminist perspective that talks of animal liberation (Gaard, 1993). As with all liberation, this requires recognition and empowerment of the views of the oppressed, animals in this case, and not just concern with perspectives of those in the position of dominance, humans in this case.

It is within this context that we need to debate whether an enclosure in a zoo can ever be sufficient to meet our obligations to the welfare of animals. Clearly, some enclosures are not sufficient. I am thinking here of the barren, concrete cages. Such an enclosure is arguably symbolised in Figure 8.1. The bars that cage the animal in are symbolic of the unmet obligation, but the symbol is one-sided, in that it is seen as such by the human and not the animal. However, when enclosures such as the one in Figure 8.1 are replaced with ones like that in Figure 8.2, the question must be asked if zoos are getting closer to meeting our obligations to animals. Yes, these animals are not free, living in the wild, but while that may be a utopian ideal, the reality is that bears in the wild are regularly targeted (legally and illegally) by hunters, and the natural environment of the orangutans is being

Figure 8.1 Bear enclosure at Alpenzoo Innsbruck, Austria (1996).
Photo by the author.

Figure 8.2 Bear enclosure at Alpenzoo Innsbruck, Austria (2013).
Photo by the author.

rapidly destroyed, leaving them with nowhere to go other than extinction. We may have an obligation to stop such processes, but we also arguably have an obligation to preserve species in high-quality zoos in the meantime: not just for human entertainment, but primarily for the preservation of individual animals and entire species.

Figure 8.3 raises additional questions about the objectification of animals in zoos. Here, an orangutan is firmly set within the gaze of numerous humans. From one perspective, this may be seen as a case of the objectification of the animal and the exposure of it to the unremitting gaze of the human. Yet there is arguably a more complex reality at play here. A conversation with Lee Durrell (Honorary Director of the Durrell Wildlife Conservation Trust, and Gerald Durrell's widow) in 2013 was particularly illuminating. There is a playground in Durrell Wildlife Park where children can burn off excess energy. Lee pointed out the playground was deliberately situated within the zoo so that the orangutans would be able to see it from their enclosure, allowing the animals to view the visitors. In this way, the visitors become the object of the gaze of the animal, a source of entertainment for the orangutans. The conclusion to be taken from this is that it can be an arrogant human-centred presumption to believe all zoos and zoo exhibits have been created for and by people to objectify animals.

Is meeting an animal in the wild as a tourist different to meeting one in a zoo within the context of our obligations to animals as sentient beings? Certainly, the two contexts of encounter can be very different for the tourist in an experiential

Figure 8.3 Who is watching whom? Durrell Wildlife Park (2013).

Photo by the author.

sense. There is simply something thrilling about encountering an animal in the wild. As such, seeing a bear in the wild on the slopes of Blackcomb Mountain in British Columbia, Canada, was far more thrilling than seeing the ones depicted in Figures 8.1 and 8.2 in Alpenzoo. This is not to say that the bears in Alpenzoo are not wonderful – far from it – but that there is just something different associated with seeing them in the wild. Thanks to the social construction of the wild animal, there is also significant social value in the form of prestige associated with witnessing an animal in the wild rather than in a zoo. However, this value is human-centric and is another example of the objectification of animals for the benefit of humans. It is in this context that there is little difference between the site of animals surrounded by people within a zoo versus in the wild. This speaks to the point made by Whatmore (2002) about the end of the wild.

Yet there are many examples of responsible animal tourism operators who enforce and abide by strict regulations to mitigate the impact of tourists on the animals they wish to see in the wild. Such rules and attempts to enforce them are arguably related to three issues: protection of the economic resources of the animal tourism industry (i.e., the animals), protection of human welfare, and protection of the animals. All of these issues may be associated with the obligations of humans to ensure the welfare of animals as sentient beings, but the final one is most clearly.

As noted in Carr (2014), dogs are increasingly seen as guests in the tourism experience, an integral part of the family holiday. Consequently, it is not uncommon to see them with their human companions in hotels. This shift in the tourism industry has been driven by the changing position of dogs within the human household, as they have journeyed from pet to companion. The notion of the dog as companion clearly infers upon the dog recognition of its sentience. As a companion, many humans reject the notion that it is acceptable to leave their dog behind while they go on holiday. To do so would be, in the eyes of such people, akin to leaving their children behind when they went on holiday. Such a decision flies in the face of social constructions of the "good parent" (Carr, 2011). In the same way, a good human companion is constructed as someone who takes their canine companion on holiday with them. Faced with the socially and personally constructed need to meet the expectations of a good human companion due to the difficulties of travelling internationally with a dog, people may turn to the emergent pet hotel industry that has grown out of the kennel industry.

The question that must be addressed is whether those who take their dog on holiday with them or place them in a pet hotel are doing so for humancentric reasons or for the welfare of the animal, or a mixture of the two. In this context, Carr (2014) has asked the question of whether pet hotels pander to the guilt humans feel at leaving their dog behind when they go on holiday or to the needs of the dog. Similarly, do those hotels that now enable humans to share a room with their dog cater to the desires of the human or the needs and welfare of the dog?

While a segment of the tourism industry has emerged to ostensibly cater to the companion dog, the reality is that they often really pander to the human owners and their desires. The humans in these situations may wish to construct an image of themselves as good dog owners caring for their dogs' needs. Or, they may be blinded by the idea that their dog is really no different from a four-legged, hairy child. Both patterns of reasoning fail to take account of humans' obligations to dogs, which include recognising and treating them as dogs – companions, perhaps, but always dogs.

As well as being companions in the tourism experience, dogs can be tourist attractions. Dog-sledding tours are perhaps the prime example of this. These tours have been accused of animal cruelty, where dogs are objectified for the financial benefit of operators and the enjoyment of tourists. The iconic example of such a situation came to light in the aftermath of the 2010 Vancouver Winter Olympic Games. A sled dog tour operator in Whistler had sought to benefit from a likely upsurge in demand during the games by significantly increasing its number of dogs. However, once the Games were over, it quickly became apparent that the operator had more dogs than was sustainable (Fennell & Sheppard, 2011). As a result, somewhere between 50 and 100 (a precise number is impossible to ascertain from media reports) were killed by the company. These dogs were seen as inconvenient objects to be used for financial gain and then disposed of when they became a burden.

Yet there are also dog sled tour operators who clearly place their obligations to their dogs at least alongside and often before their own. In these cases, the dogs are well cared for and love to run in front of the sled (or equivalent). Their owners ensure they enjoy running until such time as a decision based on the welfare of the dog must be made to have it put to sleep. Calls to ban all sled dog tours and racing are potentially guilty of failing to view the experience from the perspective of the dog and to differentiate between the pet dog and the sled dog; the two are not one in the same. Our obligations to sled dogs force us not just to look at banning sledding but to consider that dogs can benefit from it and enjoy the experience.

So far, the chapter has dealt with animals that are widely liked (and even loved) among humans. Yet to go back to the beginning of this chapter, there are also those animals that most humans hate that are present in the tourism environment. If we visit a zoo, we can often see exotic examples of these; they are, to give them their entirely unscientific name, the "creepy crawlies." They are the animals that most people prefer to not see (Lemelin, 2013), even from behind the glass of an enclosure in a zoo. They are the animals that the hospitality industry will normally do all it can to exterminate or prevent guests from seeing. People do not wish to see such animals on their hotel bed when turning on the light at night or in the hotel's swimming pool, nor do they wish to know how many bugs may lurk in the dark corners of the restaurant kitchen. These unloved animals are easily treated with a brutality that would cause uproar amongst the human populous if applied to bears, elephants, or whales, among other iconic and "attractive" animals. Yet because we have no love for them, or they have been constructed as risking the wellbeing of humans, they can be exterminated without humans feeling any guilt. However, just because we may not like a certain type of animal because it is not cute and cuddly but instead gives us the "creeps" is not in itself an automatic reason for disavowing all knowledge of any obligations to such an animal.

Conclusion

There are so many ways in which virtually every species of animal intersects with the tourism experience that to do justice to them all in one chapter is clearly impossible. Rather, the intension was to examine the obligations humans have to animals in the tourism experience. Through the examples provided, this chapter has attempted to demonstrate that how and to what extent our obligations to animals as sentient beings are met in the tourism experience is a nuanced and complex issue, but that these obligations should always be set by animals and not humans. This demands that we must listen to what animals have to say about their needs and desires. While this may be difficult, as people such as Bekoff (2007) and Horowitz (2009) have suggested, it is both possible and a rewarding experience for all concerned.

Focusing on obligations, it is not how an animal appears to be treated from the human's perspective that matters. Rather, it is the animal's perspective that matters. Consequently, it is suggested that it is not the context of the meeting of humans and animals in tourism that matters but what underlies and drives the observable behaviour. In this way, zoos, wildlife tourism operators, and dog owners all can and cannot meet obligations to animal welfare. It is not who or what they are that matters, but how they think from the perspective of the animals and then how they operationalise their obligations that matter.

If we return to the notion that all animals are sentient, though not necessarily to the same level, then it must be recognised that we have obligations to them all, no matter how humble the animal or how loathsome we find them to be, while at the same time recognising that differences in sentience that exist across species mean that the nature of the obligations similarly differs across species. Failure to recognise this is arguably demeaning to the animal.

Based on this understanding, we need to ask if animal experiences in tourism can be sustainable. The answer is "yes," if we always ensure our obligations to animals are met in an animal-centric manner. This does not necessarily entail an unreachable idyll, but instead adds a layer of thinking to the development and running of tourism experiences. In a sustainable model, it is insufficient to think only in a human-centric model, and at the same time, it is insufficient to think only in an animal-centric model. Instead, a holistic approach must be adopted that recognises the welfare needs of all and seeks to balance them in an appropriate manner. This arguably requires innovative thinking that sees the nuanced reality and does not therefore attempt to impose carte blanche thinking. In such a situation, tourism experiences for animals, about animals, and with animals can all exist. The key is understanding the welfare requirements of animals, as opposed to what humans desire the welfare needs of animals to be, and then striving to act upon the obligations that these needs entail.

To be truly sustainable within a framework that recognises all animals, human and non-human, as sentient, living together in one complex but human-dominated global ecosystem, the bi-directional nature of obligations must be examined. In other words, we must ask whether animals have obligations to humans, just as humans have obligations to animals. This is not to suggest we should go back to a traditional anthropocentric view, but that instead we must embrace all that an ecofeminist approach should entail: the empowerment of all. Through this empowerment comes a recognition of the potential for all actors, human and non-human, to have obligations. Consequently, when talking of animal welfare, we should be thinking not just of the non-human animals but all animals, a process that further dispels the myth of the existence of a distinct difference between humans and animals. This is a provocative thought to end on, one that embraces sentience and difference and potentially takes animal welfarist thinking a little further down the road towards sustainability.

References

Bekoff, M. (2007). *Animals matter*. Boston, MA: Shambhala.

Benbow, M. (2004). Death and dying at the zoo. *Journal of Popular Culture*, *37*(3), 379–398.

Bitgood, S., Patterson, D., & Benefield, A. (1988). Exhibit design and visitor behavior: Empirical relationships. *Environment and Behavior*, *20*(4), 474–491.

Bostock, S. (1993). *Zoos and animal rights: The ethics of keeping animals*. London: Routledge.

Bradshaw, J. (2011). *In defence of dogs: Why dogs need our understanding*. London: Allen Lane.

Broom, D. M. (2006). The evolution of morality. *Applied Animal Behaviour Science*, *100*, 20–28.

Carr, N. (2011). *Children's and families' holiday experiences*. London: Routledge.

Carr, N. (2014). *Dogs in the leisure experience*. Wallingford: CABI.

Carr, N. (2015). Introduction: Defining domesticated animals and exploring their uses by and relationships with humans. In N. Carr (Ed.), *Domestic animals and leisure* (pp. 1–13). Basingstoke: Palgrave Macmillan.

Carr, N. (2016a). Ideal animals and animal traits for zoos: General public perspectives. *Tourism Management*, *57*, 37–44.

Carr, N. (2016b). An analysis of zoo visitors' favourite and least favourite animals. *Tourism Management Perspectives*, *20*, 70–76.

Carr, N., & Cohen, S. (2011). The public face of zoos: Balancing entertainment, education, and conservation. *Anthrozoos*, *24*(2), 175–189.

Cohen, E., & Fennell, D. (2016). The elimination of Marius, the giraffe: Humanitarian act or callous management decision? *Tourism Recreation Research*, *41*(2), 168–176.

Curtin, S. (2005). Nature, wild animals and tourism: An experiential view. *Journal of Ecotourism*, *4*(1), 1–15.

Curtin, S. (2010). What makes for memorable wildlife encounters? Revelations from 'serious' wildlife tourists. *Journal of Ecotourism*, *9*(2), 149–168.

Cushing, N., & Markwell, K. (2011). I can't look: Disgust as a factor in the zoo experience. In W. Frost (Ed.), *Zoos and tourism: Conservation, education, entertainment?* (p. 167–178). Bristol: Channel View Publications.

Duncan, I. (2006). The changing concept of animal sentience. *Applied Animal Behaviour Science*, *100*, 11–19.

Durrell Wildlife Conservation Trust. (2015). *The Gerald Durrell story*. Retrieved March 11, 2015, from www.durrell.org/about/gerald-durrell/.

Emel, J., & Urbanik, J. (2010). Animal geographies: Exploring the spaces and places of human-animal encounters. In M. Demello (Ed.), *Teaching the animal: Human-animal studies across the disciplines* (pp. 202–217). New York: Lantern Books.

Eriksen, L. (2014). Copenhagen zoo sparks outrage by killing healthy giraffe named Marius. *The Guardian*. Retrieved February 10, 2014, from www.theguardian.com/world/2014/feb/09/danish-zoo-outrage-giraffe-marius.

Fennell, D. (2012). Tourism and animal rights. *Tourism Recreation Research*, *37*(2), 157–166.

Fennell, D. (2013). Tourism and animal welfare. *Tourism Recreation Research*, *38*(3), 325–340.

Fennell, D., & Sheppard, V. (2011). Another legacy for Canada's 2010 Olympic and Paralympic Winter Games: Applying an ethical lens to the post-games' sled dog cull. *Journal of Ecotourism*, *10*(3), 197–213.

Francione, G. L. (2004). Animals – property or persons? In C. Sunstein & M. Nussbaum (Eds.), *Animal rights: Current debates and new directions* (pp. 108–142). Oxford: Oxford University Press.

Gaard, G. (1993). Living interconnections with animals and nature. In G. Gaard (Ed.), *Ecofeminism: Women animals, nature* (pp. 1–10). Philadelphia, PA: Temple University.

Goodale, J. (2007). Foreword. In M. Bekoff (Ed.), *The emotional lives of animals* (pp. xi–xv). Novato, CA: New World Library.

Haraway, D. (2008). *When species meet*. Minneapolis, MN: University of Minnesota Press.

Herzog, H. (2010). *Some we love, some we hate, some we eat*. New York: Harper.

Horowitz, A. (2009). *Inside of a dog: What dogs see, smell, and know*. New York: Scribner.

Jamieson, D. (1985). Against zoos. In P. Singer (Ed.), *In defence of animals* (pp. 108–117). Oxford: Basil Blackwell.

Lehman, H. (1997). Anthropomorphism and scientific evidence for animal mental states. In R. Mitchell, N. Thompson, & H. Miles (Eds.), *Anthropomorphism, anecdotes, and animals* (pp. 104–115). Albany, NY: State University of New York Press.

Lemelin, H. (Ed.). (2013). *The management of insects in recreation and tourism*. Cambridge: Cambridge University Press.

Low, P. (2012). *The Cambridge declaration on consciousness*. Retrieved February 18, 2013, from fcmconference.org/img/CambridgeDeclarationOnConsciousness.pdf.

MacFarland, S., & Hediger, R. (2009). Approaching the agency of other animals: An introduction. In S. MacFarland & R. Hediger (Eds.), *Animals and agency: An interdisciplinary exploration* (pp. 1–20). Boston, MA: Brill.

Masson, J. (1997). *Dogs never lie about love: Reflections on the emotional world of dogs*. New York: Three Rivers Press.

McConnell, P. (2005). *For the love of a dog: Understanding emotion in you and your best friend*. New York: Ballantine Books.

McLean, D., & Yoder, D. (2005). *Issues in recreation and leisure: Ethical decision making*. Champaign, IL: Human Kinetics.

Moss, A., & Esson, M. (2010). Visitor interest in zoo animals and the implications for collection planning and zoo education programmes. *Zoo Biology*, *29*, 715–731.

Regan, T. (1985). The case for animal rights. In P. Singer (Ed.), *In defence of animals* (pp. 13–26). Oxford: Basil Blackwell.

Royal Society for the Prevention of Cruelty to Animals. (2012). *Frequently asked questions*. Retrieved December 31, 2012, from www.rspca.org.uk/utilities/faq/-/question/ENQ_Five_Freedoms/category/Pets/.

Rudy, K. (2011). *Loving animals: Toward a new animal advocacy*. Minneapolis, MN: University of Minnesota Press.

Sanders, C. (1999). *Understanding dogs: Living and working with canine companions*. Philadelphia, PA: Temple University Press.

Singer, P. (2004). All animals are equal. In J. Sterba (Ed.), *Morality in practice* (7th ed., pp. 474–483). London: Thomson Learning.

Small, E. (2011). The new Noah's Ark: Beautiful and useful species only. Part 1. Biodiversity conservation issues and priorities. *Biodiversity*, *12*(4), 232–247.

Small, E. (2012). The new Noah's Ark: Beautiful and useful species only. Part 2. The chosen species. *Biodiversity*, *13*(1), 37–53.

Sommer, R. (2008). Semantic profiles of zoos and their animals. *Anthrozoos*, *21*(3), 237–244.

Thio, A. (1983). *Deviant behaviour* (2nd ed.). Boston, MA: Houghton Mifflin Company.

Thomas, E. M. (2000). *The social lives of dogs: The grace of canine company*. New York: Simon & Schuster.

Ward, P., Mosberger, N., Kistler, C., & Fischer, O. (1998). The relationship between popularity and body size in zoo animals. *Conservation Biology*, *12*(6), 1408–1411.

Warkentin, T. (2010). Interspecies etiquette: An ethics of paying attention to animals. *Ethics & the Environment*, *15*(1), 101–121.

Whatmore, S. (2002). *Hybrid geographies: Natures, cultures, spaces*. London: SAGE.

9 Feral tourism

Adrian Franklin and Thomas Colas

Feral: from latin *fera* = wild animal
Adj.

1. Pertaining to, or resembling, a wild animal; fierce, savage, brutal. [Early 17th century)
2. Wild, untamed, uncultivated [Mid-17th century].
3. Chiefly of animals: belonging to or forming a wild population ultimately descended from individuals which escaped from captivity or domestication; born of such animals in the wild. [Mid-19th century]

Shorter Oxford English Dictionary (2002)

Introduction

Like wildlife documentary making, wildlife tourism typically seeks to frame nature as an idealised place beyond humanity, with wilderness as something of a gold standard against which nature experiences can be measured as authentic, real or proper. In many places, such as Australia, it also seeks to idealise and showcase native natures, as true or pure ecosystemic communities uncontaminated by feral species, whose mobilities and "invasions" shadowed naval exploration, colonialism, agriculture, scientific acclimatisations, globalisation – and tourism. Wildlife tourism also arranges tourism experiences and "outcomes" using such framings, seeking to align tourists with such values, and claiming their conversion to conservationism as a major ethical outcome. While not contesting the value of conservation, or the duty of care for our world – indeed seeking precisely to do this more realistically and effectively – this paper asks whether it is time for wildlife/eco-tourism to recognise that nature in places like Australia no longer conforms to such ideals. New configurations of "feralised natures," what Tim Low (2002) called "the new nature," now predominate across most of the continent. Australian ecologies are now typified by their mixture of native and feral with little possibility that ecological restoration back to the "native ecologies" found on first (white) settlement would ever succeed. Like Australia's society and culture, its ecologies are characterised by difference and change rather than by pure or ideal "types," despite native natures having a strong moral claim through its symbolic use in the emergence of Australian nationalism. Australia's new natures involve new becomings, new accommodations between native and feral (and humanity) and the formation of entirely new ecological landscapes. And yet, the natures we inhabit is at odds with tourism encounters that still privilege native species and bracket out the feral. At its worst, our feral natures are fraught with the same intolerance and violence we see in our own human world, as some species become precious insiders and others become outsiders and "unAustralian" monsters, to be eradicated, controlled and managed – often for very arbitrary and inconsistent reasons. This paper considers the origins of the discrepancy between Australia's ecologies and its representation as wildlife tourism, as well as the value of creating new and ethical *feral* tourism that can reveal Australia's ecological complexity as well as confront tourists with the dilemmas and tensions facing conservation biology.

As the Shorter Oxford English Dictionary shows, the word "feral" is complex and historically contingent. When used in the Australian context for example, it is also extended to wild species (of all kinds) from several places that were acclimatised from the 1860s onwards in an audacious attempt to improve the value of wildlife for hunting sports, self-provisioning and aesthetics (e.g., bird song, flowering plants). Hence they became a binary opposite to native species, and began to be positioned as opposed to national values.

Skibins (2015) defined wildlife tourism as "tourism that provides encounters with non-domesticated animals in wild *(in situ)* or captive (*ex situ*) settings" (p. 42), a view shared by many others, including Roe, Leader-Williams, and Dalal-Clayton (1997), Higginbottom (2004) and Valantine and Birtles (2004). However, across most wild settings in Australia, it would be hard to find any completely unentangled with "domestic species," "escaped captives" or the many other deliberately or unintentionally introduced "non-local" species that have been living wild for upwards of 200 years or more. This is true whether the notion of wildlife is confined to "animals" or broadened to encompass all "wild life" (all living things).

Native wildlife is among the most longstanding and important tourist attractions to Australia and yet they are rarely presented alongside these "feral" species, fauna and flora, with whom they live cheek by jowl, co-evolving in "the new nature" (Low, 2002). The new nature represents a dramatic change, properly a series of adaptive transitions towards largely hybrid ecologies, yet the nature of this change, and especially the extent of this, cannot be found in the language or the experiences offered by (almost) any form of Australian wildlife tourism.

In underlining the significance of native wildlife tourism in Australia, Fredline and Faulkner (2001) reported that 18.4% of visitors to Australia reported that the desire to see native wildlife (especially kangaroos and koolas) influenced their choice to visit Australia; that 67.5% of tourists wanted to see native animals during their visit; and that 71.1% actually did see them during their visit. However, their touristic dreams are themselves tightly framed and shaped by a privileging of native animals and the bracketing out of feral animals. Imagining that most wildlife tourists begin their journey, and form key choices, by surfing the internet, we sampled Google searches to uncover the extent to which the realities of Australian wildlife and ecology are reflected in its content. We sampled the first 200 images for the search: "Animals + Australia." Not surprisingly, native animals predominated (75% of content) with substantially less content featuring non-native species (25%). Even then a large proportion among these were farm animals such as sheep and dogs and when "feral/pest" animals appeared they tended to be animals that were subject to major extermination programs: rabbits, cats, pigs and foxes – all represented in a manner deliberately repulsive to visitors. The majority, including those that have a benign or beneficial value ecologically, are invisible.

However, when we sampled tourism-specific web sites the proportions of non-natives fell away even further, thus suggesting that a bracketing-out process has skewed the nature of Australia" s actual wildlife content as presented for consumption by tourists. We analysed the content of the first 100 Google hits for the keywords: nature tourism/eco-tours/wildlife tours/wilderness tours. Ninety-five percent of the wildlife touristic offer is focussed on native animals, and feral animals are shown only in terms of a problem to be managed, rather than something that tourists might value seeing/visiting/knowing about or as intertwined in real-life ecological settings and issues.

This is not surprising given Australian *attitudes* to the animals shown in the first 100 hits for the search: "feral animals in Australia." Here we found that negative attitudes predominate (55%) while 31% were neutral and only 14% were positive. This is a longstanding pattern. In her survey of wildlife encounters in Australia, Bulbeck (2005) discovered that 77% of visitors approved of the extermination of the fox and feral cat, a proportion that rose to 84% among tertiary educated visitors. To check these distributions against another nation with a significant number of introduced species we conducted the same search for the UK. Here however we found far more positive attitudes, with 45% expressing positive attitudes, 30% neutral but only 25% negative.

We also note from Bruce Rose's (1995) study of attitudes to native and feral animals among Aboriginal communities in Central Australia that they do not see native and feral as opposed categories, but value them by different criteria, according to whether they thrive together and together provide a nutritious landscape.

> [Bruce Rose] found that many Aboriginal people expressed the idea the Country itself shows who belongs and who doesn't. He concluded that "ethics and value judgements which support playing favourites with some species over others" do not fit easily into the views of Aboriginal Elders.
>
> (Bird Rose, 2016, no page number)

So, the binary native/feral and the ethics of privileging the former over the latter is contested and not least in recent years by critiques from animal studies, posthumanism, environmental history, environmental humanities and social and environmental anthropology (Smith, 1999; Ritvo, 2012; Trigger, Mulcock, Gaynor, & Toussaint,

2008; Haraway, 2016a). Many scholars have noted how a strong form of white nationalism in Australia drove a very close association between native species and Australian society, perhaps when the uniqueness of its wildlife proved irresistible for its semiotic recoding as a distinct new nation (Hage, 1998; Peretti, 1998; Smith, 2000; Hillier, 2016b).

However, there are other important ecological issues that arise from new entanglements that ought not to be obscured. Some demonstrate that feralised ecologies can produce new and positive forms of accommodation between host and arriving species, where new patterns of adaptation and balance become possible. They challenge older views of flora and fauna by showing how they can live in new ways and form complex new alliances and are not overdetermined by either their biology or instinct. But equally, paying attention to them, or as Haraway (2016a) suggests, "staying with the trouble," ensures that tourists are not blind to the very bad things that "feral biology" can bring into the world – as Anna Tsing (2015) shows in respect of feral tree fungi, plantation agriculture and wild forests.

The paper chapter will now expand these points in order demonstrate the scope of feral tourism to add value to our wildlife tourism experiences and engagements. It will then indicate why feral tourism might chime well with contemporary sensibilities and various ways in which feral tourism can be developed. I will show that it has conservation value, whether as dark (but thought provoking) tourism, or as counter-intuitive examples of the capacity of life to survive, surprise and delight.

Feral ecologies in Australia

While Australian wildlife as represented at major portals of internet searching and public information is heavily skewed towards native wildlife, the penetration of Australian ecologies by feral species is significantly under-represented. The scale on which Australian native species and their ecologies have been changed (or feralised) by the introduction – both by sustained scientific effort and by accident – of non-native species is extraordinary and extensive. According to the Australian Biosecurity Group, "No one has ever counted all our introduced species" and just "calculating the number of foreign insects . . . is mere guesswork" (p. 5). Many have never been identified, and new ones slip through the quarantine net each year. Even listing the numbers of known introductions is daunting (Australian Biosecurity Group, 2005).

At the turn of the 21st century, Tim Low (1999) argued that Australia's "collective ignorance about pests is remarkable" (p. 8) and all the more serious because they are "irreversible and cumulative" – by which he meant not just cumulative in the landscape but cumulative in their penetration of ecologies and as consequences for ecological and evolutionary change across the continent. In the 2001 preface to his *Feral Futures*, for example, Low conceded that the recent arrival of just one animal, the European bumble bee, had worsened our weed problems on a continental scale.

Numbers alone might not be alarming if they were highly localised and their movement containable, but they are not, which means that without actively bracketing them out there are few possibilities for the Australian zoological gaze to miss their presence – or, the consequences of their *actual* ecological relationships with other species. This is easily illustrated using the 2004 Pest Animal Control CRC publication *Counting the Cost: Impact of Invasive Animals in Australia*, which looked closely at just 11 of these species. Part of the problem for those who sought their eradication is reaching them across Australia's rugged country. Those of most "interest" to eradicators are very widely distributed and found in vast numbers, the rabbit being one of Australia's most numerous animals (20 billion even by 1920). Not surprisingly, the mouse, the fox, the rat and the cat are found throughout mainland Australia in large numbers and all of these bar the fox are in Tasmania. Feral pigs inhabit some 38% of the mainland and camels 37%, while population densities of wild dogs in New South Wales alone range between 0.1–0.3 per square km. Goats are found across all states and territories, as is the carp. There are very few rivers or lakes in Tasmania which do not have one or more species of trout in them – in great profusion. Wild Horses (brumbies) are distributed across Australia's vast cattle country in Queensland, Northern Territory, Western Australia and South Australia and also in alpine areas in Victoria and NSW (McLeod, 2004).

But these animals are not just interlopers living *outside* Australian ecological communities from where they stage destructive raids and invasions. Instead we have a patchwork of national ecologies where feral species and native species, both fauna and flora, have become irreversibly interpenetrated and interdependent in complex and wide reaching ways. Their co-presence and mutual adaptations change them biologically, leading to processes of co-evolution.

As such, even the concepts of "native" and "feral" species in Australia begin to lose all semblance of meaning and difference as they converge around evolutionary lines of flight that i) detach native species from exclusively "native Australian ecological settings," while ii) making Australia the source of incremental changes, physiological and behavioural, to the bodies of introduced species who were "only once" entirely alien to it. Put another way, Van Dooren (2011) criticised the ecological logic behind the valorisation of native species alone, suggesting that it "reifies a specific historical moment that ignores the changing and dynamic nature of ecologies" (p. 289). And the choice of moment as the baseline for ecological restoration becomes a political rather than an ecological question. Should it be the fire landscapes of Aboriginal Australia? Should it be the landscapes after Aborigines were effectively removed? And if the latter, how would it be possible to decide the right moment in the series of dramatic transformations effected since white settlement? Deciding on what we might mean by native ecosystems is very far from straightforward. The ecological reality of this and the speed with which unsettled "feralised" natures evolved, can hardly be in dispute, and is well illustrated by genetic studies of the Australian house sparrow which found that they are now biologically distinct and separate from ancestral stock (Low, 2001, p. 242). But it has also been highly problematic to exclude humanity from ecology (Ellen, 1996; Tsing, 2015) and nowhere more so than in Australia, so even the native/feral binary is an incomplete ecological reality with important touristic implications.

The increasing implications of extensive human interventions in the Australian landscape make it almost impossible for environmental threats to native species to be entirely attributed to other non-human species and yet it is they alone who are mostly made to bear the cost (Low, 1996; Hillier, 2016a, 2016b), while, as Tsing (2015) argues, it is often plantation agriculture and forestry that are the key ecological drivers of other very dangerous threats. Yet as we have seen, as *condemned* creatures and organisms that can and should be killed, they do not quite exist, cannot quite be recognised or shown. This is not new, as Ellen and Fukui (1996) note:

> Effectively all landscapes with which humans routinely interact are therefore cultural: and our environment is every bit as much what is made socially as what is not . . . How strange, then, that in another version of the biological imagination (that of classical evolutionary taxonomy) domesticated animals and non-endemics are, somehow, *not*, the real thing. The complexities of biological reality, enhanced by the insights of modern ecology and genetics, make drawing the boundary between what is cultural and what is natural, almost impossible.
>
> (p. 14–15)

The push of animal agency

To conservation biologists such as Tim Low, who have paid attention to Australia's unruly ecology, the future is feral and we had better get used to it. Low's book *Feral Future* (1999, 2001) documents an astonishing set of adaptive accommodations between native and feral species that are critical for wildlife tourists to understand – as well as fascinating. And, despite an ongoing biopolitical construction of introduced species as a threat to native species, the truth is that they do not *always* suffer from them, and in many cases, they have learned how to turn them to their own advantage. To think of native species, then, always as victims is to miss how resilient and resourceful they can be, as well as ignoring their built-in biological capacities to make connections with others. Feralised ecological narratives offer tourists a chance to learn one of the main drivers of contemporary Australian natural history and ecology – and the unique set of challenges that face conservationists – something reckoned by many to be the most valuable outcome of touristic encounters with wildlife (Fennell, 2001).

Robbed of their native habitats, largely through Australian development and farming, many endangered mammal species (e.g., the Eastern Barred Bandicoot) have learned to rely on feral plant species (aka "noxious weeds") such as lantana, blackberry and broom to protect themselves from predators. Other rare and threatened species, including "most fruit and seed eating birds in many regions" (Low, 2001, p. 241) have become "weed" dependent. The black-breasted button quail, for instance, depends on lantana for cover having lost most of its rainforest to agriculture. The "nearly extinct Norfolk Island parrot lives almost entirely on olives and cherry guavas" (Low, 2001, p. 241) and the camphor laurel feeds significant flocks of fruit pigeons who in turn distribute its seeds. The long billed and western corellas "have lost links with natural habitats and live on crop seeds and weeds" (Low, 2001, p. 241). Most Australian native birds of prey are sustained by feral animals for food, especially rabbits, rats and mice. Around Mildura, for example, 60–90% of the diets (by weight) of local eagles, goshawks, harriers, kites and falcons (eight species in all) is provided by young rabbits. Equally, outback birds of prey are now suffering as the supply of rabbits has been reduced by *calcivirus*, a virus introduced by conservation biologists to eradicate rabbits (Low, 2001). Larger non-native predators such as the fox and feral cat prevent population explosions of rabbits and rats from undermining and threatening many native bird species. Yet without a healthy population of other introduced large predators such as feral dogs and dingoes, fox and feral cat numbers can spike which may then threaten local populations of small marsupials. Again, in recent times the broad acre poisoning of feral dogs and dingos has caused huge populations spikes among foxes and cats. It is impossible not to place the actions of Australian farmers, loggers, miners or industrialists – or the conservation biologist – in the frame as potential threats and disturbances to local native species

Tim Low shows that these are not isolated or selective examples, and yet, to judge from wildlife and eco-tourism marketing and business websites, it is as if these feral animals do not exist or have any ecological or pedagogical value as subjects of wildlife tourism. As Bulbeck's (2005) study showed, they are barely present in zoos and wildlife parks or showcased in wildlife tours and ecotourism.

Although states and territories, industries and local communities are coming under pressure from the Wilderness Society (2008) to eradicate invasive species "*where possible*," it is a moot point as to whether science currently supports the feasibility of such a policy. Australia is a vast island continent, and, as Parkes (1993) pointed out, "managers should remember that if eradication is an operation that only kills 99% of the population it is a failure" (p. 47). According to Bomford and O'Brian's (1995) research, this and other necessary conditions for eradication do not exist for any introduced species.

However, it is not merely the ecological case that weighs most heavily against them but what we might call a deeply engrained sense of nativism in Australia. The next section sets out the origins of this Australian "nativism" arguing that the force of the native-feral opposition in Australia is as much driven by nationalism, politics and cultural identity as it is by ecology.

Constructing the Australian native wildlife gaze

As an early tourist to Australia in the 1890s, Mark Twain (1897) was repeatedly frustrated by his host's apparent need to demonstrate how well Australia had been modernised and how ubiquitous were its creature comforts. What Twain craved however was not railways, modern buildings of state, efficient ports or concert houses but the opposite: difference, uniqueness and the quintessentially *Australian*. As Mark Twain was travelling through Eastern Australia, the presence of

Indigenous Peoples, animals and plants had been displaced from the landscape, removed or hunted out, to a remarkable extent over the previous century:

> We saw birds, but not a kangaroo, not an emu, not an ornithorhynchus [platypus], not a lecturer, not a native. Indeed, the land seemed quite destitute of game. But I have misused the word native. In Australia it is applied to Australian-born whites only. I should have said that we saw no Aboriginals – no "blackfellows." And to this day I have never seen one.
>
> (Twain, 1897, p. 57)

Franklin (2006, 2014) traced the extraordinary story of native animal depletion prior to this time, and their replacement with British and other so-called "choice" species – which paralleled an equivalent project to remove Indigenous Peoples from their land and to erase them from memory (Healy, 2008). The extent of this colonial acclimatisation, a process propelled by Acclimatisation Societies established in every colony from 1861 onwards, is hard to grasp, especially the extent to which Australian ecologies today remain essentially restructured by it.

Twain was travelling through Australia just as a new tide of nationalism and nationhood was emerging, as new generations of white Australian born settlers began to identify themselves very strongly with Australian native species. Twain's observation that white settler society had just then begun to claim "nativeness" was therefore a prescient observation because in many ways they went on to deepen the claim by championing native animals over those acclimatised by their forefathers. As the new custodians of the land, white settlers began to privilege all things "Australian" in a national branding process achieved by conflating themselves and their body politic with what they took to be the continent's ancestral species. This is the root of the enduring tension balance between native and feral, for the latter threatens the very integrity of Australianness. Twain was both too late and too early to see native animals.

By the time of Federation in 1901, a positive aestheticisation of Australian nature and an inclination to protect and preserve it from further extirpation was already underway. Australian culture quickly mantled itself in symbols of Australian nature which became metonymic of their lives and their aspirations to assert their dominion over Australia and the value of Australian-ness. This transition, completed within thirty years, from a Britainised to an Australianised polity and ecology is richly documented by Cozzolino (1987) using records of changing trademarks and other registered symbols. Few other countries deployed so much native wildlife in the semiological construction of its identity.

In these ways, therefore, visitors as well as migrants and citizens came to associate native species with what it was to be "properly" Australian. As Ghassan Hage (1998) put it, "the ecological fantasy is part of the nationalist fantasy and vice versa" (p. 169). And, to be seen to be ruthlessly upholding the naturally given place of native animals against the encroachment of animals that were out of place, ecologically speaking, was an activity that also reinforced their national legitimacy and values and a much-feared migration of Asian peoples (Hage, 1998).

Indeed, through Australia's "White Nation" policies, the political project of national boundaries closing to unwanted human migrants could be narratively enriched through pointing up the dangers of all forms of unAustralianess as a form of pollution. Here is yet more dark tourism, where nature meets culture. Each new scientific campaign or policy announcement that promoted native animals or sought the eradication of introduced animals simultaneously reinforced national values – a favourite trope that has been routinely exploited by generations of Australian politicians (Smith, 2011). Feral species have become a useful anomaly, then, for those "who want to uphold a state of anxiety about belonging and not-belonging in Australia" (Franklin, 2011, p. 203). Given the ubiquitousness of national discourses, it is not surprising that these messages and values overlaid the marketing messages in Australian tourism and influenced how Australia wishes to present itself and thus how it was visited.

Killing feral species

Paradoxically, while non-native or feral animals are obscured, underplayed, and, widely under-appreciated in wildlife representations to tourists, within scientific, environmental and political discourses across Australia their ecological presence is acknowledged as "overwhelmingly significant" though largely framed in negative terms. According to Hillier (2016a), this was no accident. Hillier has shown in great detail how a deliberate statistical and psychologically formulated scare campaign to misrepresent the actual level of threat posed by feral species has been orchestrated in order to garner ethical support for their extermination. Hillier's (2016b) Foucauldian analysis of the feral cat demonstrates how significantly they are subjectivated and objectified through political and policy narratives. As Donna Haraway (2016b) noted in a recent discussion with Cary Wolfe, ecological and species recovery is "never entirely innocent" (p. 235).

The ways in which feral animals are aligned in negative ways and framed by environmental concerns, management and discourses can be revealed using new software developed by Sciences Po Paris Medialab (directed by Bruno Latour at the Ecoles Normales Superior, Paris). Using this, we traced and measured the connectedness of concepts and their use in political and public policy language and discourse. The software takes "root articles" featured on Wikipedia and then scrolls though all connected articles by the mention "See Also." A "tension vector" treatment permits graphs to be produced from this data showing both the nature and direction of the associations between keyword nodes: the more connected a keyword node is to a corresponding article, the closer it is and the more distant it is for the non-related articles. Colours of lines denote on how far from the root articles the keyword nodes are. "Level -1" means that the "roots articles" belongs to the "See Also" list of the node. "Level 0" means that the node is in the "See Also" list of the "roots articles." "Level 1" means that the node belongs to the "See also" list of a "level 0" node and so on.

Figure 9.1 shows the results from using the roots "Fauna of Australia." Here, we can see the extent to which invasive species are subjectivated as a central issue

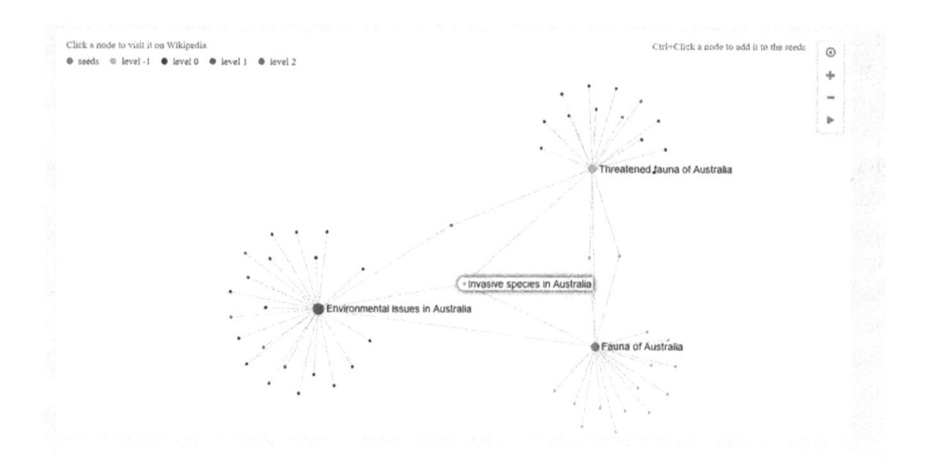

Figure 9.1 Invasive species, a central environmental issue in Australia.

for Australian wildlife management. The scrolling of the associated articles by the software makes three clusters appear, linked by one article: "Invasive species in Australia." The main cluster, which represents the "Environmental issues in Australia," is connected to the "Threatened fauna of Australia" by the "Invasive species" node. While the link between threatened species and environmental issues could have been made by questions such as global warming, drought and changing fire regimes, the main issue comes directly from the "Fauna of Australia" cluster itself: specifically, its invasive species.

In Figure 9.2, the root articles are "Invasive species in Australia" and "Fauna of Australia." We can see from this graph how invasive and native species form an opposed dichotomy and also how invasive species have become a central issue for environmental issues in Australia.

Then, taking the root article "Introduced Species in Australia," Figure 9.3 shows very clearly how "introduced species" are systematically associated with "Invasive species" and negatively depicted, with such normative and negative terms as "pollution," "invasion" and "contamination." Here is how they "appear" in Australia.

In recent years, however, as environmental change has put greater pressure on more remnant populations of small native marsupials, the spectre of a dramatic series of extinctions is focussing attention on protection measures and changing the ecological narrative of native and feral species in interesting ways. It is recognised that even the most vilified feral cat can live in some kind of ecological balance with native species. It is not so much their presence that matters as how their prodigious rates of breeding can be kept in check by predators. As Chris Johnson (in Groche, 2014) put it: "There are no extinctions of wildlife in Tasmania that we can blame on the feral cat but there are on mainland Australia" (no page number).

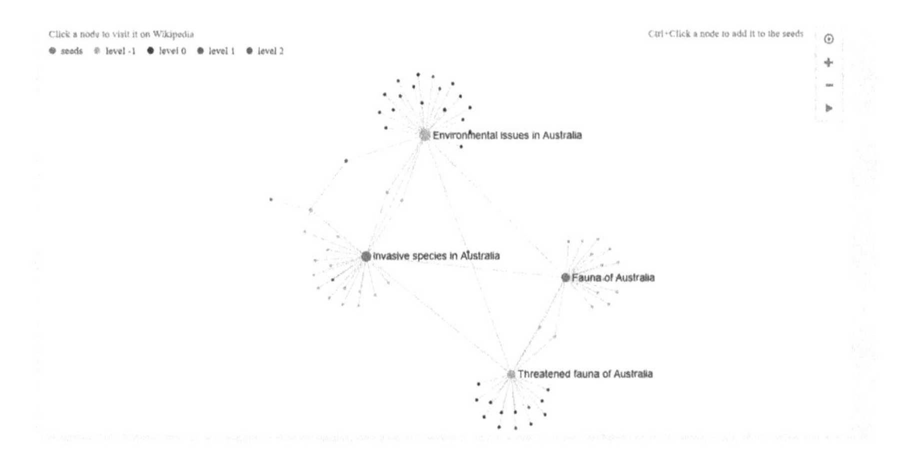

Figure 9.2 The native/invasive opposition.

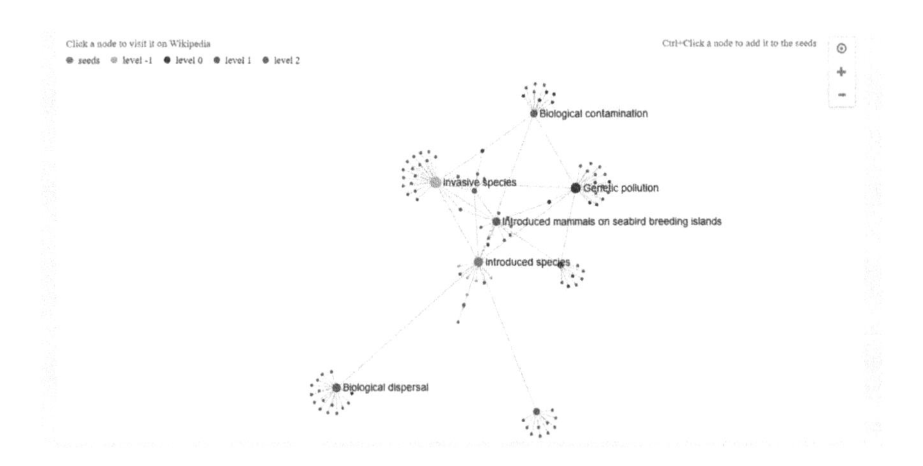

Figure 9.3 Introduced species understood as invasive species.

So their threat is entirely contingent on the life chances of those animals that hunt them, and these have largely been affected by anthropogenic changes, often by ecologists themselves. The feral cat has been in Tasmania for over 200 years. This means that the conservation goal is now to effect the right balance between introduced and native, which if successful would remove the ecological case against feral animals and their place in wildlife tourism. Henceforth, only their elevated and dangerous populations levels would require adjustment through anthropogenic killing or the introduction of predators. Johnson, for example, is in favour of reintroducing the Tasmanian Devil to Victoria. So it makes no sense to continue the pretence of an exclusive native wildlife since clearly, the truth of their lives as well as their futures cannot be told in the absence the feralised ecologies and feral species that co-constitute their world.

Developing feral tourism

The tourism industry thrives on finding new ways to engage publics and to narrate new and compelling stories. Richards and Wilson (2006) have pin-pointed "repetition" and "serial copying" as one of the biggest problems in the industry, creating jaded and bored visiting publics. By over-representing native species and distorting the nature of so many feralised Australian ecologies, the wildlife tourism industry is missing a significant opportunity to refresh and broaden wildlife tourism narratives, as well as educate their public through advances in conservation and natural historical research. While there is insufficient space to develop a fully formed sense of the potential for feral tourism, the remainder of this paper is used to outline some emerging issues and potential forms.

Extending wildlife tourism into the "new nature"

Feral tourism is feral in two senses. First, it is more ecologically representative than native wildlife tourism. It is interested in ecological specificities and promiscuities in the real world rather than the contrived, managed, purified albeit well-meaning and vital sanctuary set ups or fenced-in arks. It is not that the former should replace the latter so much as build on them to provide a more mature, scientifically valid, reflexive and exhaustive tourism offer across the sector. Second, it is feral in the sense that it is wild, unruly and unpredictable. It does not correspond to any narrative of ecological balance or stability but is formed from essentially open-ended, disordered processes shaped by historic and recent introductions and management regimes, post-colonialism, climate change, the vicissitudes of globalising markets, free trade, hypermobilities and agriculture; by accelerating rates and directions or forms of mobility (Urry, 2007). Neither does it restrict the spatial focus of wildlife tourism to wilderness-type settings, thus opening up a greater range of wildlife spaces from national parks to national capitals – knowing that cities and hinterlands can be both rich in biodiversity and important refuges for endangered species (Franklin, 2016; Kirkpatrick, 2007; Low, 2002). As Haraway (2016a) observed: "Learning to stay with the trouble of living and dying together on a damaged earth will prove more conducive to the kind of thinking that would provide the means to building more livable futures" (back cover book description). Here, forms of tourism engagement that challenge people to think about rather than merely absorb information from sources of authority may prove invaluable. Perhaps we should place more trust in visitors' reflexive capacity to gauge the moral and ethical implications of feral futures?

Previous and contemporary feral tourisms

Some forms of feral tourism date back a long time and, along with the species they were focussed on, now accrue paradoxical forms of "heritage" value. Most of these focus on specific feral animals rather than their ecology, although trekking forms often follow wildlife safari formats and take visitors deep into country inaccessible by other means. Examples of the former might include, in the colonial era, buffalo hunting tourisms in the country around Darwin and Kakadu, on what Robinson (2005) called "the feral frontier of Australia's Northern Territory" (p. 887). We might also include the so-called "Shannon Rise," a dry fly trout fishing phenomenon centred on the brown trout of Great Lake in Tasmania (from the 1930s to the 1960s), which grew to extraordinary sizes and drew fly fishing tourists from all around the globe.

Those feral species that evoke historical associations with national military campaigns and nation building, and who have a popular urban following, such as the brumby, have had aggressive actions against them (e.g., the aerial shooting of mares and foals in Guy Forkes River National Park (GFRNP), NSW in 2000) condemned through public protest and kerbed through ministerial directive. Subsequent to this case, brumbies were deemed to have "heritage value" with steps taken to protect and conserve them – though they were banished from GFRNP. Increasingly, brumbies provide tourists with opportunities to trek through very rugged country, while the opportunity to see wild brumbies is regularly singled out as a highlight for them (New South Wales Government, 2006).

Outback camel trekking in the central deserts has been in operation since the mid-1970s while horse trekking in the East Kimberley has been growing steadily since the mid-1980s. The dingo is another ambiguous category, at once an introduced feral dog and a naturalised native. The fact that it predated white settlement seems to be the rather arbitrary, but telling, reason. It has been a drawcard for wildlife tourism on Fraser Island since the 1970s, though being fed by tourists reduced their natural reserve and resulted in more intimidating behaviour and numerous serious attacks and subsequent culls.

Indigenous wildlife tourism

Indigenous wildlife tourism is arguably a long overdue and potentially very important, alternative wildlife tourism owing to the ethics and valorisation of "country," a landscape cared for so as to conserve its nutritional affordances for the people who live there (Bird Rose, 1996). Aboriginal knowledge about the nutritional capacities of Australian ecologies was gathered for, and deployed by, the Australian Army in assembling a survival guide. Its principal author, Major Les Hiddins, turned this into a highly popular and long running ABC TV show called *Bush Tucker Man* (1988–1996), at once, demonstrating its value both as important knowledge and as touristic infotainment across a very broad demographic. This was one of several initiatives that prompted Indigenous Australians to develop tourism on their lands. Aboriginal tours of Country have operated since at least 2000 with the establishment of *Animal Tracks*, a wildlife safari first operated out of Kakadu National Park. The emphasis of their seven-hour tour is on hunting and gathering, where spotting and observing wildlife under the tutelage and constant guidance of local

Aboriginal guides is combined with gathering foods in order to have a "cook-up" as the sun goes down.

> We gather all kinds of foods such as turtles, snakes, grubs, fruits, yams, various native tubers, bulbs and corms etc. It's a very hands-on experience in a small group . . . Daily campfire cooking at sunset can include any of the foods mentioned above and magpie geese [and] buffalo.
>
> (*Animal Tracks*, 2017, np)

The tours include experience of feral and native species living together in Kakadu and regularly include wild pigs [their term], buffalo and dingo. Mindful that they are repackaging engagements with wildlife for those who often visit the area with largely white "low impact" conservation values, their website suggests it is suitable for "broadminded people."

The scope for Indigenous leadership in establishing feral tourism is clear, not only because they pay scant regard to white moral taxonomies of "good" and "bad" wildlife but because potentially they could open up a wide variety of Aboriginal Country across Australia, thus injecting an inexhaustible source of ever changing experiences for visitors, features that enhance repeat tourism. Aboriginal Peoples in Central Australia have hunted the feral cat for a very long time, and still do, a practice that keeps feral cat numbers in check. Recent evidence also shows that prior to being removed from their homelands into reserves/missions/stations. Aboriginal Peoples in Queensland used to hunt feral cats, and it was only after their removal to reserves and missions that the cat population became unchecked and small mammals became at risk. Wildlife tourism that acknowledges the place and value of human hunting in Australia generally has an important educational role to play in identifying the possibility of utilising feral animals as food. For example, Australian Kaye Keesing began experimenting with wild feral meat from cats, camels and rabbits, figuring that hunting and developing a stream of tourism cuisine to Asian tourists would be both profitable and ecologically useful (Edwards, 2007).

Feral zoos and wildlife parks

The logic of feral tourism in wild settings could be extended to zoos and wildlife parks for those on shorter itineraries but also for residents. Clearly, as conservation issues vie with those of exhibition and entertainment, it makes no sense to use the close-up format of zoos to narrate conservation narratives and challenges without a representative collection of animals that feature in their stories. Including specimens of feral animals provides a resource for recognition as well as ecological connection. Breeding colonies of rabbits and mice in the zoological collection might be connected to native raptors and small carnivores. Enclosures might be constructed so as to show connections between native animals and invasive plant species that provide food and protection. Clearly, zoos are thinking about this: Healsville Sanctuary, Victoria, has begun to think about introducing feral animals into their collection, because to do otherwise, in their view, was not providing an authentic picture of the challenges and value of their conservation mission (personal communication between Franklin and Healsville Sanctuary).

Feral tourism and climate change

Brief mention should be made of the future of the feral/native binary under conditions of climate change. Ethical considerations of animal conservation are driving demands to move affected species into new geographical locations when their historical habitats/territories are no longer capable of sustaining them. In an article entitled "Translocation of species, climate change, and the end of trying to recreate past ecological communities," Thomas (2011) argued that "the only viable option to maintain populations of these species in the wild is to translocate them to other locations where the climate is suitable" (p. 216) and where they will have to adapt to new plant and animal communities. In the event that climate change accelerates, we could face a prospect where nature conservation switches to a new era of scientific acclimatisation of species on a global scale. In time, this would mean that criteria for the reckoning of eco-systemic boundaries and membership would disappear, resulting in the collapse of any formal recognition of native and feral species.

Conclusion: feral times?

While the ecological justification for feral tourism is compelling, to what extent is feral tourism compatible with contemporary sensibilities? At a symposium entitled "The Feral Among Us," the architect/artist Richard Goodwin (2015) bemoaned the continuity and vigour (in Australia) of long-outdated modernist binaries such as native/feral. For Goodwin, these terms belonged to a previous, modern age in which taxonomy, differentiation, territorialisation, secularisation, belonging, rationality and "purification" were defining characteristics of a modern world order – one that once defined science as much as it did society. The modern world re-organised itself around these concepts, steadily purifying/purging the pre-modern world of its in-built heterogeneities, blurred categories and hybrid forms. However, over the past fifty years or so, many modernist boundaries have been questioned, breached, transgressed and dispensed with, and so while anti-feral attitudes still run high in Australia, Goodwin suggested that a new structure of feeling is emerging. The contemporary world is increasingly de-differentiated, mobile, flexible, liquid and multicultural, while fixed boundaries whether social, sexual, ethnic, biological, urban or cultural are giving rise to a proliferating range of transgressive hybrid forms. So, for Goodwin, ferality was itself fast becoming a metaphor for life in contemporary times (see also Ingold, 2010). In some circumstances, the term feral connotes positive qualities, as for example when is applied to anti-logging protesters who live in wild and primitive conditions in the forest. Here it can mean courageous, anti-authority, free-ranging, activist, free-thinking (St. John, 1999). So, Goodwin suggests that contemporary tourists may be far more invested in a world where anthropogenic impacts, "new natures" and the cultural/political dynamics of wildlife conservation can be considered and experienced "together." Perhaps we should take tourists into the thick of feralised Australia and trust them to cope with and enjoy its complexities and face the moral conundrums it poses, rather than censor it.

References

Animal Tracks Tours. (2017). *Animal tracks wildlife safari*. Retrieved February 2017, from www.animaltracks.com.au/tour-highlights/wildlife-safari.html.

Australian Biosecurity Group. (2005). *Invasive weeds, pests and diseases. Solutions to secure Australia*. Canberra, Australia: CRC for Pest Animal Control, CRC for Australian Weed Management and WWF.

Bird Rose, D. (1996). *Nourishing terrains: Australian Aboriginal views of landscape and wilderness*. Canberra: Australian Heritage Commission.

Bird Rose, D. (2016). *Love at the edge of distinction*. Retrieved October 24, 2017, from http://deborahbirdrose.com/tag/lyn-watson/.

Bomford, M., & O'Brian, P. (1995). Eradication or control for vertebrate pests? *Wildlife Society Bulletin, 23*, 249–255.

Bulbeck, C. (2005). *Facing the wild*. London: Earthscan.

Cozzolino, M. (1987). *Symbols of Australia*. Ringwood, Victoria: Penguin.

Edwards, L. (2007). Wild cat is pot luck for hunters and collectors. *The Age*. Retrieved October 23, 2017, from www.theage.com.au/news/national/wild-cat-is-pot-luck-for-hunters-and-collectors/2007/08/29/1188067191856.html

Ellen, R., & Fukui, K. (Eds.). (1996). *Redefining nature: Ecology, culture and domestication*. Oxford: Berg.

Fennell, D. A. (2001). A content analysis of ecotourism definitions. *Current Issues in Tourism, 4*(5), 403–421.

Franklin, A. S. (2006). *Animal nation*. Sydney: University of New South Wales Press.

Franklin, A. S. (2011). An improper nature? Species cleansing in Australia. In B. Carter & N. Charles (Eds.), *Human and other animals: Critical perspectives* (pp. 195–216). London: Palgrave Macmillan.

Franklin, A. S. (2014). The adored and the abhorrent: Nationalism and feral cats in England and Australia. In G. Marvin & S. McHugh (Eds.), *Routledge handbook of human-animal studies*. London: Routledge.

Franklin, A. S. (2016). The more-than-human city. *The Sociological Review, 65*(2), 202–217. doi:10.1111/1467-954X.12396/full.

Fredline, E., & Faulkner, F. (2001). *International market analysis of wildlife tourism*. Wildlife Tourism Research Report Series: No. 22. Gold Coast, Cooperative Research Centre for Sustainable Tourism, Australia. Retrieved October 23, 2017, from https://eportal.stust.edu.tw/eshare/EshareFile/2015_3/2015_3_4ff10d81.pdf

Goodwin, R. (2015). *The feral among us*. Siteworks, Bundanon Trust, September 26. Illaroo: NSW. Retrieved from https://bundanon.com.au/whats-on/siteworks-2015/.

Groche, N. (2014). Scientists call for Tasmanian devils to be reintroduced as mainland predators to combat feral cats. *ABC News*. Retrieved October 12, 2014, from www.abc.net.au/news/2014-10-12/tas-devils-to-prey-on-feral-cats-holder/5806242.

Hage, G. (1998). *White nation*. London: Pluto Press.

Haraway, D. (2016a). *Staying with the trouble: Making kin in the Chthulucene*. Durham. NC: Duke University Press.

Haraway, D. (2016b). *Manifestly Haraway. The cyborg manifesto. The companion species manifesto. Companions in conversation (with Cary Wolfe)*. Minneapolis, MN: University of Minnesota Press.
Healy, C. (2008). *Forgetting aborigines*. Sydney: University of New South Wales Press.
Higginbottom, K. (2004). *Wildlife tourism: Impacts, management and planning*. Altona: Common Ground Publishing.
Hillier, J. (2016a). Cat-alysing attunement. *Journal of Environmental Policy and Planning, 19*(3), 327–344.
Hillier, J. (2016b). Is extermination to be the legacy of Mary Gilbert's cat? *Organization, 23*(3), 387–406.
Ingold, T. (2010). *Bringing things back to life: Creative entanglements in a world of materials*. NCRM Working Paper, Realities, Morgan Centre, University of Manchester.
Kirkpatrick, J. (2007). Collateral benefit: Unconscious conservation of threatened plant species. *Australian Journal of Botany, 55*(3), 221–224.
Low, T. (1996, Autumn). Feral cats: Scoundrels or scapegoats? *Nature Australia*.
Low, T. (1999). *Feral future*. Ringwood, Victoria: Penguin.
Low, T. (2001). *Feral future* (2nd ed.). Ringwood, Victoria: Penguin
Low, T. (2002). *The new nature*. Ringwood, Victoria: Penguin.
McLeod, R. (2004). *Counting the cost: Impact of invasive animals in Australia 2004*. Canberra, Australia: Cooperative Research Centre for Pest Animal Control.
New South Wales Government. (2006). *Guy Forkes River National Park horse management plan*. Retrieved from www.environment.nsw.gov.au/pestsweeds/GfrnpHorseMgmtplan.htm.
Parkes, J. P. (1993). *National feral goat control plan for New Zealand*. Unpublished Landcare Research Contract Report, LC9293/41, Christchurch, NZ.
Peretti, J. H. (1998). Nativism and nature: Rethinking biological invasion. *Environmental Values, 7*, 183–192.
Richards, G., & Wilson, J. (2006). Developing creativity in tourist experiences: A solution to the serial reproduction of culture? *Tourism Management, 27*, 1209–1223.
Ritvo, H. (2012). Going forth and multiplying: Animal acclimatization and invasion. *Environmental History, 17*, 404–414.
Robinson, C. (2005). Buffalo hunting and the feral frontier of Australia's Northern Territory. *Social and Cultural Geography, 6*(6), 885–901.
Roe, D., Leader-Williams, N., & Dalal-Clayton, B. (1997). *Take only photographs, leave only footprints: The environmental impacts of wildlife tourism*. London: International Institute for Environment and Development.
Rose, B. (1995). *Land management issues: Attitudes and perceptions amongst Aboriginal people of Central Australia*. Central Land Council Cross Cultural Land Management Project: 7.
Skibins, J. C. (2015). Ambassadors or attractions? Disentangling the role of flagship species in wildlife tourism. In K. Markwell (Ed.), *Animals and tourism: Understanding diverse relationships* (pp. 256–273). Bristol: Channel View Publications.
Smith, N. (1999). The howl and the pussy: Feral cats and wild dogs in the Australian imagination. *The Australian Journal of Anthropology, 10*(3), 288–305.
Smith, N. (2000). *Nature, native and nation in the Australian imaginary*. PhD Thesis, School of Sociology, La Trobe University.
Smith, N. (2011). Blood and soil: Nature, native and nation in the Australian imaginary. *Journal of Australian Studies, 35*(1), 1–18.
St. John, G. (1999). Ferality: A life of grime. *UTS Review, 5*(2), 101–113.

Thomas, C. D. (2011). Translocation of species, climate change, and the end of trying to recreate past ecological communities. *Trends in Evolution and Ecology*, *26*(5), 216–221.

Trigger, D., Mulcock, J., Gaynor, A., & Toussaint, Y. (2008). Ecological restoration, cultural preferences and the negotiation of "nativeness" in Australia. *Geoforum*, *39*, 1273–1283.

Tsing, A. (2015). *Feral biologies*. Paper for Anthropological Visions of Sustainable Futures Conference, University College London.

Twain, M. (1897). *Following the equator: A journey around the world*. Hartford, CT: Samuel Clemens.

Urry, J. (2007). *Mobilities*. Cambridge: Polity Press.

Valantine, P., & Birtles, A. (2004). Wildlife watching. In K. Higginbottom (Ed.), *Wildlife tourism: Impacts, management and planning* (pp. 15–34). Altona: Common Ground Publishing.

Van Dooren, T. (2011). Invasive species in penguin worlds: An ethical taxonomy of killing for conservation. *Conservation and Society*, *9*(4), 286–298.

Wilderness Society. (2008). *Wildlife policy*. Retrieved February 2008, from wilderness.society.org.au.

10 Toward a participatory ecological ethic for outdoor activities

Reconsidering traces

Philip M. Mullins

There is a tension between the dominant Leave No Trace (LNT) ethic designed to protect wilderness from visitors and an emerging sustainability paradigm intended to help participants and operators in outdoor and nature-based recreation, education, and tourism understand and take responsibility for their social, economic, and ecological entanglements on wider scales and longer terms (Brymer, Downey, & Gray, 2009; Buckley, 2009; Cachelin, Rose, Dustin, & Shooter, 2011; Hill, 2013; Hill & Brown, 2014; Leung, Marion, & Farrell, 2008; Mullins, 2014a). This tension speaks to the need to develop, share, and reflect on outdoor travel and living skills that embrace and enable various lived socio-ecological relationships with places, landscapes, and environments.

Given the aggressive promotion and ubiquity of LNT, along with the lack of clearly presented alternatives, in this chapter, I examine the LNT movement and ethic and then sketch for comparison a different outdoor ethic based on the participatory ecological approach. In so doing, I hope to speak back to the dominance of LNT, and in particular highlight its guiding ideology, which I see as limiting and problematic. To elucidate the participatory ecological approach to outdoor activities (Mullins, 2011, 2014b), I introduce a set of nine tenets based on the works of Tim Ingold (2000, 2007a, 2007b, 2008, 2011). I then provide and explain a set of eight principles for enacting a participatory ecological ethic. I hope these tenets and principles will give readers (a) a stronger understanding of the limitations of LNT by providing a comparator, and more importantly, (b) a positive way to actively, creatively, and reflexively build relationships in support of sustainable social and ecological communities through their outdoor travel practices.

I suggest an outdoor ethic is needed that can help prevent local negative ecological impacts *and* contribute to (and leave room for) diverse, healthier, and more-sustainable societies locally, regionally, and globally. Along the way, in sum, I hope to make clear that LNT involves a problematic hidden curriculum (Lynch, 1989) and outline an analogous ethic that starts from a position of belonging and that enables positive, creative, socioecological participation.

Leave No Trace

According to Turner (2002), the need for and rise of outdoor recreation practices that left minimal impact in wilderness areas came about following the resolution of debates during the 1960s within the American wilderness preservation movement about whether or not, to what degree, and how to restrict human access in order to maintain "a pristine wilderness system little-used by the public" (Turner, 2002, p. 471). By the 1970s, according to Turner, it became clear that the wilderness advocacy community had decided in favour of wilderness areas with compromised biological integrity that prioritized recreational use, and which thereby might maintain political popularity and enable future expansion of the system, rather than holding a hard line on wilderness areas as non-human biological reserves, which might undermine public support. Yet, with either option, the point of reference remained a realist understanding of wilderness as pristine nature (see Shultis, 2012), a bounded space, an object apart from humanity (see Haila, 2000), that would, ideally, remain untouched by humans whose presence was assumed to be necessarily detrimental.

A tool was needed to negotiate the tension between maintaining both the non-human biological health of an area and a very specific cultural and social aesthetic experience of it enabled by recreational and touristic activities that threatened to degrade these same biological and aesthetic qualities. The assumed biology being pristine environments untouched by humans. The assumed aesthetic being the "wilderness experience" that continues to reflect romantic, transcendentalist, and frontier values of solitude and self-reliance in the presence of sublime nature. These values which flow from earlier anti-modern reactions to the "march of progress," closing of the American frontier, and industrialized urban life of the late 19th and early 20th century America were used to justify the creation of wilderness areas, but also to promote outdoor recreation (Cronon, 1996; Fox, 2000; Hull, 2000; Mullins, 2011). Rather than taking a regulatory approach, LNT educational programming was developed in the early 1990s through a partnership between the National Outdoor Leadership School (NOLS) and the US Forest Service (Simon & Alagona, 2009; Turner, 2002). LNT built on earlier efforts to promote minimum impact camping, but added a new embrace of consumer technology (Turner, 2002). The original partnership also lead to further partnerships and sponsorship with major outdoors industry associations in order to create an organization to administer the program (Simon & Alagona, 2009). Within the historical context of American wilderness preservation, it makes sense that the resulting authoritative version of such an "ethic" is called Leave No Trace.

The Leave No Trace Center for Outdoor Ethics (LNTCOE) states that it "teaches people of all ages to enjoy the outdoors responsibly, and is the most widely accepted outdoor ethics program used on public lands"; their mission is "to protect the outdoors by teaching and inspiring people to enjoy it responsibly" (Leave No Trace, 2012a). The organization has the rather aggressive goals of having LNT "in every park", "integrated into every youth and school program that takes kids outside", and that "every person who ventures outside puts leave no trace practices into action" (Leave No Trace, 2012a).

LNTCOE accomplishes its goals through partnerships. Formally, the Leave No Trace Seven Principles, education, and marketing effort become institutionalized, promoted, and enforced by government agencies such as parks services, but also shared widely via marketing and education campaigns with other affiliate partners that include corporations, educational institutions, non-profit organizations, as well as outdoor service and retail providers (Leave No Trace, 2012c; Leave No Trace Canada, 2009). The development and promotion of LNT programming and materials are also financially supported by partners (e.g., Subaru) in exchange for visibility, marketing, and access/links through LNT (Leave No Trace, 2012c; Leave No Trace Canada, 2009).

Informally, the LNT ethic and versions of its principles are voiced and further marketed through promotional consumer products such as stickers, water bottles, patches, posters, and baseball caps produced by LNT. For example, they have set of 19 "Tech Tips" stickers, sponsored by Keen Footwear, for use by advocates and educators, and for sale in their online store. Some of these tips provide sound advice for reducing ecological impacts such as negative wildlife encounters. Yet, the very first sticker in the set, titled "Refuse the Makeover," states there is "no need for a major remodel of nature. Bring you own lightweight camp furniture and conveniences such as camp gas stoves, sleeping pads, chair and lanterns. When you leave, it should look as though you were never there" (Leave No Trace, 2012b). The ideas promoted by LNT are further spread and supported outside of the organization by popular slogans such as "pack it in, pack it out," "walk softly," and "take only pictures, leave only footprints." Together, using commercial marketing techniques, these products and slogans keep messages present and operating in the public sphere.

The pedagogy and content of the ethic centre on the Leave No Trace Seven Principles, which are described in their literature and web content in brief, but also in depth with supporting research (Leave No Trace, 2012d). Furthermore, LNT provides awareness workshops, trainer courses, and master educator courses to teach the ethic and practices. The principles are:

1. Plan ahead and prepare.
2. Travel and camp on durable surfaces.
3. Dispose of waste properly.
4. Leave what you find.
5. Minimize campfire impacts.
6. Respect wildlife.
7. Be considerate to other visitors.

The principles provide instruction on trip planning, safety, and minimizing local impacts in the backcountry. The basic concept of each principle appears prima facie as a respectful way to practice outdoor activities, particularly in heavily visited areas where cumulative impacts can be substantial and hard for travelers to recognize and respond to.

The approach has been very successful, in a traditional North American park management kind of way. Simon and Alagona (2009) summarized how LNT has mitigated against site-specific impacts of high volume visitation such as pollution, erosion, and soil compaction, as well as helping with recovery of denuded backcountry sites. Furthermore, authors suggest that the use of education to establish social norms and target moral development, as well as appealing to participants' self-interest greatly contribute to the effectiveness of LNT, with the important managerial benefit of requiring minimal enforcement (Marion & Reid, 2007; Simon & Alagona, 2009). However, within the descriptions of the Seven Principles are specific prescriptions for practice and corresponding rationales that demonstrate the priorities, limitations, allegiances, and capitulations of LNT.

The wilderness ideology of LNT

Crucial to this paper are the notions of setting, land, and participants assumed and apparently desired in the LNT ethic. The name *Leave No Trace* describes the ethic and organization's core purpose and approach, but also implicates a notion of the land or setting, which LNT usually refers to as "the outdoors," as well as a notion of people as visitors or temporary occupants. The outdoors is presented as a space for recreational experiences in capital "N" "nature," imagined to be without human influence and distanced from society, usually in the backcountry, bounded by trailheads, put-ins and take-outs, and park borders. The outdoors also constitutes the somewhat-arbitrary self-imposed limits of the ethic (Simon & Alagona, 2009). Clearly, the ethic and organization assume that leaving no human trace on the land or in the outdoors is both possible and desirable.

The outdoors, with no human traces, would be the ideal wilderness; but as Cronon (1996) so clearly articulated:

> The trouble with wilderness is that it quietly expresses and reproduces the very values its devotees seek to reject. The flight from history that is very nearly the core of wilderness represents the false hope of an escape from responsibility, the illusion that we can somehow wipe clean the slate of our past and return to the tabula rasa that supposedly existed before we began to leave our marks on the world. The dream of an unworked natural landscape is very much the fantasy of people who have never themselves had to work the land to make a living – urban folk for whom food comes from a supermarket.
> (Cronon, 1996, pp. 16–17)

Cronon described well the core ideology of LNT with which I take issue. Though valuing the opposite side of the same nature-culture dualism, the exaltation of pristine wilderness remains mired in the structure of a problematic Western environmental worldview from 19th and 20th centuries, not the realities of life and pressing issues today, be that in cities or in remote regions (Butler & Menzies, 2007; Cronon, 1996; Haila, 2000).

Green, Hebron, and Woodward (1990) described an ideology as "the complex system of perceptions and representations through which we experience ourselves and come to make sense of the world" (p. 30), and McLennan described it as "sets of ideas, assumptions and images, by which people make sense of society, which give a clear social identity, and which serve in some way to legitimize power relations in society" (as cited in Baldock, Mitton, Manning, & Vickersaff, 2012, p. 128). Many practices within LNT's Seven Principles are common courtesy, such as leaving a place cleaner than you found it. However, the principles and rationales also express and allow for experiences in reality of the wilderness ideology by characterising the land, people, and their interrelation in three particular ways. Moreover, social marketing of LNT and by LNT then works to normalize and export the ideology while legitimizing the power relations established by state, land managers, corporations, and recreationists.

First, wilderness is framed as being distanced from and damaged by society, and the development of "outdoor" identities are tied to respectfully experiencing wilderness aesthetically (and not more) as a visitor (and not inhabitant). Fox (2000) showed that privileging wilderness experiences as leisure (a) denies real histories of people and the land while focusing on, and naturalising, the present and (b) reinforces notions of the self as an isolated individual free of responsibility. LNT self-imposes an arbitrary boundary, limiting its concern largely to backcountry wilderness settings (Simon & Alagona, 2009); as such humans are framed as transient, isolated visitors, and not as belonging within or inhabiting the outdoors. The principles offer little if any advice pertaining to non-outdoor places or activities "back home" except in preparation for a visit. On the land, evidence of human presence or human-induced changes are framed negatively, becoming "scars" (from trails, fires, campsites). For people, LNT strives to choreograph aesthetic experiences of solitude through disciplining social activities as well as direct and indirect interactions by limiting group size, suggesting people stay shielded from view, remain quiet, and use muted colours.

Second, LNT relies on technology and promotes consumerism within a global economy, yet remains silent on the impacts of mass consumption globally and on participants' engagement with wild places (Simon & Alagona, 2009; Turner, 2002). Turner (2002) described LNT as relying on and increasing consumption of technology in the outdoors, while simultaneously turning away from using and interacting with local ecologies and renewable resources. In so doing, LNT aligns with the capitalist consumer economy, gives up social environmental critique that had previously been part of outdoor ethics, and fails to address social and ecological impacts of the globalized trade on which it relies (Simon & Alagona, 2009; Turner, 2002). Authors have also consistently described participants as experiencing a technological "bubble" that insulates them from their surroundings, with implications for environment, safety, and personal development (Ryan, 2002; Shultis, 2001). The result is that people come to "occupy" an outdoor setting as a visitor, but the place becomes a leisure commodity, and the people become less likely and able to interact with non-human environments in direct and meaningful ways (Ryan, 2002; Sandilands, 2000; Turner, 2002).

Third, within LNT, there is little attention to the positive impacts of outdoor activities, such as using recreation to support conservation and generate employment or the benefits of social and cross-cultural encounters during a trip (Buckley, 2009; Mullins, 2009; Mullins & Maher, 2007). Nor is there recognition of management or human action as a positive approach to interacting with and making places and people; for example, through trail building, habitat protection, advocacy, or harvesting for sustenance.

Although LNT tends to be referred to as an educational approach to management, it quite clearly has evolved into a sophisticated and ongoing social marketing campaign aimed at behaviour change according to its ideology. Social marketing is the practice of adapting commercial marketing techniques for use in the public sector with the express purpose of creating behavioural change for a perceived social (or ecological) good; and it has been used successfully in local environmental campaigns (Andreasen, 1994; Jamal & Watt, 2011). Granted, LNT was intended, and has succeeded, as a management tool to change and promote ecologically and aesthetically sensitive behaviours during leisure in backcountry wilderness settings (Marion & Reid, 2007). Andreasen (1994), however, recognized the serious ethical implications of social marketing, and warned that it "can be used by anyone who claims (or believes) that it is being used for [the social good]" (1994, p. 113), and so it should generally only be used for action on issues of broad public concern and consensus.

This social marketing of LNT is largely driven by the good as determined by LNTCOE and enacted through its partnerships. LNT takes a universal and normative approach to behaviour change based on a Western wilderness ideology. Establishing prescriptive, codified, state-sanctioned norms for outdoor behaviour creates an in-group of compliant and "responsible outdoors people" who identify as visitors to Nature and coercively sets them against a potentially phantom out-group of delinquent "others" (Ryan, 2009; Sandilands, 2000). Indeed, Ryan described that "today, LNT and minimum impact camping are . . . the basic standard against which backcountry users are measured" (2009, p. 38). Thus, the process used by LNT naturalizes and privileges dominant Western and particularly white urban American wilderness ontology and identities (Cronon, 1996; Guha, 1989).

Moreover, LNT exports the ethic and campaign internationally, guided and sanctioned by private businesses, organizations, and state institutions (rather than a wider public or local consensus). In so doing, LNT occludes other predominant yet nuanced ethics, ideologies, and histories,[1] as well as those that are less dominant but persist on the land in developing, rural, and Indigenous communities around the world, and which continue to struggle with privileged Western understandings of wilderness, humanity, and their relationship (Butler & Menzies, 2007; Cronon, 1996; Guha, 1989; Mullins, Lowan-Trudeau, & Fox, 2016). Through its global partnerships and social marketing, the content and methods used by LNT appear to follow a "cultural myth that encourages us to 'preserve' peopleless landscapes. . . [which] can become an unthinking and self-defeating form of cultural imperialism" (Cronon, 1996, p. 18). More than "preserving" these landscapes, LNT continues to privilege, reify, and create them (imperfect as they always will be) on the land and in imaginations (see Owens, 2011). Thus, the marketing and ethic leave little room to recognise or respond to the contested terrain (real not metaphorical) and diverse socioecological approaches, experiences, or communities in which they work to shape behaviour.

Grounding and limiting the outdoor field's dominant environmental ethic in this wilderness ideology and set of principles is now, I would suggest, constraining progress towards embracing practices and contributing to communities that are socially and ecologically diverse, just, and responsible. It is worth asking whether the content and approach to teaching environmental ethics for the outdoors is enabling participants to grow in relation to their environment, or simply visit in isolation from it? I fear the ideology of LNT encourages the latter in the name of wilderness preservation. I do not advocate or want to be misunderstood or misrepresented as rationalizing practices that are irresponsible, wasteful, or damaging to outdoor places. At the same time, from a sustainability perspective, the deliberate building, recognition, and taking further responsibility for social and ecological relationships is crucial.

A participatory ecological approach

An ecological approach situates human development, activity, and experience in relation with an environment that is always already social and biophysical (Beringer, 2004; Gibson, 1986; Ingold, 2000). The purpose of the participatory ecological approach is to challenge the Western nature-culture dichotomy so as to shift understandings in outdoor fields from being based on Western notions of wilderness, as a first principle, to being based on inhabitation, as a first principle, and for sustainability (Mullins, 2011, 2014b). The approach and purpose in no way devalues the necessity of large and small areas of land and sea that are predominantly characterized by non-human elements, forces, and inhabitants. The approach recognizes and embraces – with concomitant responsibility – that people interact with and develop in relation to dynamic environments, whatever the type.

This participatory ecological approach was developed through attempts to understand the implications of the work of anthropologist Tim Ingold for the theory and practice of outdoor adventure recreation and travel (Mullins, 2011). "The production of life," Ingold (2005) pointedly wrote, "involves the unfolding of a field of relations that crosscuts the boundary between human and non-human" (p. 504). No one, he argued "has made the crossing from nature to society, or vice versa, and no-one ever will. There is no such boundary to be crossed" (Ingold, 2005, p. 508). Human beings, he described, are "in the first place, organisms . . . as such, they are born and grow within the current of materials, and participate from within in their further transformation" (Ingold, 2011, p. 29). Wayfaring, according to Ingold (2000, 2011), is movement/travel that requires attention and interaction with one's surroundings; he argued that "the path, and not the place, is the primary condition of being, or rather of becoming. . . [and] that wayfaring is the fundamental mode by which living beings inhabit the earth" (Ingold, 2011, p. 12). Though wayfaring and other skills, as well as stories heard, people come to know, find meaning in, and shape the world they inhabit. Skills and practices bring forth meaning in the surroundings, establish webs of social and ecological relations, and shape both the people and the environments and landscapes engaged; at once making people and places (Ingold, 2000). The name "participatory ecological approach" is meant to imply that people participate in shaping diverse environments and landscapes and that environments and landscapes shape people. I happen to be particularly interested in how this occurs through outdoor activities.

A set of nine descriptive tenets for this approach are provided in Table 10.1. The principles inform one another, and are presented beginning from one's extended surroundings (1) in order to contextualize the personal position (9) as a locus of growth and action at the centre of a web of socioecological relations (Ingold, 2000). Hence, the approach is both "participatory" and "ecological." The order is not intended to imply any hierarchy, sequence, or process.

So, the skills we learn and teach (such as LNT) establish webs of social, economic, ecological relations within landscapes and environments that are supportive, active, and interconnected, rather than doomed, static and isolated. In this sense, enskilment and skilled practice are crucial processes of socialization and biophysical interaction that contribute to shaping places and people. Furthermore, life and travel are interpretive and expressive, stories inform our lives and our travels, and stories result from them, and these stories further characterize and inform ourselves, others, places, and the activities we love (Mullins, 2015). If we are to live sustainable lives in sustainable communities, taking pause to carefully consider the skills embraced and the stories told is crucial; few practices and stories are as fundamentally important to outdoor recreation, outdoor education, and outdoor adventure and nature-based tourism as those that express, frame, and enact the relationship between humans and the world they inhabit.

A participatory ecological ethic

The reconciliation of a tension between an emerging sustainability paradigm, on one hand, and normalized ethics and practices of LNT, on the other hand, requires further research and scholarship. I try in this section to sketch a tentative, first pass, at an alternative ethic or set of principles that can inform outdoor activities, and which make applicable tenet nine in Table 10.1. The principles are meant to respond to and contrast with (and therefore show) what is being normalized and accepted in LNT. The principles also, hopefully and more importantly, instruct and inspire different ways to think and do outdoor activities in recreation, education, and tourism contexts. It is my hope that this ethic can help re-invigorate socio-environmental critique, encourage intentionality regarding socioecological relationships, and support action for sustainable societies through outdoor activities and experiences.

As relational corporeal beings, human action shapes the actor and affects the socioecological environments and communities in and through which she, he, or they act. Food, water, instruction, and equipment manufacturing enable skilled practice, and skilled practice itself leaves traces and makes places. Suggesting that participants ought to and can "leave no trace" is to ostensibly deny or ignore human corporeality and ecology; at the same time, accepting human corporeality does not justify unsustainable human ecology and behaviours.

Table 10.1 Nine tenets of a participatory ecological approach.

1	Environments are active.	Outdoor activities occur out in the open while interacting with flows, features, and inhabitants (human and non-human) in dynamic environments that influence participant's movement as well as social and environmental relationships.[a]
2	Landscapes are interconnected.	Landscapes of various types provide opportunity for travel and learning. Multiple flows interconnect landscapes, which are shaped to different degrees and proportions by both human and non-human forces. Outdoor activities and travel need not be restricted to a type of landscape or typology based on an urban-wild continuum.
3	Activities occur in contexts and create context.	Adventure travel activities, experiences, and skill are situated within larger personal and socio-environmental (social, ecological and economic) contexts and histories. Skilled travel activities, daily tasks, and routes also provide a context in which participants understand surroundings.
4	Activities are multiple.	An outdoor activity is comprised of multiple choreographed practices and tasks that require skill, occur at various stages of a trip, and are coordinated among people within and beyond the group of participants. Activities are situated within multiple traditions and have various typical and atypical patterns of practice.
5	Skilled performance expresses environmental knowledge.	Through skilled outdoor activities, participants share and embody forms of socio-environmental knowledge. They develop, express, and share meaningful relationships with elements of their surroundings that are salient to their activities. Tools and technologies shape the skills and environmental knowledge developed.[b]
6	Relations are mobilized and managed.	Participants are positioned within social, ecological, and economic relationships that they mobilize and manage and which extend beyond their immediate surroundings to interconnect diverse landscapes and environments.
7	Movement is fundamental.	Outdoor activities occur primarily as modes of movement in or between places and regions. Movement along a route is fundamental to knowing, engaging, and interconnecting inhabitants, places, landscapes, and environments.[c] The choreography of different modes of movement over the course of a trip influences how travellers relate to and interconnect regions. The combination of activity and landscape as well as the chosen route and itinerary enable and constrain movement.

(*Continued*)

Table 10.1 (Continued)

8	Learning and growth occur in places and along routes.	Participants' learning and growth occur in places and along routes by developing and practicing outdoor living and travel skills while exchanging substances and knowledge with other participants, local inhabitants, and their shared surroundings.[d] Prevalent traditions and discourses in the activity may influence how travellers understand and experience themselves as being with others in an environment.
9	Travellers and local residents inhabit and participate in environments.	An ethic of sustainability is consistent with active, respectful, and self-reflexive participation in the continuing lives of places, landscapes, environments and their human and non-human inhabitants.

Note: Table adapted from Mullins (2011). [a]See Ingold (2007a, 2008) regarding life in the open. [b]See Ingold (2000) regarding skill, tools, and technology. [c]See Ingold (2000, 2007b, 2011) regarding movement, place, landscape, and environment. [d]See Ingold (2000, 2008, 2011) regarding exchanges of knowledge and substance, learning, and growth.

Rather than a universal ethic or etiquette of practice, a sustainability paradigm for adventure travel requires practices that can respond to, address, and improve local social, economic, and ecological realities within the context of larger global processes. Moreover, ethics of sustainability cannot be limited to individual participants' behaviour as though they are lone actors. Ethical considerations of sustainability must extend to the patterns, practices, pedagogies, equipment, and institutions that structure outdoor activities and experiences, and participants' ecological relations. It is within this context that I present the eight principles of a participatory ecological ethic for outdoor activities.

Please,

1 *Remember you're not the first or only one here, you won't be the last. Learn from and respect those you meet.*

First and foremost, this attempts to contribute to decolonization. Be a good guest, ask permission and know your neighbours. Respect Indigenous claims, management, connections, and activities on the land. Recognize settler culture, management, activities that characterize the place. Respect wildlife that inhabit the area. Interpersonal and inter-species encounters occur, and should be welcomed respectfully as opportunities for learning, sharing. Act in ways that support the sustenance and sustainability of communities, human and non-human, for future generations.

2 *Choose carefully the stories that motivate and shape your trips and that you tell about your trips and their settings.*

Reflect on the stories that frame and motivate your participation (e.g., environmental change, activism for a cause, heroic quest, exotic others, escape). These stories give your trip meaning, do not simply follow overdetermined narratives; consider how stories shape your route choices, travel practices, and other types of engagement (social, political, ecological). Use your travels to explore and act on stories and issue that might inform and contribute to conservation and sustainable places and communities. Consider the tales you tell about your trip to be political; they characterize places and people and can perpetuate, challenge, or ignore contemporary and historic myths, issues, and realities.

3 *Learn and use ecologically responsive and responsible techniques to travel along environmental flows, through diverse landscapes, across park boundaries.*

Consider where your route will take you, and why (don't be afraid to start close to home). Follow environmental flows (e.g., rivers, pipelines, roads, ridgelines, beaches, and currents) that interconnect wild, rural, urban, industrial, and/or extractive landscapes. Adapt your modes of travel to the health and usage of the settings you will visit. Incur as little negative and as much positive ecological impact as possible; traditional, Indigenous, and Western scientific ways of knowing can help determine appropriate practices. Doing so will allow you to (a) connect ways of life with social and ecological impacts/resources, (b) challenge the traditional distinctions within outdoor fields between society and nature, and (c) contextualize "the outdoors," "wilderness" and parks, as well as other landscapes and activities (agriculture, industry) ecologically and in your experience.

4 *Learn to attend to your surroundings rather than devices. Use tools and technologies as ways of learning and engaging further with places, processes, and issues.*

Try to recognize how technology demands your attention and can prevent you from learning environmentally engaged skills. When this happens, elements of the environment have little chance to work into you during enskilment, and you may be unable to act (e.g., wayfind) independent of the technology (e.g., GPS). Technology can also be used to learn and teach more about skills, places, ecology, and issues encountered. However, it can also engage people in "hard fascination" and prevent the "soft fascination" that people benefit from in natural settings (Kaplan, 1995; Wright & Mathews, 2015). Tools for travel, like paddles or skis, help you engage environments in different ways, enabling you to travel and know your surroundings differently and for these environments and activities to shape your development.

5 *Fuel your journey responsibly; you consume; you are not "human powered."*

Recognize and celebrate the productivity (food, wood, water) and animacy (wind, current, waves, gravity) of environments within your travel, experience, skills, stories, and becoming. Consider how you relate socially and ecologically through the fuels and foods you choose and use, and to where your impacts are (re)located – at what costs and benefit, and to whom? Can you reduce fossil fuel consumption needed for your trip? Use sustainable modes of travel; reduce and offset carbon emissions. Can you grow, trade for, hunt or gather food? Are there locally produced goods that reduce lasting negative impacts, support local communities, and allow you to know your surroundings as productive and supportive? Try to reduce and eliminate packaging – consider buying in bulk and using reusable containers in which to pack food for a trip. Dispose of waste in ecologically and socially responsible ways. Respect and reciprocate the generosity of the environment by not over harvesting and by supporting sustainable conservation, agriculture, energy, and development efforts.

6 *Use economies to positively impact communities in and around your route.*

Reciprocate your hosts' generosity by sourcing locally-produced goods and services (supplies, equipment, accommodation, guides) in communities along your route. Enable people and communities to value and benefit from outdoor recreation, education, and tourism as well as resource stewardship and conservation. In this way, participants come to know and rely on people who inhabit the lands traveled, adding to their knowledge of place. Moreover, this helps maintain access, public support, social license, and social/environmental justice by benefiting the communities most likely to bear the costs.

7 *Support, engage, and improve social, environmental, and activity-related stewardship and justice.*

Recognize that conservation and other environmental issues require management, civic/political engagement, public support, and are a reflection of society. Work to establish respectful and equitable social norms. Contribute to other people's responsible learning and participating in outdoor activities, which depend on social relations. Consider using your outdoor activities and experiences to engage politically for more sustainable societies. Critique and improve the ways in which your activity is performed, taught, and accessed.

8 *Reduce consumption and increase accessibility by sharing equipment and clothing.*

Demand socially and environmentally responsible production of clothing and equipment that is long lasting. Purchase less equipment and clothing, maintain what you buy, and consider making them as a way of connecting to place and others (human and non-human). Learn to sustainably use goods and materials that occur along the way. Establish, support, and contribute to clubs and equipment trade or sharing programs.

Conclusion

The interconnected nature of the world's ecologies and economies now mean that outdoor activities are shaping landscapes in less-obvious ways. The LNT ethic is problematic to the extent that it is complicit in, silent on, and perhaps willfully ignorant in two broad ways. First, LNT does not recognize the negative socio-cultural impacts of ignoring or erasing other human traces in "the outdoors." Second, LNT is silent on the social, cultural, and ecological impacts, effects, and traces incurred by outdoor recreation, education, and tourism beyond the areas and ideals of the outdoors. As such, LNT presents little challenge to, and likely reaffirms, the dominant Western environmental worldview within or beyond wilderness areas. Such a worldview may clash to different degrees and in different ways with the peoples being reached by LNTs ever-expanding education and social marketing campaign. To point, park services and other public agencies might consider the intersection of their efforts at decolonization and the environmental ethics they officially adopt, profess, and teach.

LNT was never intended to be a broad environmental ethic, rather it is a code of conduct for local management supported by highly successful social marketing. We in the outdoor field should be clear about what LNT is. I feel deeply ambivalent about LNT and critiquing its approach because I, too, practice minimum impact camping and because LNT has been successful in minimizing damage to wild landscapes. But, the central premise of LNT – that we can and should leave no trace – is flawed, and it limits practitioners' and participants' understanding of their inescapable individual and collective engagement, ownership of impacts (good and bad), and power to act positively. We need to be asking what sorts of traces are we leaving and want to be leaving? What social and ecological relations support me, and how might I improve these, nurture them, and give back? What traces am I leaving, where, and at what cost and with benefits to whom?

Leave No Trace includes a not-so-hidden and pervasive curriculum regarding "society" and "wilderness" that distorts and does not respond to current socio-ecological realities in which outdoor activities are situated. Humans are always place-making, and so, thankfully, there remain various histories and ideologies shaping landscapes. In outdoor, nature-based, and adventure recreation, education, and tourism we can and should reflect on ideologies that underlie the codes of conduct that guide our practices, as well as their roles in shaping people, places, and socio-environmental issues on various scales. Using a participatory ecological approach, I have tried to put forward principles that (a) recognize and make opportunity for the land, environment, and inhabitants to contribute more fully and directly to participants' experience, development, and becoming; (b) recognize and position outdoor activities within larger social and environmental realities and histories; (c) strive to "own" negative impacts through, for example, chains of production and consumption; but also (d) foster and act on social, economic, and political relations in ways that leave positive traces of our humanity.

Note

1 See Gelter (2000) on Scandinavian Friluftsliv; Lugg (2004) on Australian outdoor education; and Potter and Henderson (2004) on Canadian outdoor traditions.

References

Andreasen, A. (1994). Social marketing: Its definition and domain. *Journal of Public Policy & Marketing, 13*(1), 108–114.

Baldock, J., Mitton, L., Manning, N., & Vickersaff, S. (Eds.). (2012). *Social policy* (4th ed.). Oxford: Oxford University Press.

Beringer, A. (2004). Toward an ecological paradigm in adventure programming. *Journal of Experiential Education, 27*(1), 51–66.

Brymer, E., Downey, G., & Gray, T. (2009). Extreme sports as a precursor to environmental sustainability. *Journal of Sport & Tourism, 14*(2–3), 193–204.

Buckley, R. (2009). Evaluating the net effects of ecotourism on the environment: A framework, first assessment and future research. *Journal of Sustainable Tourism, 17*(6), 643–672.

Butler, C., & Menzies, C. (2007). Traditional ecological knowledge and Indigenous tourism. In R. Butler & T. Hinch (Eds.), *Tourism and Indigenous Peoples: Issues and implications* (pp. 15–27). Burlington, MA: Butterworth-Heinemann.

Cachelin, A., Rose, J., Dustin, D., & Shooter, W. (2011). Sustainability in outdoor education: Rethinking root metaphors. *Journal of Sustainability Education, 2*. Retrieved from www.jsedimensions.org/wordpress/wpcontent/uploads/2011/03/CachelinEtAl20111.pdf.

Cronon, W. (1996). The trouble with wilderness: Or, getting back to the wrong nature. *Environmental History, 1*(1), 7–55.

Fox, K. (2000). Navigating confluences: Revisiting the meaning of wilderness experience. In S. F. McCool, D. N. Cole, W. T. Borrie, & J. O'Loughlin (Eds.), *Proceedings from the wilderness science in a time of change conference – Volume 2: Wilderness within the context of larger systems* (pp. 49–58). Missoula, MT: U.S. Department of Agriculture, Forest Service, Rocky Mountain Research Station.

Gelter, H. (2000). Friluftsliv: The Scandinavian philosophy of outdoor life. *Canadian Journal of Environmental Education, 5*(1), 77–92.

Gibson, J. (1986). *The ecological approach to visual perception*. Hillsdale, NJ: Lawrence Erlbaum Associates. Retrieved from http://site.ebrary.com/id/10713812.

Green, E., Hebron, S., & Woodward, D. (1990). *Women's leisure, what leisure?* Basingstoke, Hampshire: Macmillan.

Guha, R. (1989). Radical American environmentalism and wilderness preservation: A third world critique. *Environmental Ethics, 11*(1), 71–83.

Haila, Y. (2000). Beyond the nature-culture dualism. *Biology and Philosophy, 15*(2), 155–175.

Hill, A. (2013). The place of experience and the experience of place: Intersections between sustainability education and outdoor learning. *Australian Journal of Environmental Education, 29*(1), 18–32.

Hill, A., & Brown, M. (2014). Intersections between place, sustainability and transformative outdoor experiences. *Journal of Adventure Education and Outdoor Learning, 14*(3), 217–232.

Hull, R. (2000). Moving beyond the romantic biases in natural areas recreation. *Journal of Leisure Research, 32*(1), 54–57.

Ingold, T. (2000). The perception of the environment: Essays on livelihood, dwelling and skill. New York: Routledge.
Ingold, T. (2005). Epilogue: Towards a politics of dwelling. Conservation and Society, 3(2), 501–508.
Ingold, T. (2007a). Earth, sky, wind, and weather. *Journal of the Royal Anthropological Institute*, *13*(1), S19–S38.
Ingold, T. (2007b). *Lines: A brief history*. New York: Routledge.
Ingold, T. (2008). Bindings against boundaries: Entanglements of life in an open world. *Environment and Planning A*, *40*(8), 1796–1810.
Ingold, T. (2011). *Being alive: Essays on movement, knowledge and description*. New York: Routledge.
Jamal, T., & Watt, E. (2011). Climate change pedagogy and performative action: Toward community-based destination governance. *Journal of Sustainable Tourism*, *19*(4–5), 571–588.
Kaplan, S. (1995). The restorative benefits of nature: Toward an integrative framework. *Journal of Environmental Psychology*, *15*(3), 169–182.
Leave No Trace. (2012a). *About us*. Retrieved February 26, 2017, from https://lnt.org/about.
Leave No Trace. (2012b). *Leave no trace tech tips*. Retrieved April 2, 2017, from https://lnt.org/learn/techtips.
Leave No Trace. (2012c). *Our partners*. Retrieved March 24, 2017, from https://lnt.org/about/our-partners.
Leave No Trace. (2012d). The Leave No Trace seven principles. Retrieved March 2, 2017 from https://lnt.org/learn/7-principles.
Leave No Trace Canada. (2009). *Current partnerships*. Retrieved March 24, 2017, from www.leavenotrace.ca/partnership.
Leung, Y.-F., Marion, J., & Farrell, T. (2008). Recreation ecology in sustainable tourism and ecotourism: A strengthening role. In S. F. McCool & R. N. Moisey (Eds.), *Tourism, recreation, and sustainability: Linking culture and the environment* (pp. 19–37). Cambridge, MA: CABI.
Lugg, A. (2004). Outdoor adventure in Australian outdoor education: Is it a case of roast for Christmas dinner? *Australian Journal of Outdoor Education*, *8*(1), 4–11.
Lynch, K. (1989). *The hidden curriculum: Reproduction in education, a reappraisal*. New York: Falmer Press.
Marion, J., & Reid, S. (2007). Minimising visitor impacts to protected areas: The efficacy of low impact education programmes. *Journal of Sustainable Tourism*, *15*(1), 5–27.
Mullins, P. (2009). Living stories of the landscape: Perception of place through canoeing in Canada's north. *Tourism Geographies*, *11*(2), 233–255.
Mullins, P. (2011). *A phenomenological approach to canoe tripping: Applicability of the dwelling perspective*. Unpublished PhD dissertation, University of Alberta, Edmonton, AB.
Mullins, P. (2014a). A socio-environmental case for skill in outdoor adventure. *Journal of Experiential Education*, *37*(2), 129–143.
Mullins, P. (2014b). Conceptualizing skill within a participatory ecological approach to outdoor adventure. *Journal of Experiential Education*, *37*(4), 320–334.
Mullins, P. (2015). Getting into it: Qualitative research in outdoor recreation. *International Leisure Review*, *4*(2), 56–82.
Mullins, P., Lowan-Trudeau, G., & Fox, K. (2016). Healing the split head of outdoor recreation and outdoor education: Revisiting Indigenous knowledge from multiple

perspectives. In B. Humberstone, H. Prince, & K. A. Henderson (Eds.), *Routledge handbook of outdoor studies* (pp. 49–58). New York: Routledge.

Mullins, P., & Maher, P. (2007). Paddling the big sky: Reflections on place-based education and experience. *Science and Stewardship to Protect and Sustain Wilderness Values*. Retrieved from www.fs.fed.us/rm/pubs/rmrs_p049/rmrs_p049_402_410.pdf.

Owens, L. (2011). Burning the shelter. In A. H. Deming & L. E. Savoy (Eds.), *The colors of nature: Culture, identity, and the natural world* (pp. 211–214). Minneapolis, MN: Milkweed Editions.

Potter, T., & Henderson, B. (2004). Canadian outdoor adventure education: Hear the challenge – learn the lessons. *Journal of Adventure Education & Outdoor Learning, 4*(1), 69–87.

Ryan, S. (2002). Cyborgs in the woods. *Leisure Studies, 21*(3–4), 265–284.

Ryan, S. (2009). *A critical analysis of the paradoxical nature of the discourses of ecology (1913–2000) and outdoor recreation (1960–2008)*. Library and Archives Canada = Bibliothèque et Archives Canada, Ottawa.

Sandilands, C. (2000). A flâneur in the forest? Strolling Point Pelee with Walter Benjamin. *TOPIA: Canadian Journal of Cultural Studies, 3*, 37–57.

Shultis, J. (2001). Consuming nature: The uneasy relationship between technology, outdoor recreation and protected areas. *The George Wright Forum, 18*(1), 56–66.

Shultis, J. (2012). The impact of technology on the wilderness experience: A review of common themes and approaches in three bodies of literature. In D. N. Cole (Ed.), *Wilderness visitor experiences: Progress in research and management. USDA Forest Service Proceedings* (pp. 110–118). Fort Collins, CO: U.S. Department of Agriculture, Forest Service.

Simon, G., & Alagona, P. (2009). Beyond leave no trace. *Ethics, Place & Environment, 12*(1), 17–34.

Turner, J. (2002). From woodcraft to "Leave No Trace": Wilderness, consumerism, and environmentalism in Twentieth-Century America. *Environmental History, 7*(3), 462.

Wright, P., & Mathews, C. (2015). Building a culture of conservation: Research findings and research priorities on connecting people to nature in parks. *PARKS, 21*(2).

11 The Anthropocene

The eventual geo-logics of posthuman tourism

Mick Smith

A geological tour

In a geological sense, everything is transient, even mountains grow and move, flow, shrink, and perish – eroded by water and ice, exploding in volcanic ecstasies, melting and slipping back into the torrid heat of the Earth's mantle. The very ground we stand on shifts, sometimes violently as the earth quakes, sometimes so very slowly that we would never dream of questioning its permanence. Yet rocks are the earth's continental drifters, continually travelling across the planet in the very act of constituting that thin lithospheric crust, just a few kilometres in depth, on which all life, all earthlings, are entirely dependent.

Over eons of time, (and technically an eon is one of the longest geological periods, spanning billions of years) these earthlings – the once living but now extinct creatures that moved across land surfaces and swam through waters, that burrowed and crawled in mud and sand; the forest stands and sedentary corals, the algae, arthropods and molluscs – contributed themselves, quite literally, to rock and mountain formations, to limestones and chalks, to reefs and cliffs. Even the Himalaya, like, but so very unlike, the Derbyshire peaks of my birth and my current glacier-scraped home ground in Ontario, are a cooperative venture between plate tectonics and marine or lacustrine organisms, a venture that required no capital, "natural" or financial. Yet, now, in our strange times, a global economy, built on the most impermanent foundations and guided only by an invisible hand, is busy inscribing its effects into the Earth's crust.

Of course, these "inscriptions" more usually take the form of excisions. Of mountain-top removal, massive opencast mines, and a sudden absence of species from any future fossil record; a sixth great extinction, this time of those "written off" by capitalism. Posterity will also be gifted a thin layer of radioactive dust and ample lithospheric evidence of climatic, and for many species, climactic, changes. Perhaps, then, before we get ahead of ourselves in dedicating a new epoch (technically, a more dramatic shift or longer period than a mere geological "age," but still hardly an eon) to our own anthropogenic contributions, we might consider the Anthropocene in geological terms, not as an epoch stretching out into the future, but as an *event* now happening. After all, an event is (relatively speaking) a momentary occurrence, a sudden conjunction of unexpected forces bringing about radical change; more like the meteor impact that extinguished the dinosaurs, ammonites, and so many other taxa ending the Cretaceous era some 65 million years ago. In this sense, and in others, the Anthropocene would be something of a misnomer, since what happens in the period following such an event will probably be entirely out of human hands. The only anthropogenic agency we actually have is in determining *now*, and politically, how destructive we allow this event to be.

Thinking about responsibilities for, and responses to, changes on such immense scales is daunting. Perhaps, though, attending more closely to the geological remnants of past ages, to those rock bourn souvenirs, petrified and carried forward into our present world, memorials of the world's previous "natural histories," might help. Here we might employ what Benjamin (1992, p. 246) refers to as our "weak Messianic power," an ability to re-call something of the past back into the life of the present. Not to resurrect past creatures, as in the genetic fantasies of Jurassic Park, but to let past lives matter in ways that are potentially "redemptive." We might attend to creations and creatures that have literally composed the earth and can, despite their extinction, still play very different roles in re-composing our world. After all, the oil that powers global tourism and feeds global climate change is also just a matter of a carboniferous afterlife. It is a "fossil" fuel.

Natural heritage on the Jurassic Coast

Some of what has gone before, one could discover in a brief trip to a museum, like those in Lyme Regis on Britain's southern coast. Dinosaurland Fossil Museum, (not at all as the name might imply, a Disneyland like theme park, but a serious collection of thousands of fossils housed in a converted Congregational Church), or the towns' Philpot Museum, closely associated with the author John Fowles, its curator and archivist for many years before his death in 2005.

Lyme Regis was, of course, the location of Fowles's meta-historical novel *The French Lieutenant's Woman* (1969) set in the late 1860s, that is, just a few years after the publication of Darwin's *Origin of Species* (1859). As Fowles noted, this is not a historical fiction but a *novel*, a making of something new out of a particular reading, an interpretation, indeed interlocution, of the past in the present. Smithson, the book's male protagonist visits the town (and his fiancée) while collecting fossils from the surrounding cliffs and beaches and exploring the aptly named "Undercliff," site of the massive Bindon landslip that had carried away many acres of pasture, cottages, and crops on Christmas Eve 1839. Here, his chance encounters with Sarah, the book's eponymous "heroine," compromise his settled plans in unexpected ways. Fowles even offers alternative "endings" to the book, in which different relations between Sarah, Smithson and his fiancé survive while others fall apart, each conclusion depending upon events and their interpretation by the author, the characters, and the reader.

Smithson is a fictional successor to many actual fossil hunters, eminent and amateur, who travelled to, or lived in, the area around Lyme Regis. William Buckland and Rev. William Conybeare, for example, were both present at the time of the Bindon landslip (Conybeare was vicar of Axminster) and together published a detailed account of it in 1840 illustrated by Mary Buckland, William's wife.

The continual erosion, movement, and slippage of the land and cliffs on this coast exposes fossils from the Jurassic and Cretaceous periods, held captive in various depositional layers dating from approximately 200 to 100 million years ago. Here, on the surrounding beaches, one can find "serpent stones" (ammonites), "devil's fingers" (belemnites), and crinoids, all once residents of a subtropical shallow sea that covered the area where these rocks formed. Along this coast in 1811 Mary Anning and her brother Joseph discovered the head and then the remainder of the first complete Ichthyosaur skeleton. In 1823, she found the first recognized plesiosaur and in 1828 the first pterosaur uncovered in Britain (described by Buckland as *Pterodactylus macronyx*) (Torrens, 1995). In 1833, while fossil hunting, her terrier, Tray, was buried by a landslide that nearly killed her too, a great sorrow for her, a fatal and anachronistic internment for him.

Buckland, Conybeare, and Richard Owen, the last a controversial figure and opponent of Darwin's evolutionary theories and now best known for coining the term "dinosauria," had gone fossilizing together with Mary Anning earlier in 1839. Other prominent local fossil hunters included Henry Thomas De La Beche (pronounced beach, says Fowles in his *A Short History of Lyme Regis*) and the three Philpot sisters. They had encouraged Mary Anning in her fossil hunting and themselves amassed a very significant collection of local fossils that now resides in Oxford University. Publicity around Anning's discoveries and their scientific descriptions led to an influx of fossil hunters, buyers, and collectors, from Europe and beyond. Her visitors included the American geologist, George William Featherstonhaugh in 1927, the Swiss (later American) paleontologist Louis Agassiz, in 1834, and, in 1844, the King of Saxony (Torrens, 1995). Agassiz named two fossil fish after Anning and one after Elizabeth Philpot.

Holidaying children now roam the summer beach at low tide with plastic buckets and geological hammers bought in local fossil shops; commercial descendants of Anning's own family business, "Annings Fossil Depot" which was at one time close by the site of the current Philpot museum. If lucky, these tourists might stumble across a near perfect ammonite, or an eroded ichthyosaur vertebra. Since 2001, a 155-km stretch of this coastline in Dorset and East Devon has been designated *The Jurassic Coast*, recognized as a World Heritage Site by UNESCO for its paleontological and geological importance. Needless to say, this title, with its filmic as well as geologic connotations, is used to market the area as a tourist destination. As its official website notes "The Jurassic Coast is a Walk Through Time" (Jurassiccoast, 2017), and it is, quite literally, in the sense that the long-distance South-West Coast footpath runs through the area (and also through the Undercliff, now a nature reserve). You can also cycle, enjoy tram rides, visit museums, or, of course, collect fossils.

Here, then we have a geographic area and a tourist destination officially defined by, and historically, literarily, and economically indebted to its paleontological past. The heritage status of the Jurassic Coast is consequent upon the unpredictable afterlife of fossilized beings in terms of the interest generated in visitors. But rather than considering the fossil as a novelty item, as the temporary focus of touristic attention or an interesting holiday souvenir, the focus here is on what fossils occasionally offer in terms of experiential encounters that shift our understandings of *relations between* (*inter-esse*) *beings* in ways that matter. Can the experiential possibilities harbored or sheltered within a momentary encounter with all that remains of an evolutionary "dead-end" help re-envision links between traces of past being(s), intensities of present experiences, and future oriented ecological concerns regarding the Anthopocene?

It is the fossils' being able to affect us in the here and now, its *presenting* itself (making its *presence* felt *now*) in a *novel* way, that affords possibilities to imagine different worlds, past, present, and future, here on Earth. In this sense, the fossil encounter might situate us in a larger context that (like Fowles's novel) lacking a single, predetermined conclusion reveals a future that is, as yet, undecided. So understood, the fossil encounter is very much an "event" in Walter Benjamin's, rather than a geological, sense; that is, a suddenly emergent "image" of the relation of "what-has-been to the now" (Benjamin, 1999), an event which precipitates novel constellations of meanings and ethico-political possibilities.

To consider fossils in this way obviously differs from most work on geotourism. The usual focus of such literature is on employing geological encounters to spark interest in the conservation of geologically and culturally significant locations, whilst also, of course, generating tourist revenues. This, after all, is also the main rationale behind the UNESCO designation of the Jurassic Coast. As T. H. Hose (2012), a pioneer in this rapidly expanding academic field notes, "The main reason for the original UK development of geotourism was to promote and provide some funding for geoconservation" (p. 3; see also Barettino, Wimbledon, & Gallego, 2000).

Such approaches often express laudable concerns with "sustainable tourism" (Newsome & Dowling, 2010) and sometimes gesture toward the touristic generation of a wider ethics of sustainability. They tend, though, to focus on ways to contribute educationally and economically to the present while preserving evidence of the past. An emphasis on the encounter as a "Benjaminian" event is quite different. In this case, the emphasis lies on how the event precipitates a change in our worldly understandings with cascading ethico-political consequences. Its main concern is not with unearthing that causally linked chain of beings stretching back behind us, nor with re-constituting or preserving a natural historical line of descent. Rather it focuses on a historical discontinuity that becomes apparent through the re-insertion of a singular relic of an almost entirely lost (historically overlain) past world, into the present moment. The event is the "presentation" (in all the senses of, the appearance, the making present, the making its presence felt) of a fossil's residual agency, it marks the possibility of a form of "material" afterlife. Of course, we cannot, actually "resurrect" past lives, we can only metaphorically "breathe new life" into the fossil. However, in conjunction with the encounter, we can afford it a certain novel historical agency it would otherwise lack, an agency where the disjunction of its past life with its current appearance can also present a shock to what we currently take for granted. In other words, the fossil encounter can offer an exemplary opening into past, present, and future that changes our understanding of all.

The occurrence of such an event depends upon inserting the material and phenomenological appearance of the instantiated past "object" (its novel sensory impressions) and the interpretations it generates (its hermeneutic effectivity) into a contemporary ethico-political context. Such an emphasis on phenomenology and hermeneutics is not itself unique: There are certainly cases in the geotourism literature where both are taken very seriously. Gordon (2012), for example, traces how early touristic encounters at Fingal's Cave and the Falls of Clyde in Scotland, reveal how "geological features and places inspired a *sense of wonder* that was conveyed through contemporary literature and art" (p. 66). But even here, Gordon's main concern seems (quite understandably given its frame of reference) to be to employ new iterations of this phenomenological/interpretative experience of the sublime "to develop a broader constituency of support for geoconservation and enable people to reconnect with their geoheritage" (p. 66).

However, regarding fossils as just another, as yet relatively under-developed, tourism resource (Laws & Scott, 2003), even one that might contribute to the conservation of something of intrinsic value, would only take us so far. By contrast, the suggestion here is that our experiences of the fossil record, of a visit to a museum, a casual stroll on the beach, or simply holding a fossil in the palm of our hand, might also, in certain contexts, act to reorient our thinking and concerns in ways that elicit an ethics and a politics of resistance to the Anthropocene. Our being in touch with the relics of past extinctions, with previous life turned to stone, might help make us aware of the ecological and ethical disaster now threatening to frame and define the future existence of all earthlings.

Is this so ridiculous an idea? After all, the fossil discoveries of Anning and the Philpot sisters did indeed contribute to very profound effects on our understanding of our place in the world. In conjunction with other events, discoveries and theories, they affected a cosmological, as well as cultural shift that promised a novel way of decentering, but also biologically re-attaching, humanity in relation to the Earth's pre-history. Over the course of the 19th century (such a brief span of geological time) evolutionary understandings of the Earth and its natural, rather than super-natural, history became widely adopted, dependent upon an increasing appreciation of "deep time" and the impermanence of landscapes that had previously, with the exception of dramatic events like the Bindon landslip, seemed almost unchanging (Hose, 2005; Rudwick, 2008).

Even the meanings of rocks themselves altered. Mary Anning, for example, noted that the cylindrical bezoar stones, previously regarded as magical antidotes to all poisons, were often found within ichthyosaur remains, and suggested their origins might be more prosaic, namely that they were the fossilized feces of ichthyosaurs. They were, in terms of Buckland's neologism, "coprolites." Indeed, when broken open they contained the bones of species of fossil fish commonly found in the area. Even their dark color could now be explained by their hosts having eaten "the ink sacs of squid like animals to which the fossil belemnites (also common in the Lias [rock formations around Lyme]) were now attributed"

(Rudwick, 2008, p. 155). Quite suddenly, the pre-historic "ecology" of an age before humanities existence could be envisaged, and De La Beche's 1830 illustration of this primeval environment (Figure 11.1) based largely on Anning's fossil finds, had immense cultural reverberations.

Few would have regarded this picture as an accurate rendition of the past (Rudwick, 2008), but it still illustrated, in dramatic terms, how very different this earlier Jurassic world had been to ours. When interpolated into an ethico-political context, this realization had equally profound effects. Those seeking social change noted that if species were not essentially pre-ordained but had evolved, if geology was impermanent, and if entire worlds had passed, then there could be no justification for a fixed social and economic order. The radical religious, cultural, and social, implications of such changes were obvious to many geologists and natural historians too, including Darwin, which may explain his reluctance to make his proposals concerning the idea of natural selection public for so many years (Desmond & Moore, 1991). The ethico-political implications of this fossil generated cultural event (which also inform the setting of Fowles's novel) are still not fully apparent today. Indeed, the idea of the Anthropocene is itself indicative of a failure to recognize the extent of this radical geo-temporal decentering of the human species. For in one sense, the Anthropocene is just the latest attempt to recuperate a central role in the Earth's natural history for humanity.

Perhaps, then, a felt awareness of the accidental and intended intersections of timescales and life-histories, of phenomenology and hermeneutics, stone and flesh, life and death, might help foster what Cohen's (2015) subtitle refers to as "an ecology of the inhuman" requiring a "Long Ecology" (p. 41) that acknowledges

Figure 11.1 Henry De La Beche (1830) Duria Antiquior, a more ancient Dorset.

a more-than-human scale of "temporal and spatial entanglement" (p. 41) with profound ethical implications.

The ammonite and the appearance of fossil tourism

In my hand, I hold an ammonite, purchased from a fossil shop close by the Philpott museum in Lyme Regis. As already noted, the last ammonites, a taxonomic group that had been present since the Devonian era some 400 million years ago, were extinguished in the same Cretaceous-Paleogene extinction event that destroyed the dinosaurs.

This ammonite fossil is a lustrous pale yellow, almost translucent in appearance. On one side, it is still held tight in the matrix of smooth, grey rock from which it was partially chipped. This specimen is only a couple of centimetres across, perhaps a juvenile, but some species were smaller still and others grew to be larger than cartwheels. (The largest specimens known are over two meters in diameter.) The size might also relate to its sex, since ammonites were strongly dimorphic, the male being much smaller than the female. My fingertip can trace the ridged fossil whorl beginning near its centre, spiralling round anti-clockwise three times until it finishes where the very end of the fossil was sheared off during its extraction. Here, a darker circle, filling the space within the yellow circumference, indicates the hollow body cavity of the shell. Ammonite shells were internally divided into chambers by walls (septa) and the living creature, looking somewhat like that extant relative of the squid, the nautilus (but actually more closely related to octopi and squid), would have inhabited only the last chamber, its eyes and many thin arms protruding from it as it swam and fed. As the creature grew the chambers behind filled with gas or fluids for buoyancy, allowing the animal to rise or fall through the water column by altering their contents. The ammonite shell depicted, bottom left, in De La Beche's illustration, shows the entrance to the shell pointing upwards (as became standard in scientific depictions) but the direction would actually have depended upon the creature's body length and position in the shell (Monks & Palmer, 2002). When living, it probably fed on small planktonic creatures, foraminifera, bryozoa, crustaceans, and so on.

This ammonite glows faintly; others have a metallic sheen or lustre. Some still seem to have the mother of pearl appearance of the nacre that originally constituted one of the layers of their tough protective shells. Some are heavily eroded, smoothed by waves, grey as the rocks on which, or in which, they are found. To tempt tourists some are polished smooth to reveal where the crinkled septa walls joined the shell, or even cross-sectioned to reveal inner patterns of septa and chambers. Their appearance today, then, depends upon the species, age, sex, the process of fossilization, the degree and kind of mineralization, for example, pyritization, involving iron and sulphur [there is an entire science, taphonomy, that studies the different ways and settings in which fossils form (Martin, 1999), and, of course, the subsequent interventions by human sellers and collectors].

I believe this ammonite to be a specimen collected close by Lyme Regis; however, lacking expertise, I might be completely mistaken. The fossils for sale today are part of a global trade. One can buy fossils from Brazil, Utah, Mongolia, Madagascar, just about anywhere they occur and ammonites had a worldwide distribution. Many fossils command high prices, well beyond most tourists' pockets. Some of the more nefarious online sites have fossils for sale such as ammonites from the legally protected Walsh River area in Queensland. Indeed, the pillaging of fossil sites for saleable artifacts exactly mirrors the destruction of those cultural and archaeological sites that tourism has played (and continues to play) a well-documented role in facilitating (Clottes, 2008; Vella et al., 2015).

Of course, the kinds of fossil collecting tourism encourages are certainly not all destructive, as the case of Mary Anning shows. Most fossils near Lyme Regis would otherwise, in any case, only be left to erode on today's seashore, and sales in museums and shops no doubt do continue to "help to promote palaeontology as a science" (Donovan & Lewis, 2004, p. 367). As students of tourism might expect, tourism has conflicting roles in paleontological terms: sometimes encouraging and financing conservation and museum work, helping to maintain what is, as the museums in Lyme Regis attest, both a matter of natural *and* cultural heritage; at other times playing a more destructive role, opening previously inaccessible areas to despoliation and financing the haphazard extraction of historically important fossil artifacts from their original strata and interpretative contexts, that is, from fossil beds that are sometimes irretrievably damaged in the process. Interestingly, it was recognition of visitors vandalizing the Triassic fossil trees and looting petrified wood that was "the sole reason for establishing the Petrified Forest National Monument" [Arizona] (Lubick, 1996, p. 4) as long ago as 1904.

We also need to recognize that appearances can be deceptive. There is a thriving industry in faking fossils for tourists and collectors. Only a real expert could tell if the fossil trilobite I have from Morocco is genuine or simply resin mounted on stone (Koppka, Sonntag, & Burkard, 2003). As with so many other cases in the tourist and heritage industry, it seems there are many potential issues around the "authenticity" of any fossil purchased. This is nothing new. One of Mary Anning's customers, Thomas Hawkins, was notorious for "enhancing" the fossils he then sold on to major institutions, including the British museum. Many of the fossil bones of his "sea dragons" turned out to be made of plaster, much to the consternation of Buckland who had recommended the museum should purchase Hawkins collection.

If there are issues concerning what we might term a fossil's "material" authenticity, then there are also matters of "staged authenticity" to consider. Tourist encounters with fossils are often mediated by interpretative exhibits that, rather like De La Beche's lithographs, are often as much the products of imaginative license as scientific evidence. This too, is nothing new, as the anatomically inaccurate dinosaurs produced by Waterhouse Hawkins for the relocated Crystal Palace of the Great Exhibition of 1851 and based on Richard Owen's opinions reveal.

As Doyle and Robinson (1993) note "Crystal Palace Park in southeast London was the site of the first geological 'theme park'" (p. 181) opening in 1854, as an explicit attempt "to bring complex geological concepts to the paying public" (p. 181). This included not only the dinosaurs (Owen hosted a famous dinner party partly inside the mold of an iguanodon on New Year's Eve 1853) but old red sandstone, lias, coal formations, and limestone "mountains" of rocks imported and reconstructed to suggest fossil bearing geological strata.

The dinosaurs (some, like the ichthyosaur and plesiosaur, drawing upon Mary Anning's earlier fossil finds) were placed on, or near, artificial islands in a lake, supposed to represent the habitats and vegetation associated with different geological periods. This themed park, like the Jurassic Coast, might also have been described as "a walk through time" since the visitor footpath led them back in time from the Tertiary period (the so-called age of mammals) past the ichthyosaur and plesiosaur in the lake, across a bridge to the island occupied by earlier dinosaurs, like the iguanodons and the megalosaurus.

The staging of the dinosaurs certainly worked to make the park a major tourist attraction. Unfortunately, the Park never really recuperated the costs of translocating Joseph Paxton's Crystal Palace building and of developing the gardens. Within a few decades, the dinosaur reconstructions had also come to be recognized as inauthentic in other ways. The iguanodon, for example, stood on four feet rather than two and had a horn on its nose that should really have been a claw on its front limb. Yet, ironically, when a cataclysmic event occurred on 30th November 1936 and Paxton's Crystal Palace building was entirely destroyed by fire, only the dinosaurs survived! Later, in 1962, "the Mountain Limestone was destroyed by blasting during the redesign of the watercourse as a rockery and watergarden" (Doyle & Robinson, 1993, p. 185) although, in 2002, it was "rebuilt" with yet more imported Derbyshire limestone during the dinosaur's "restoration."

Inaccurate or not, and despite the educational intent of the parks makers, which under Owen's tutelage, and prior to Darwin's publication of *The Origin*, was not designed to represent evolution but to celebrate God's "digressions" – that is, his earlier creations/creatures – these tourist encounters with cement dinosaurs and imported geological strata could still have very real and unforeseen aftereffects:

> Intended to point visitors toward Creationist conclusions about history predicated on man's central role in God's scheme, the park thematized a divinely ordained progress of civilization of which Victorians were the final heirs. Yet despite such attempts at rigid hermeneutical control, the park nevertheless presented profoundly disturbing evidence of degeneration and extinction, thereby denying the verity of human progression and suggesting that the primitive and the civilized – the ancient and the modern – were intimately related.
>
> (Marshall, 2007, p. 286)

Walking backwards through time, the visitor could not help but recognize the short span of human existence, the alien forms of earlier creatures, and the overwhelming evidence of extinction. In "this type of time travel, human grandeur dissipated and indeed humanity itself disappeared as one progressed through the exhibit" (Marshall, 2007, p. 296).

To be clear: although planned as part of an educational visitor entertainment, following directly on from the most impressive and successful exhibition of technical progress and colonial prowess then produced, these artificial dinosaur reconstructions, actually subverted this "anthropocentric" self-assurance. Their presence suggested quite different interpretations on just how the past, in all its depth, connected to, and jutted through into, the present. For some visitors and commentators at least the "geological illustrations" at Crystal Palace raised troubling questions about cosmology, religion, and the transitory nature of human existence here on Earth (Marshall, 2007). They exemplified the ways that fossils in general, even before they were interpreted in terms of Darwinian natural selection, troubled civilizational certainties about linear temporal progress.

Now the ammonite in front of me, like the ichthyosaur, is not one of those extant when the meteor smashed into the Earth wiping out seventy-five percent of all known species, dinosaurs included. This particular species may have evolved into other forms and/or become extinct for many other reasons long before. That, though, is not what matters now, or in Benjamin's terms. The point, after all, is not to re-live an extinction event in the past, but to consider how attending to such relics might help stop a similar event happening in the present. What matters, and what is troubling, is that such fossils are all that remains of this previous life-form and all of its progeny, that the Earth was unexpectedly changed so very suddenly, making it impossible, after a span of more than 200 million years, for ammonites to continue to survive and evolve. This ammonite signifies the end of an "evolutionary" story that cannot be re-written, one without the possibility of any alternative ending. The fossils effects are no longer, or hardly at all, ecological, but only cultural. This specimen, like those cement models only indirectly related to Anning's fossilized ichthyosaurs and plesiosaurs, now has only a vicarious life in terms of the ways it might intrude into our understandings of its, and our, very different places in very different worlds. The phenomenological, hermeneutical, and ethico-political issues that arise concern what kind of heritage the fossil ammonite re-presents to us, and more importantly, what kind of heritage we will leave behind us.

Fossil "Heritage," posthumanism and the Anthropocene

There is, of course, a long-standing scepticism in tourism studies about the very concept of heritage. Heritage experiences can epitomize the worst kinds of staged authenticity and can easily be derided as misplaced forms of "nostalgia" for an idealized past. In this sense, they might be said to fail to pay due attention to both past realities and the present. Wood in Urry (1990), for example, claims that "now that the present seems so full of woe . . . the profusion and frankness of our nostalgia . . . suggest not merely a sense of loss . . . but a general abdication, an actual desertion from the present" (p. 105).

The current world is certainly full of ecological woe, but Wood's remark hardly rings true for the petrified ammonite. Certainly, the ammonite might generate a sense of loss; of the loss of the individual creature's life, the loss of this species, the loss of all ammonites, of the loss of an entire world. However, it is difficult (though perhaps not impossible) to feel "nostalgic" for a world that was entirely lacking in any human presence. We could never have actually gone "Walking with Dinosaurs." The ammonite's marine world was, if anything, even less familiar than that of its land-based contemporaries. Like Anning's dinosaurs, the ammonite fossil provides only a petrified glimpse of a hitherto unsuspected and strange world, a curious world certainly, and a world that inspires curiosity, but hardly one that can be idealized in a comfortable or comforting way as an alternative residence to the present.[1] The ammonite's world troubles us because, even though it prefigures our own it remains so intractably alien, and also because our world, now threatened in its turn, is a world entirely predicated on the destruction wreaked on that of the ammonites. So, if "nostalgia" plays any role at all here, it is surely to articulate a recognition of an irretrievable past event that effected our accidental emergence, rather than its allowing us to wallow in a mythologized past.

Perhaps, though, some might argue, we should not exaggerate the "troubling" nature of these (dis)continuities between past and present worlds? After all, the tourism industry itself does much to make dinosaurs and their contemporaries a familiar part of our present cultural world. Their images are everywhere (Mitchel, 1998): in films, children's toys, advertisements. Ammonites too appear in the most unsuspected places on the Jurassic Coast, as ornamental lampposts, publicity brochures, and so on. Even the fictional Jurassic Park was intended as a "tourist trap." No doubt, the shock of Owen and Hawkins Crystal Palace dinosaurs has receded; they are now largely curiosities (and architecturally they are grade one listed buildings). However, there does remain a phenomenal and hermeneutic gap between the culturally familiar imagery of the Jurassic and close encounters with the fossilized bones, shells, and bodies of actual pre-existing beings. By and large, and insofar as we resist inhabiting entirely fictional worlds, these calcareous and lithic events have the potential to elicit more profound repercussions. We touch, and are touched by, these "rocks," in ways that generate different response-abilities. Of course, some of these responses might still be diverted into consumerism but others bring us to consider how the now inanimate past articulates with past and present lives. In Cohen's words (2015), "The tactility of cognition: hand upon stone triggers epistemological shift, spurs an insight about nonhuman imbroglios, about being as a hazardous doing, about nonseparability and irreducibility" (p. 43).

If this still seems far-fetched, consider how, *despite the familiarity of skeletal images*, something similar occurs in encounters with dead and transformed human bodies. Take the skull or mummified body in a museum display, or the "plastinated" bodies of individuals in Gunther Von Hagens "Body Worlds" exhibition (see, e.g., https://en.wikipedia.org/wiki/Body_Worlds), itself a major "dark tourist" attraction (Stone, 2011). Such encounters can provoke profound ontological discomfort in visitors (Davidson et al., 2009). In certain contexts, the "preserved" remains of once living persons, now displayed before us as a spectacle, can affect us emotionally and interpretatively in many ways, as uncanny, unnerving, sad, improper, curious. They draw attention to what little we know of that individual's life and death, to our own mortality, and to more general questions of the nature of existence and our place in the world. Such exhibits also directly raise cultural, ethical, and political concerns, for example, in terms of the potentially (in)voluntary donation of bodies or objections to the collection and display of the remains of Indigenous ancestors under the guise of Western anthropology (Hamilton, 2010). Even stuffed animals in museum display seem to have phenomenal, hermeneutic, and political, afterlives (Alberti, 2011), some aspects of which elicit something of that specific animal's life history. Others, as in a taxidermic exhibition of now extinct creatures like the passenger pigeon, the thylacine, or the dodo, almost inevitably provoke thoughts of anthropogenic extinctions, of bodies and beings the world now lacks.

In such situations, we can hardly be unaware that there is also a gap, a difference that is ontological, experiential, meaningful, and material, between encountering a petrified relic of a past being and being in actual community with still living beings. This gap troubles us, it can even force recognition of their and our (our shared) impermanence. Benjamin went so far as to suggest that we have a responsibility, a secret redemptive agreement with those past generations (although, of course, he was referring only to past human generations) now buried by history, to conserve and re-articulate something of the lives they gave in ways that make a material difference in the present. For, "every image of the past that is not recognized by the present as one of its own concerns threatens to disappear irretrievably" (Benjamin, 1992, p. 247. He was also clear that "[t]o articulate the past historically does not mean to recognize it 'the way it really was' . . . It means to seize hold of a memory as it flashes up at a moment of danger" (p. 247). It should not need to be said that we, earthlings, are *all* in a moment of grave danger.

Mary Anning's fossils appeared in the cultural context of early modern Britain, replete with the sudden landscape and social changes induced by the industrial revolution, the interpretative changes wrought by the rise of Romanticism, the cultural aftershocks of the Enlightenment (and its effects on religious beliefs), and the emergence of a new "scientific" emphasis on natural history and geology.[2] This context, which cannot be separated from the political changes also taking place, might be glossed as part of the development of a "progressive humanism." Yet, as we have seen, the appearance of these fossils in this context remained strangely ambiguous. On the one hand, these "geological illustrations" represented the triumphs of new scientific understandings of a natural history that was increasingly at variance with previous religious cosmologies but, on the other, this triumph also left humanity decentred. It fundamentally challenged human exceptionalism.

Over subsequent years, and with certain exceptions, including some aspects of ecological, geological, and evolutionary thought, this decentring of humanity from Earth's natural history has remained culturally, ethically, and politically marginalized. To say this might seem odd given the acceptance of these "sciences" in most intellectual circles. However, even in this milieu, which no longer regards humanity as an exceptional being made in God's image, or the world being gifted to us by God, this humanism still envisages the Earth as "ours," to do with what we will. It treats human sovereignty over the non-human world as an unquestionable given (Smith, 2011), reducing diverse ecologies to nothing more than a (human) resource, a global system of ecosystem services (Sullivan, 2010). Even those aspects of popular culture that treat evolution as a fact still seem to assume that humanity is its natural and processual telos and apogee. That is to say, the story of the Earth is still regarded as a linear narrative that has humanity as its natural and historical end, albeit an end we bizarrely expect "to be continued" in much the same progressive vein in the following installment.

In this world, nature's agency, perhaps especially its lithographic agency, is given little weight. We build nuclear power stations on coasts near seismic fault lines, and holiday hotels right on the beach, and never expect for a moment an earthquake-generated tsunami. Such events are assumed to appear on different time scales to our own brief period of residence so the intersection of these temporalities comes as an unwelcome, and often fatal, surprise. We continue to burn fossil fuels despite their climate changing effects, to travel more frequently and more widely in order to add experiences to our personal accounts, and so on. A volcanic eruption in Iceland is now regarded as little more just an irritating interruption to the traveller's flight plans. And, as airlines and satellites provide the kind of global coverage international tourism relies upon, who but an environmentalist could now doubt that human technology has placed us in control of our lives, the unelected governors of the increasingly complex artificial systems we devise, and masters of what remains of the planets increasingly denuded ecologies?

No doubt, as the inauguration of the Anthropocence epoch is itself intended to convey, our contemporary context is very different from that of Mary Anning's. We are witnessing, many social theorists also argue, a move from a humanist to a post-humanist situation where nature and human beings and technology are, to all effects and purposes, inextricable (Wolfe, 2010; Braidotti, 2013; Haraway, 2016). However, despite a plethora of posthumanist discourses, the recognition of these inescapable relations does not necessarily lead to a sense of ethical/political responsibility for the more-than-just human world. Quite the contrary, many theorists are more interested in arguing that this means there is no such thing as "nature" to concern ourselves with anymore, just systems, networks, and/or processes of distributed agency (Latour, 2004) that are all now more or less anthropogenically affected and driven. There are even forms of "posthumanism" that engage in an unconstrained celebration of the technologically sublime. Here, humans will extricate themselves still further from a nature now past by becoming integrated into increasingly sophisticated (information) technology (Hayles, 1999). Some suggest we might even separate ourselves completely from both our bodies and planet Earth, escaping the rigours of mortality and human extinction. Such science fiction is really just a form of hyper-humanism, an extension of anthropocentrism.

Similarly, the Anthropocene might also be regarded as a form of hyper-humanism; more of a continuance of progressive humanism rather than a radical break from it. Acceptance of the term might even suggest that recognizing this systemic involvement requires our changing from the "accidental" to the "purposive" geoengineering of the entire planet's climate and lithosphere. Serious (and seriously worrying) proposals include pumping particles into the stratosphere to mimic the atmospheric cooling effects of volcanic eruptions, pumping liquid CO_2 into the depth of the lithosphere or seeding the oceans with iron particles to encourage algal uptake of CO_2. Any, or all of these, might have planet-wide ecological consequences that will only add to the extinctions already being caused. Geo-engineering, we might say, is just an extreme example of an anthropocentric *and* Anthropocenic ideology that suggests that humans should be in the driver's seat of global historical changes. To these advocates even catastrophic risk-taking seems preferable to the possibility of consciously altering the trajectory of the global economy that drives such changes!

We are indeed, in Benjamin's terms, at a moment of extreme danger, and so, unfortunately, are all the other species with which we "share" this planet. The danger we all face is not that of an impending meteor strike, but an economic system with the potential to wreak comparable global damage. Studies suggest that 15–37 percent of all land plants and animals could become extinct due to climate change by 2050 (Thomas et al., 2004). In terms of marine effects, "one-third of reef-building corals face elevated extinction risk from climate change and local impact" (Carpenter, 2008, p. 560). The only ethical stance to take to the declaration of the Anthropocene is to concern ourselves with our more than just human contemporaries whose very existence is now threatened by the activities of certain (but certainly not all) human beings. Some versions of post-humanism certainly recognize that we need to "stay with the trouble" and with our sometimes very strange kin (Haraway, 2016). We need to make sure the Anthropocene in terms of its destructive anthropocentrism lasts as short a time as possible.

Perhaps attending to the petrified but still wonder-full remains of a past life, even one we just happened to pick up on the holiday beach, might just begin to make a difference. It might just open us to a realization that, rather like Fowles's book, different endings are possible and, as yet, undecided. These endings too will depend upon novel interpretations, and involvements, on ethics and unexpected passions, and chance encounters. Such events might make us realize that fossils are not just a matter of fuels to extract, burn and exhaust. This is just what we have made of them in our current economic age. Very different fossil after-lives attest to the dangers of such a narrow, short-term, approach and its existential perils. In this sense, these "relics" from past ages might harbor a contemporary lithic agency that will eventually help us reflect on a world that might become "posthuman" in one of two very different senses, that is humanly uninhabitable or, preferably, humanly decentred. There is a possibility of redemption here through an understanding that we have response-abilities and responsibilities that go far beyond the presentism of mindless consumerism. We need to stop behaving like planetary tourists and start acting as though the Earth, as fossils reveal, has always has been our home, and that of every other single being, living and dead, that has ever existed. Like the ammonite, we are all earthlings.

Notes

1 Although, Mitchel (1998) suggested that Rudolph Zallinger's giant fresco 'The Age of Reptiles' at Yale's Peabody Museum "envisions a dinotopic refuge from World War II" (p. 188).

2 William Whewell coined the term "scientist" in 1833 in a review of Mary Somerville's book *On the Connection of the Physical Sciences*. He also coined the terms "catastrophism" and "uniformitarianism" relating to understandings of geological history as a matter of sudden massive or long-term gradual changes.

References

Alberti, S. (2011). *The afterlives of animals*. Charlottesville, VA: University of Virginia Press.

Barettino, D., Wimbledon, W. A. P., & Gallego, E. (Eds.). (2000). *Geological heritage: Its conservation and management*. España: Instituto Tecnológico Geominero de España.

Benjamin, W. (1992). Theses on the philosophy of history. In *Illuminations: Essays and reflections*. London: Harper Collins.

Benjamin, W. (1999). *The arcades project*. Cambridge, MA: Harvard University Press.

Braidotti, R. (2013). *The Posthuman*. Cambridge: Polity.

Carpenter, K. E. (2008). One-third of reef-building corals face elevated extinction risk from climate change and local impact. *Science*, *321*, 560–563.

Clottes, J. (2008). Rock art: An endangered heritage worldwide. *Journal of Anthropological Research*, *64*(1), 1–18.

Cohen, J. J. (2015). *Stone: An ecology of the inhuman*. Minneapolis, MN: University of Minnesota Press.

Darwin, C. R. (1859). *On the origins of species*. London: John Murray.

Davidson, J., Huff, L., Bridgen, J., Carolan, A., Chang, A., Ennis, K., Loynes, K., & Miller, J., (2009). Doing gender at body worlds: Embodying field trips as affective educational experience. *Journal of Geography in Higher Education*, *33*(3), 303–314.

Desmond, A., & Moore, J. (1991). *Darwin*. London: Michael Joseph.

Donovan, S. K., & Lewis, D. (2004). Palaeoecology in the museum gift shop. *Proceedings of the Geologists' Association*, *115*(4), 367–370.

Doyle, P., & Robinson, E., (1993). The Victorian 'geological illustrations' of Crystal Palace Park. *Proceedings of the Geologists' Association*, *104*(3), 181–194.

Fowles, J. (1969). *The French Lieutenant's woman*. London: Jonathan Cape.

Fowles, J. (2012 [1982]). *A short history of Lyme Regis*. Stanbridge: The Dovecote Press.

Gordon, J. E. (2012). Rediscovering a sense of wonder: Geoheritage, geotourism and cultural landscape experiences. *Geoheritage*, *4*, 65–77.

Hamilton, M. A. (2010). *Collections and objections: Aboriginal material culture in Southern Ontario*. Montreal and Kingston: McGill-Queen's University Press.

Haraway, D. (2016). *Staying with the trouble: Making kin in the Chthulucene*. Durham, NC: Duke University Press.

Hayles, K. N. (1999). *How we became posthuman: Virtual bodies in cybernetics, literature, and informatics*. Chicago: University of Chicago Press.

Hose, T. A. (2005). Geo-tourism – appreciating the deep time of landscapes. In M. Novelli (Ed.), *Niche tourism: Contemporary issues, trends and cases* (pp. 27–37). London: Elsevier.

Hose, T. A. (2012). Editorial: Geotourism and geoconservation. *Geoheritage*, *4*, 1–5.

Jurassiccoast. (2017). Retrieved February 1, 2017, from http://jurassiccoast.org/.
Koppka, J., Sonntag, H., & Burkard, H., (2003). *How to identify fake trilobites*. Retrieved February 13, 2017, from www.fossilmuseum.net/collect/faketrilobites3.htm.
Latour, B. (2004). *Politics of nature*. Cambridge, MA: Harvard University Press.
Laws, E., & Scott, N. (2003). Developing new tourism services: Dinosaurs, a new drive tourism resource for remote regions? *Journal of Vacation Marketing*, *9*(4), 368–38.
Lubick, G. C. (1996). *Petrified Forest National Park: A wilderness bound in time*. Tuscon, AZ: University of Arizona Press.
Marshall, N. R. (2007). A dim world, where monsters dwell: The spatial time of the Sydenham Crystal Palace Dinosaur Park. *Victorian Studies*, *49*(2), 286–301.
Martin, R. E. (1999). *Taphonomy: A process approach*. Cambridge: Cambridge University Press.
Mitchel, W. J. T. (1998). *The last dinosaur book*. Chicago: University of Chicago Press.
Monks, N., & Palmer, P. (2002). *Ammonites*. Washington, DC: Smithsonian Institute Press.
Newsome, D., & Dowling, R. K. (Eds.). (2010). *Geotourism: The tourism of geology and landscape*. Woodeaton: Goodfellows Publishing.
Rudwick, M. J. S. (2008). *Worlds before Adam: The reconstruction of geohistory in the age of reform*. Chicago: University of Chicago Press.
Smith, M. (2011). *Against ecological sovereignty: Ethics, biopolitics and saving the natural world*. Minneapolis, MN: University of Minnesota Press.
Stone, P. R. (2011). Dark tourism and the cadaveric carnival: Mediating life and death narratives at Gunther von Hagens' Body Worlds. *Current Issues in Tourism*, *14*(7), 685–701.
Sullivan, S. (2010). Ecosystem service commodities: A new imperial ecology? Implications for animist immanent ecologies, with Deleuze and Guattari. *New Formations*, *69*, 111–128.
Thomas, C. D., Cameron, A., Green, R. E., Bakkenes, M., Beaumont, L. J., Collingham, Y. C. . . . Williams, S. E. (2004). Extinction risk from climate change. *Nature*, *427*, 145–148.
Torrens, H. (1995). Mary Anning (1799–1847) of Lyme: 'The greatest fossilist the world ever knew'. *British Journal for the History of Science*, *28*, 257–284.
Urry, J. (1990). *The tourist gaze*. London: SAGE.
Vella, C., Bocancea, E., Urban, T. M., Knodell, Alex, R., Tuttle, C. A., & Alcock, S. E. (2015). Looting and vandalism around a World Heritage Site: Documenting modern damage to archaeological heritage in Petra's hinterland' *Journal of Field Archaeology*, *40*(2), 221–235.
Wolfe, C. (2010). *What is posthumanism?* Minneapolis, MN: University of Minnesota Press.

12 Indigenous methodologies revisited

Métissage, hybridity, and the Third Space in environmental studies

Gregory Lowan-Trudeau

Introduction

In this chapter, I explore approaches to research that explicitly consider the relationships between Western and Indigenous methodologies. In so doing, I engage with various interpretations of Homi Bhabha's (1994) Third Space, métissage, and other articulations of hybridity as discussed by a variety of scholars from distinct cultural and epistemological perspectives in relation to Indigenous methodologies. I reflexively revisit some of my own past work in this context as a Métis scholar in Canada of mixed Indigenous and European ancestry as well as that of several leading and emerging Indigenous scholars. This line of inquiry concludes with presentation of inspiring examples and discussion of the implications for research in Indigenous environmental studies with a specific focus on the interconnected areas of natural resource management, land-based tourism, outdoor leadership, and education. Through this discussion, I aim to contribute to the relatively limited (Neilsen & Wilson, 2012), but growing, collection of Indigenous voices in tourism studies and related fields.

Indigenous methodologies

Over the past several decades, an increasing array of propositions has emerged regarding what it means to conduct Indigenous research within the Western-dominated Academy. As Indigenous research has become more commonplace in institutions across North America and around the world, so to have its conceptions and variations in practice. Building on the foundational work of scholars such as Linda Tuhiwai Smith (2012) from Aotearoa (New Zealand) and others, Indigenous scholars continue to expand and demonstrate what is possible through various interpretations of Indigenous research in theory and in practice. As tourism scholars, Chambers and Buzinde (2015) suggest, while such developments are undeniably inspiring, research in the Academy is far from decolonized – many Indigenous research projects still fail to create or facilitate meaningful changes in the lives of Indigenous Peoples.

A range of complexities and varying viewpoints of what counts as Indigenous research have also arisen. One central preoccupation in Indigenous research circles is the relationship between Western and Indigenous methodologies; important questions persist in this regard, such as:

- Is it acceptable to use Western methods in the service of Indigenous social and/or environmental justice?
- Or, should all Indigenous research be carried out exclusively using Indigenous traditions for knowledge collection and interpretation?
- If not, how/can Western and Indigenous methodologies come together in respectful ways to produce hybrid/convergent methodologies?
- Or perhaps there are different applications for a variety of methodological approaches that all still serve Indigenous interests in one way or another?
- And how might place be authentically incorporated into contemporary Indigenous environmental research?
- And finally, but not exhaustively, what sort of ethical concerns might one expect to encounter in these various scenarios?

As might be understandably predicted, a range of responses has arisen in response to such questions. As Australia-based Cree scholar Shawn Wilson (2001) suggested some time ago, in order for Indigenous researchers to conduct truly Indigenous research, a paradigm shift is required which, I would suggest, has been occurring slowly, but steadily, over the past several decades. Chambers and Buzinde (2015) also describe this transformative process as an "epistemic de-linking" (p. 3) and note that it is vital for researchers to carefully consider the nuances and implications of their own positioning. While Indigenous researchers continue to explore and expand possibilities for research conducted through a variety of methodologies and methods, both traditionally-grounded and otherwise, non-Indigenous researchers are also becoming increasingly aware of and adept at seeking respectful ways to engage with Indigenous Peoples in research while still using primarily Western methods through responsive attention to Indigenous concerns and protocols for research.

In the following, I provide an interpretation of some of the main streams of Indigenous methodologies based on the articulations of leading and emerging Indigenous scholars with particular reference to environmental studies and a focus on those who explicitly consider Bhabha's Third Space and other related epistemologies, ontologies, and methodologies. I then close with specific examples of and considerations for Indigenous and non-Indigenous researchers working in land-based Indigenous contexts with a specific focus on natural resource management, tourism, and education. In so doing, I respond to the editors' invitation to revisit with fresh eyes some of my own work in this area along with that of others that has and continues to influence my understanding.

Reconsidering métissage and the Third Space

During the early stages of my doctoral work, I engaged with Métis scholar Catherine Richardson's (2004) interpretation of Homi Bhabha's (1994) Third Space, which she describes as a "Métis Space" situated between Western and Indigenous cultures, languages, identities, and methodologies. Richardson's adaption of Bhabha's insights stuck with me and greatly informed my doctoral journey. However, while Richardson conceived of the First Space as European with the second being Indigenous and the Third as a hybrid Métis space in-between, I took the advice of an astute audience member during a conference presentation who observed that it "should" in fact be the other way around. Thus, the First Space in my work became Indigenous with the second being the colonial European and the Third persisting, as Bhahba suggests, as a sometimes uneasy, but ultimately productive meeting place of the two as expressed through identity, language, culture, and, in my case, methodological approaches and ecological philosophies and practices (Lowan-Trudeau, 2014, 2015).

Influenced by the work of Bhabha, Richardson, and others, I conceived of the related concepts of ecological and methodological métissage. Ecological métissage considered the possible relationships between Western Science, other knowledge systems rooted in Euro-Western contexts such as Deep Ecology and Bioregionalism, as well as Indigenous and other culturally related ecological knowledges and practices. While I acknowledged and considered the distinctions between culturally rooted approaches, my primary focus was on the potential congruences in these areas. As such, I identified the key tenets of ecological métissage to include:

- Respecting and recognizing cultural and ecological diversity,
- Acknowledging the inherent value of all beings and spiritual forces,
- Long-term multigenerational thinking,
- Understanding the embedded and relational position of human beings in the circle of life,
- Locally focused and responsive living,
- Practical application of theoretical principles,
- Respecting and maintaining local traditions, and
- Acknowledging Indigenous territories and sacred landmarks (modified from Lowan-Trudeau, 2014, 2015).

The development of my methodological métissage occurred more organically as I moved through my doctoral studies. In conversation with my supervisor, Dr. Gail Jardine, I came to realize that what I was attempting to articulate and enact methodologically required careful consideration of both the commonalities and distinctions between critical, interpretive, and Indigenous methodologies. As such, key questions that I developed to guide my study and ascertain its validity included:

- Was the research reciprocal?
- Was it explicitly positioned?
- Was there participant review?
- Was a narrative approach employed?

- Was the research reflexive?
- Has community accountability been satisfied?
- Was it place-based/contextualized?
- Have critical issues been problematized?
- And, were tribal customs followed and respected [if appropriate given the individual participant's preferences]? (Modified from Lowan, 2012, p. 77)

As with ecological métissage, I sought points of overlap between Western and Indigenous traditions, philosophies, and practices with reference and theoretical influence from leading Indigenous and non-Indigenous scholars. Several years on now into my scholarly career, I remain influenced by métissage as a general concept that can be viewed through several lenses and continue to use it at times in both theoretical scholarship and empirical research. At its most etymological, métissage simply means, "to mix" in French with strong connections to cultural, racial, and linguistic interpretations. Indeed, the term "Métis" is related; it also has roots in classical Greece with connections to the Greek Goddess Metis (note the lack of accent) who was known for cunning, intuitive, and oblique wisdom (Dolmage, 2009). Métissage has also recently become a popular metaphor for composing metaphorically braided narratives amongst life writing scholars such as Cynthia Chambers, Carl Leggo, Erika Hasebe-Ludt (2009), and others such as Dwayne Donald (2010) who employs what he describes as "Indigenous métissage," a more critical stance which juxtaposes Western and Indigenous narratives to highlight persistent colonial influences on our understandings of particular places.

As alluded to in subsequent work (see, for example, Lowan-Trudeau, 2015), I have come to realize that my doctoral project was deeply personal; it was a reckoning of my own cultural and ecological identity as a Métis person in Canada of mixed Indigenous and European ancestry on both sides of my family in conversation with the experiences of the participants and the scholars with whom I engaged. However, through further scholarly, pedagogical, and personal experience along with changing political landscapes on both sides of the Medicine Line (US-Canada border), I have also come to recognize the somewhat overly idealistic stance that I adopted in my earlier engagement with both ecological and methodological métissage.

As my research program has taken a turn to focus on, explore, and respond to the political dynamics at play in Canada over the past five to six years, including, but not restricted to, the grassroots Indigenous movement Idle No More and other instances of social and ecological activism (Lowan-Trudeau, 2016a, 2016b), as well as inspiring developments such as the rise of renewable energy projects in Indigenous communities across Canada (see www.indigenousenergy.ca), my views have hardened somewhat. I have also witnessed and been part of an inspiring surge in Indigenous initiatives in the Academy, which has inevitably influenced my scholarly preoccupations.

As such, I have been led to reconsider the earlier conception of both ecological and methodological métissage as a metaphorically comfortable meeting and mixing points between Western and Indigenous environmental philosophies, knowledge systems, practices, and research methodologies (Lowan-Trudeau, 2015). Given my own increasing critical awareness and the growth in Indigenous voices both in Turtle Island (North America) and around the world, I have been nudged towards a more critical stance from which I wonder if such a pastoral mix is indeed possible. This shift has also led me to reconsider my perceptions of the Third Space.

The Third [sovereign] Space

Given this turn towards an increasingly critical stance, like Amoamo (2011), I have been led to revisit Bhabha's conception of the Third Space and hybridity in general. As such, I find resonance with Bruyneel's (2007) more critical interpretation of the Third Space as a manifestation of Indigenous sovereignty wherein Indigenous Peoples rightly step into contemporary, arguably Western-dominated, life in accordance with the United Nations Declaration of the Rights of Indigenous Peoples' affirmation of Indigenous Peoples' right to simultaneously maintain rights to their traditional territories and land-based practices while also participating in contemporary society beyond their communities both physically and existentially. In relation to her studies of Maori people's engagement with tourism activities, Amoamo (2011) astutely notes that such dynamics also inform the personal experiences of contemporary Indigenous People who must constantly navigate and negotiate personal identities amidst a range of mis- or underinformed external perceptions of Indigenous Peoples; as I have experienced myself at times, Amoamo emphasizes that hybridized identity assertions in such contexts are themselves socio-culturally disruptive acts. What implications then, do such notions hold for Indigenous research?

Bruyneel's (2007) conception of the Third Space from the perspective of a non-Indigenous scholar seems to fit well with the views of Indigenous scholars such as Bagele Chilisa (2012) from Botswana, who emphasizes the persistent connection between Indigenized research agendas and critical theory. Chilisa provides several descriptions of what this looks like in research practice; for example, she highlights the work of Latin American scholars who engage with Borderland-Mestizaje feminism as a, "hybrid and multidimensional mode of thinking [and conducting research]" (p. 270). She describes Borderland-Mestizaje feminism as both an active form of cultural, linguistic, gender-based, and anti-colonial resistance, while simultaneously recognizing its inherent "rhizomatic and integrative framework for synthesizing postcolonial Indigenous methods" (p. 270). In this manner, Chilisa, like Bruyneel, recognizes the inherent hybridity of a contemporary Third-Space approach, that may draw from multiple cultural traditions and frameworks while also, without apology, simultaneously assuming an actively critical stance. Similar streams of tension and consideration exist in the past and present work of other Indigenous scholars, both explicitly and implicitly, as discussed below.

Considering strategic methodologies

In an insightful exploration of Indigenous methodologies, Anishnaabe scholar Lana Ray (2012) proposes that there are two main methodological families at present. She describes the first as "strategic methodologies." According to Ray, strategic methodologies take a stance inspired by critical theory and as such are focused on resistance and achieving social [and environmental] justice for Indigenous Peoples. She suggests that they are typically carried out unapologetically using Western research methods and may be influenced by Indigenous and traditions for knowledge exchange and exploration but often are not. Ray suggests that this is fine, as such projects often also create space for further consideration and exchange of traditional Indigenous Knowledges.

Ray's proposition may seem controversial to some, as it does not emphasize Indigenous knowledge and practices, though other Indigenous scholars such as the well-known Cree and Saulteaux academic Margaret Kovach (2010) also recognize that, at times, Western methods and even methodologies are the most appropriate choices for projects that may still focus on Indigenous Peoples and issues. However, one may be left rightly wondering about those instances wherein an Indigenous researcher may wish to more explicitly incorporate cultural influences into their work. What then?

Convergent and hybrid methodologies: indigenizing Western research?

Another common family of Indigenous research methodologies includes what Ray (2012) describes as "convergent methodologies." These represent a meeting, but not necessarily mixing, place between Western and Indigenous methodologies and are more explicitly guided by Indigenous knowledge traditions and practices while still utilizing Western methods with careful intention. Much contemporary Indigenous scholarship falls into this stream and, as such, many other Indigenous scholars discuss such approaches using a variety of terms and conceptual starting points. For example, Chilisa (2012) considers such approaches through a lens of Indigenizing research methodologies. In Chilisa's view, Indigenized research maintains an existential connection to critical theory, but, echoing Ray, she also suggests that such an approach requires that: "Researchers with an indigenization focus . . . combine theoretical approaches and methodologies borrowed from the literature and knowledge archives of the West with Indigenous perspectives" (p. 101). Indeed, much of my own scholarship, whether explicitly described as métissage or not, fits within a convergent and/or Indigenized framework, as I most often strive to explicitly incorporate Indigenous principles and protocols as appropriate along with common Western research methods.

While perhaps not as explicitly critical as strategic methodologists, like Amoamo (2011) suggests in reference to hybridized identities, Ray (2012) emphasizes that convergent methodologists are also taking an active stance in relation to the Academy. Such an approach is reminiscent of Bruyneel's (2007) description of the Third Space as an active site of Indigenous sovereignty wherein Indigenous Peoples maintain a connection to traditional practices and/or rights while also employing contemporary Western approaches to best serve their agenda. While convergent approaches are now quite commonplace, Ray also notes the remaining potential for researchers to go further in exploring Indigenous methodologies grounded more exclusively in traditional Indigenous knowledge and practices. Questions regarding the role of non-Indigenous researchers also persist.

Collaborative, community-based approaches

Many strong examples of collaborative, community-based approaches to environmental research, planning, tourism, and other related endeavours led by and in partnership with Indigenous communities are also emerging. The persistent work and thoughtful theorizing of both Indigenous and non-Indigenous scholars in these areas has led to the development of practices which often align well with Indigenous community practices and protocols for sharing and validating knowledge. Such approaches often bring together Western research methods, both qualitative and quantitative, with local practices for knowledge sharing and preservation while also creating opportunities to consider and give voice to social, ecological, and/or cultural justice concerns (Lane, 2006).

As an edited collection by Menzies (2006) demonstrates, Traditional Ecological Knowledge is increasingly recognized and included as an equal partner with Western Science in a variety of natural resource management activities ranging from fisheries to forestry and land mammal conservation. Others also advocate for community based approaches to environmental planning and monitoring that may include a range of activities that encompass Western methods as well as approaches that acknowledge and enact community appropriate methods for gathering and making sense of environmental knowledge (e.g., Natcher & Hickey, 2002; Tsetta, Gibson, McDevitt, & Plotner, 2005). As Natcher and Hickey (2002) emphasize, such approaches also serve to support and engage with the plurality of voices and perspectives both within and between particular communities, challenging, as Bishop (1998) would suggest, overly general narratives that ignore inter and intra-Indigenous nuances and diversities. However, important questions continue to be raised related to the role and perceptions of Indigenous Peoples in such research and practice.

For example, tourism scholars Wearing and Wearing (2006) trouble the ethnocentricity and hegemonic superiority present in many initiatives that bring non-Indigenous tourists into contact with Indigenous Peoples. Like Amoamo (2011), who emphasizes the plurality of Indigenous identities, Peters and Higgins-Desbiolles (2012) also challenge oppressive assumptions through disruptive discussion of the contemporary experiences of Indigenous tourists in Australia.

Non-Indigenous tourism and experiential education scholars Grimwood (2011) and Mullins (2009), acknowledge and ponder on the importance of considering and respecting Indigenous territories in the context of canoe-based expeditions and related inquiries. Other Indigenous (Simpson, 2002; Lowan, 2009) and non-Indigenous (Root, 2011; Scully, 2012) scholars have also critically considered the interaction of Western and Indigenous knowledge systems and colonial dynamics as they relate to personal, pedagogical, and methodological positioning in outdoor and environmental education research and practice.

Such considerations are also increasingly embodied in the practices of Indigenous communities and their non-Indigenous partners and formalized through co-management agreements pertaining to existing and proposed national and provincial parks. For example, Holmes, Grimwood, King, and notable co-author Lutsel K'e Dene First Nation (2016) discuss the development of a code of ethics for visitors to their territory, which includes the Thelon Wildlife Sanctuary and proposed Thaidene National Park Reserve, in keeping with local protocols as part of their efforts to assert and maintain socio-ecological sovereignty. As described by the authors, such efforts in research and practice also challenge commonly held romantic notions of the North as a vast, largely uninhabited, "wilderness" and, as Amoamo (2011) suggests, force researchers and visitors to consider the contemporary existence of Indigenous Peoples in a more nuanced manner.

As Brown (2002) suggests, guides and educators have great facilitative power in experiential learning contexts to guide group discussions with clients and students. Such an approach could be used to bring to light, for example, contrasting narratives of place in line with Donald's (2010) Indigenous Métissage, wherein Western narratives of particular places may be explicitly or implicitly juxtaposed with one another. Such an approach may serve to encourage thoughtful discussion that transcends the anthropocentric/biocentric stakeholder dichotomy present in so many contemporary land use disputes.

While strategic, convergent, and collaborative methodologies continue to do important work in the Academy and, at times, Indigenous communities, one might still be left wondering if we can go further to truly revive and perhaps reimagine research methodologies through Indigenous lenses and practices. We might even ask if research, as it is commonly conceived of in the Western academic tradition, aligns with Indigenous traditions for knowledge sharing and exploration?

Towards Indigenous paradigms and relational validity

Wilson (2001) suggests that what is truly required is a shift towards an Indigenous paradigm. Wilson's conception of a paradigm involves congruence between the epistemological (ways of knowing), ontological (ways of being), axiological (moral and ethical guidelines), and methodological aspects of a research endeavour. In Wilson's view, all of these must be grounded in Traditional Indigenous knowledge practices for truly Indigenous research to occur. In a similar spirit more specific to tourism studies, Chambers and Buzinde (2015) posit that even Indigenous researchers must be reflexively aware of the complex and, at times contradictory, relationship between social positioning and epistemological understanding – due to the colonial influences of the Academy, Indigenous researchers themselves may still be operating in colonized ways despite personal understanding of and experience with indigeneity in general and their own culture in particular. How might we then, as Indigenous and non-Indigenous researchers alike, address such complexities?

Kovach (2015) shares what she considers to be key aspects of Indigenous research: legitimizing Indigenous knowledge systems and research methods, the centrality of relationships, and individual and community reciprocity. Her emphasis on the crucial importance of relationships resonates with Chilisa's (2012) discussion of *Ubuntu*, an African worldview that recognizes and places great importance on understanding and respecting the intricate relationships between people and with other inhabitants of the natural world. As discussed in the following, Tuck and McKenzie (2015) also allude to relational validity as a central tenet in their proposition for critical place inquiry.

Critical place inquiry

As in my conception of both ecological and methodological métissage, many other Indigenous authors emphasize the centrality of place in Indigenous methodologies. Some, such as Eve Tuck and her non-Indigenous co-author Marcia McKenzie (2015), have spent extensive time considering and articulating just what this might mean in contemporary research. They have developed what they call "critical place inquiry" to describe a move towards increased emphasis on place not only in explicitly Indigenous research, but studies of all kinds.

Tuck and McKenzie (2015) propose that critical place inquiry involves a nuanced and interactive understanding of place that considers shifting human and other species' actions and experiences; acknowledges social, economic, gender, sexuality, and culturally related disparities in terms of how places are experienced; addresses the effects of colonization on places; moves beyond anthropocentric understanding of landscapes; generates critical and relational politics related to particular places; and, finally, seriously acknowledges "Indigenous epistemologies of land" (p. 636–637). As leading Maori scholar Russell Bishop (1998) also notes, we must be cautious with overly general grand narratives that ignore local nuances and specificities.

Taking critical place inquiry seriously along with Wilson's (2001) more general call for a paradigm shift in Indigenous research, and Kovach's (2015) emphasis on relationships, are there then examples in the past and present to which we might look for inspiration?

Inspiring examples

One might rightly wonder if examples exist of research carried out that fully embodies an Indigenous paradigm and traditions of knowledge exchange and exploration. As described above, many projects do indeed embody aspects of Indigenous paradigms, however, in my explorations, I have yet to come across a study that does so completely. However, this could be a simple blind spot on my part or perhaps a sign of the limits of the Western Academy. Despite such challenges, there are many inspiring examples of Indigenous scholars truly pushing the boundaries of what is considered possible in terms of enacting Indigenous paradigms and practices in the Academy with both explicit and implicit connections to land, culture, language, and environmental considerations; three particular examples initially come to mind from the work of Indigenous graduate students.

The first is the doctoral work of the late Dale Auger (2001) a Cree scholar, artist, and storyteller who completed his studies at the University of Calgary. Auger's doctoral study took the form of a scripted play that he wrote himself and then directed and produced. Cast members lived in tipis for seven days of rehearsals prior to the opening of the show during which time they, "engaged in a process of traditional First Nations education through their experiences" (Auger, 2001, p. iii). Auger's doctoral committee was invited to attend the performance that demonstrated his doctoral level understanding of issues in Indigenous education. As a respected ceremonialist, he also welcomed his committee into his sweatlodge, wherein he further demonstrated his cultural knowledge through traditional protocols. As he states in the abstract for his dissertation, "Through this experience, my committee members were placed in a position to connect in both the physical and spiritual sense with Land and the Beings at the sweatlodge site" (p. iii). While Auger's work did not completely embody an Indigenous paradigm in every possible way, it certainly pushed the boundary of what was/is acceptable in the academy. While the work was presented in English, it still reflected an extensive amount of effort to enact Indigenous epistemologies, ontologies, axiologies, and, to a certain extent, methodologies.

Another more recent example of a different kind comes from the University of British Columbia. Patrick Stewart (2015) who initially endeavoured to compose his doctoral dissertation in Nisga'a, the language of his people; however, he was met with opposition from members of his supervisory committee (Hutchinson, 2015). They finally reached a compromise, however, and he agreed to compose his dissertation in a manner reflective of the oral tradition in lowercase letters without significant use of English punctuation. This iteration was also met with scepticism by some, but Dr. Stewart persisted and successfully defended his dissertation. We can see in this case an attempt by the student to embody an Indigenous paradigm in his work despite significant pressures from within a well-established institution.

However, other Indigenous scholars have successfully composed and defended dissertation in Indigenous languages. For instance, in 2010, Alfred Metallic defended his dissertation in the Faculty of Environmental Studies at York University in Toronto that was composed entirely in Mi'kmaq. Metallic was also supported and examined by a doctoral committee composed of both academics and respected Indigenous community leaders (McLean, 2010). Given the use of an Indigenous language to conduct the research and the inclusion of cultural leaders on his committee, this work appears to be an exemplary demonstration of an Indigenous paradigm at work in the academy.

As described above, collaborative and community based methodologies are also increasingly embraced by Indigenous and non-Indigenous researchers and practitioners alike as another approach for respectfully responding to and embodying Indigenous considerations.

Final thoughts

Whether or not articulated as such, a growing number of Indigenous research endeavours in the related fields of environmental studies, tourism, and education enact many of the principles, dynamics and tensions described above. While explicitly naming such endeavours as strategic, convergent, collaborative, métissage, hybrid, decolonized, or Indigenized can be useful at times, I would propose that it is also important to look to the larger picture to recognize when such initiatives do embody such principles whether described as such or not. Indigenous practices for collecting, sharing, and interpreting knowledge often lend themselves well to community-based environmental research, and it behooves researchers, Indigenous and non-Indigenous alike to seek opportunities for congruence with and departure from Western methods as appropriate given individual and community preferences. Indigenous researchers may also seek to lead projects that challenge Western norms by structuring and carrying out research with intention through Indigenous paradigms. Both Indigenous and non-Indigenous supervisors can also contribute by supporting graduate students to consciously engage with intention in strategic, convergent, and paradigm-shifting approaches as appropriate dependent on project focus and researcher positioning. These more nuanced and critically aware approaches will serve to not only enhance critical awareness of Indigenous socioecological issues, but also the ongoing decolonization and transformation of Indigenous research.

References

Amoamo, M. (2011). Tourism and hybridity: Re-visiting Bhabha's third space. *Annals of Tourism Research, 38*(4), 1254–1273.

Auger, D. (2001). *First Nations education: Sharing of knowledge*. Unpublished doctoral dissertation, University of Calgary, AB.

Bhabha, H. K. (1994). *The location of culture*. London: Routledge.

Bishop, R. (1998). Freeing ourselves from neo-colonial domination in research: A Maori approach to creating knowledge. *International Journal of Qualitative Studies in Education, 11*(2), 199–219.

Brown, M. (2002). The facilitator as gatekeeper: A critical analysis of social order in facilitation sessions. *Journal of Adventure Education and Outdoor Learning, 2*(2), 101–112.

Bruyneel, K. (2007). *The third space of sovereignty: The postcolonial politics of U.S.-Indigenous relations*. Minneapolis, MN: University of Minnesota Press.

Chambers, D., & Buzinde, C. (2015). Tourism and decolonisation: Locating research and self. *Annals of Tourism Research, 51*, 1–16.

Chilisa, B. (2012). *Indigenous research methodologies*. Thousand Oaks, CA: SAGE.

Dolmage, J. (2009). Metis, mêtis, mestiza, Medusa: Rhetorical Bodies across Rhetorical Traditions. *Rhetoric Review, 28*(1), 1–28.

Donald, D. T. (2010). Forts, curriculum, and Indigenous metissage: Imagining decolonization of Aboriginal-Canadian relations in educational contexts. *First Nations Perspectives: The Journal of the Manitoba First Nations Education Resource Centre*, *2*(1), 1–24.

Grimwood, B. S. R. (2011). "Thinking outside the gunnels": Considering natures and the moral terrains of recreational canoe travel. *Leisure/ Loisir*, *35*(1), 49–69.

Hasebe-Ludt, E., Chambers, C. M., & Leggo, C. (2009). *Life writing and literary métissage as an ethos for our times*. New York: Peter Lang.

Holmes, A., Grimwood, B. S. R., King, L., & The Lutsel K'e Dene First Nation. (2016). Creating an indigenized visitor code of ethics: The development of Denesoline self-determination for sustainable tourism. *Journal of Sustainable Tourism*, *24*(8–9), 1177–1193.

Hutchinson, B. (2015, May 8). UBC student writes 52,438 word architecture dissertation with no punctuation – not everyone loved it. *National Post Online*. Retrieved March 27, 2017, from http://news.nationalpost.com/news/canada/ubc-student-writes-52438-word-architecture-dissertation-with-no-punctuation-not-everyone-loved-it.

Kovach, M. (2010). *Indigenous methodologies: Characteristics, conversations, and contexts*. Toronto: University of Toronto Press.

Kovach, M. (2015). Emerging from the margins: Indigenous methodologies. In S. Strega & L. Brown (Eds.), *Research as resistance* (2nd ed., pp. 43–64). Toronto: Canadian Scholars' Press.

Lane, M. (2006). The role of planning in achieving Indigenous land justice and community goals. *Land Use Policy*, *23*(4), 385–394.

Lowan, G. (2009). Exploring place from an Aboriginal perspective: Considerations for outdoor and environmental education. *Canadian Journal of Environmental Education*, *14*, 42–58.

Lowan, G. (2012). Expanding the conversation: Further explorations into Indigenous environmental science education theory, research, and practice. *Cultural Studies in Science Education*, *7*, 71–81.

Lowan-Trudeau, G. (2014). Considering ecological métissage: To blend or not to blend? *Journal of Experiential Education*, *37*(4), 351–366.

Lowan-Trudeau, G. (2015). *From bricolage to métissage: (Re)thinking intercultural approaches to Indigenous environmental education and research*. New York: Peter Lang.

Lowan-Trudeau, G. (2016a). Protest as pedagogy: Exploring teaching and learning in Indigenous environmental movements. *Journal of Environmental Education*, *48*(2), 96–108.

Lowan-Trudeau, G. (2016b). Gateway to understanding: Indigenous ecological activism and education in urban, rural, and remote contexts. *Cultural Studies of Science Education*, *12*(1), 119–128.

McLean, S. (2010, November 24). PhD student defends thesis in Mi'gmaw language, a York first. *yFile, York University Online News*. Retrieved April 11, 2016, from http://yfile.news.yorku.ca/2010/11/24/phd-student-defends-thesis-in-migmaw-language-ayork-first/.

Menzies, C. R. (Ed.). (2006). *Traditional ecological knowledge and natural resource management*. Lincoln, NE: University of Nebraska Press.

Metallic, A. G. (2010). *Ta'n teligji'tegen 'nnuigtug aq ta'n goqwei wejgu'aqamulti'gw*. Unpublished doctoral dissertation, York University, ON.

Mullins, P. M. (2009). Living stories of the landscape: Perception of place through canoeing in Canada's North. *Tourism Geographies*, *11*(2), 233–255.

Natcher, D., & Hickey, C. G. (2002). Putting the community back into community-based resource management: A criteria and indicators approach to sustainability. *Human Organization, 61*(4), 350–363.

Neilsen, N., & Wilson, E. (2012). From invisible to Indigenous-driven: A critical typology of research in Indigenous-tourism. *Journal of Hospitality and Tourism Management, 19*, 1–9, e5.

Peters, A., & Higgins-Desbiolles, F. (2012). De-marginalising tourism research: Indigenous Australians as tourists. *Journal of Hospitality and Tourism Management, 19*, 1–9, e6.

Ray, L. (2012). Deciphering the "Indigenous" in Indigenous research methodologies. *AlterNative, 8*(1), 85–98.

Richardson, C. L. (2004). *Becoming Metis: The relationship between the sense of Metis self and cultural stories*. Unpublished doctoral dissertation, University of Victoria, Victoria, BC.

Root, E. (2011). This land is our land? This land is your land: The decolonizing journeys of White outdoor environmental educators. *Canadian Journal of Environmental Education, 15*, 103–119.

Scully, A. (2012). Decolonization, reinhabitation and reconciliation: Aboriginal and place-based education. *Canadian Journal of Environmental Education, 17*, 148–58.

Simpson, L. (2002). Indigenous environmental education for cultural survival. *Canadian Journal of Environmental Education, 7*(1), 13–35.

Stewart, P. R. R. (2015). *Indigenous architecture through Indigenous knowledge: Dim sagalts'apkw nisiḿ [together we will build a village]*. Unpublished doctoral dissertation, University of British Columbia, BC.

Tsetta, S., Gibson, G., McDevitt, L., & Plotner, S. (2005). Telling a story of change the Dene way: Indicators for monitoring in diamond impacted communities. *Pimatisiwin: A Journal of Aboriginal and Indigenous Community Health, 3*(1), 59–69.

Tuck, E., & McKenzie, M. (2015). Relational validity and the "where" of inquiry, place and land in Qualitative Research. *Qualitative Inquiry, 21*(7), 633–638.

Tuhiwai Smith, L. (2012). *Decolonizing methodologies: Research and Indigenous Peoples* (2nd ed.). New York: Zed Books.

Wearing, S., & Wearing, M. (2006). 'Rereading the subjugating tourist' in neoliberalism: Postcolonial otherness and the tourist experience. *Tourism Analysis, 11*(2), 145–162.

Wilson, S. (2001). What is Indigenous research methodology? *Canadian Journal of Native Education, 25*(2), 175–179.

13 Conclusion

In the forest

Kellee Caton

We are born into a world filled with others. From the moment of arrival, we are always already *among*. Our psyches, however, are slow to clue in. Compared to the young of other animals who share our planet, human babies are notoriously helpless, requiring years of parental investment to survive and flourish in their environment. We can do almost nothing for ourselves, and so our first awareness of others appears through the lens of their service to us. Warm, animated shapes, hopefully with soothing voices and a gentle touch, move about ministering to our needs (Nussbaum, 2010). As our minds develop, those shapes take on greater identity. But years go by before we are truly able to see them as creatures like ourselves – with depth and complexity, capable of experiencing joy and suffering, and deserving of respect and dignity and the right to pursue their own dreams and desires in ways not immediately related to our interests. It is a *moral accomplishment* to grow to see others as full beings in their own right (Nussbaum, 2010).

If we succeed developmentally, we are able, at a fairly young age, to empathize, respect, and behave in caring ways toward the people in our immediate environment: parents, siblings, friends, teachers. We struggle more with expanding our circle of care to encompass those at greater distance from ourselves – physical distance, or alternatively, perceptual distance, for those we consider "different" from ourselves (Berreby, 2005; Singer, 2009). Social psychology's notion of *propinquity* captures this dual conceptualization of distance from others. Much suffering in our human world has the propinquity problem at its root (Singer, 2009; Berreby, 2005). Conflicts between cultural or ideological groups lead to violence, bigotry harms people on the basis of superficial characteristics that happen to be in or out of acceptance at a particular time and place, and lack of basic resources results in entirely preventable suffering for some, while others throw away the same resources in excess.

But the propinquity barrier of *species* is arguably even firmer. As Carr (Chapter 8) explores in this volume, we sometimes transcend this barrier with other mammals, as in the case of people who consider their domesticated dogs to be full companions. Some visionaries take things even further. Robert Frost's (1928) poem "Tree at My Window" captures the story of a man who finds a kindred spirit in the tree growing near his bedchamber. He recognizes the differences between his own nature and that of the tree, but expresses his experience of their inter-species solidarity, noting the way they have stood by each other through the interior and exterior storms of life. "But tree," says the poet, after first acknowledging their differences, "I have seen you taken and tossed,/And if you have seen me when I slept,/You have seen me when I was taken and swept/And all but lost." The two have ended up together, Frost concludes, thanks to fate's lively imagination – the tree's "head so much concerned with outer," the poet's with "inner, weather."

Probably much more often than finding true kindship as Frost did, however, we humans simply *fail to regard* the non-human beings with which we share our planet. For many of us, the moral accomplishment of seeing ourselves as *among* is partial at best.

A moral gaze?

The notion of *the gaze* has long been of importance in tourism studies. After Urry's (1990) early work pinpointed tourism's role in creating regimes of regarding and relating to peoples and places away from our home environments, a raft of theory followed, elucidating mechanisms of the tourist gaze (Strain, 2003), exploring the mutuality of its nature (i.e., between tourists and hosts) (Maoz, 2006; Moufakkir & Reisinger, 2013), contextualizing it sociopolitically (Morgan & Pritchard, 2000; McAlister, 2001; Echtner & Prasad, 2003), and delving beyond ocularcentrism to explore how we also "gaze" with our other senses and capacities (Everett, 2008; Picard & Robinson, 2012). Speaking from around the bend of tourism's moral turn (Caton, 2012), a different question arises: What might a *moral gaze* look like?

In his book-length study *Assholes: A Theory*, philosopher Aaron James (2012) argues that the vast majority of humans don't fit his titular description. We can readily identify habitually bad behavers (assholes and otherwise) and theorize their actions precisely because there is such a large normative backdrop of "good" behaviour against which these aberrations stand out; in other words, there is much about "the good" that we can agree on. Assuming that most of us, in the reasonably mature stages of our life, share in valuing care, compassion, and authentic and meaningful engagement with beings outside ourselves, it becomes philosophically fruitful to consider the idea of a moral gaze. We spend a lot of time talking about how we *do* gaze at others, in tourism and beyond. How *should* we?

Bruce Springsteen (1978) leads us toward perhaps the most basic answer to this question near the end of "Badlands," when, speaking as he often does in the voice of hard working folks society has left behind, he presses a particularly poignant line: "I wanna find one face that ain't looking through me." This line captures not the injustices of poverty or unequal opportunity, not the frustrations of failure in a system one cannot control, not even the pain of judgement by the others one is among. Instead, it articulates something much more fundamental: the indignity of invisibility within the gaze of others. A moral gaze then, first and foremost, requires recognition of the other.

How much of life escapes our awareness completely?

In Canada, where the three editors of this volume live and work, most of us know of the balsam fir. It is ubiquitous here, growing from the Great Lakes area, north to the shores of James Bay, eastward up into the Maritimes, and westward all the way into portions of northern Alberta. We readily recognize other creatures, such as eagles and squirrels, which share its ecosystem; they trigger emotional responses, like awe or endearment, as we watch them soar above the forest canopy, or hunker within, nibbling a snack navigated with tiny paws. Probably less often do we consider the ground beneath the trees. And yet the boreal soil out of which the balsam fir rises – composed of fallen needles, broken roots, and other corpse matter, but also of living microbes – is, by some calculations, the world's largest carbon repository, sequestering three times as much carbon as the more attention-grabbing green things growing above the surface (Haskell, 2017).

Cold winters and soggy summers have conspired to favor carbon storage, but climate change is warming the boreal forest. Increasingly frequent fires release carbon directly, but more insidious are changes in the soil's microbial communities, as cold-adapted, slow-moving microbes are replaced by more active decomposers, fit to function in warmer environments. As Haskell (2017, p. 56) explains it, "The biological fire [of decomposition] makes no smoke, but is all-pervasive and therefore more important to the global flow of carbon than the drama of flame." Also important are the fungi, which live cooperatively with balsam fir roots. Working in partnership, the roots and fungi scavenge nitrogen which, in their absence, would be available for capture by microbes to power decomposition (and, hence, more carbon release). Warming is making boreal areas more hospitable for joint tree-fungi ventures from more southerly climates to expand their range, and these partnerships lack the same nitrogen-pulling effect (Haskell, 2017).

Deep beneath the forest canopy, our cold-sluggish microbial allies, our nitrogen-greedy fungus comrades, all toil away, in lives of invisible labour that inadvertently safeguard the well-being of *Homo sapiens* – us. How often do we stop to say hello? Does their presence register in our gaze? How many such creatures, dwelling here with us on planet earth, fall into this category of non-acknowledgement by human beings, the category Carr, in Chapter 8 of this volume, calls the "invisible ones"?

Regarding the Other

If "looking through" another – failing to register its presence – is one end of a spectrum that ends in its opposite, receiving the other in its fullness, then there is surely lots of room in the middle. One place in the middle is acknowledgment of the other motivated by self-interest: when others come into view because of the benefits they can provide for ourselves. Much of our awareness of other species proceeds through such an instrumentalist lens. At a basic level, human societies are built upon the exploitation of other species as resources: animals and plants for food, timber and grasses for building materials and fuel. In wealthy, contemporary societies, free of material want but starved for meaning, other species continue to serve as important resources (Fennell, 2012) in the "experience economy" (Pine & Gilmore, 1998), of which tourism is a driving force. Animals are locked in enclosures, sometimes required to perform for tourists, sometimes even disposed of in ways that create a show (see again Carr's discussion in Chapter 8 of this volume). Still-living trees are carved open to give motoring tourists, for a $5 price tag, the thrill of driving right through a giant redwood.

The movement toward vegetarianism – and even more so, veganism – represents a substantive practice of resistance to an instrumental gaze by humans toward nonhuman animals. Many arguments can be made for vegetarianism, including ones centering on land use efficiencies, waste management, and human health, but as both Bertella (Chapter 6) and Kline and Rusher (Chapter 7) explore in this volume, more fundamental arguments can also be made about the place nonhuman animals should occupy in the human conscience. Bertella, for example, considers vegetarian ecofeminism as a framework for contextualizing the eating of nonhuman flesh as unjustified speciesism. Such interventions are difficult in a tourism industry that so readily capitalizes on "traditional" food cultures for enormous profit (Scarpato & Daniele, 2003), but they are not impossible, as Bertella demonstrates. Even in Italy, heartland of slow food, where culinary tourism fantasmatics place not only ravioli di zucca and sangiovese, but also Parmigiano Reggiano, cream, and Prosciutto di Parma, on the imagination's authentic table, committed entrepreneurs are finding ways to influence the institutional field of Italian food tourism to include vegetarian and vegan offerings – and therefore to make room for experiences of touristic gustatory pleasure not rooted in instrumental relations between human and nonhuman animals. Changing social norms in heavy tourist-sending regions like North America may help. Kline and Rusher tell us that vegetarianism is on the rise there, with more than one in ten members of the Millennial generation opting for this lifestyle. Perhaps this is one example of humans acting to transcend the instrumental gaze.

There is also another risk in trying to navigate along the spectrum toward appreciating others in their fullness: the problematic relationship between knowledge and power (Foucault, 1980). There is an inevitable gap between the mind of a human subject and that which lies outside it, and this gap can only be crossed by interpretation generated by that subject (Gadamer, 1975). There is no unmediated access to the other, nor can the other present itself fully on its own terms; Other has, at best, incomplete agency over Self's interpretive process. At worst, Other has no agency at all, pinned to the page and sorted into the taxonomy of Self's system of knowing.

Knowledge-as-mastery has a strong history in the Western tradition, particularly in the aftermath of the Enlightenment. Science, positioning itself in opposition to the messiness of metaphysics (Gould, 2003), was in the business of knowing via observing, and then isolating, taxonomizing, controlling, manipulating, and deductively reasoning about, the phenomena of the physical world. Its character was reductionist (and largely still is, to the chagrin of systems thinkers across the sciences today). Study of the social world followed suit, with scholars optimistic that methodological approaches developed for the study of the physical world would transfer effectively into the realm of the social (Baronov, 2004). Early anthropologists and geographers, for example, set out to map and categorize the earth's people in the same way natural historians and biologists sorted insects and plants. That a shared logic was sought is visible in anthropological metaphors drawn from biology: People were part of "trees" of ancestry and hailed from "motherlands" and "fatherlands" (Malkki, 1992). If "each nation is a grand genealogical tree rooted in the soil that nourishes it," then "by implication, it is impossible to be part of more than one tree" (Malkki, 1992, p. 28); similarly, by definition, a person can have but one biological father or mother. These nature-based metaphors thus constituted people as something fit for taxonomic ordering.

Such projects of knowing did not arise purely from innocent curiosity, but rather from imperialist desires of domination and control (Malkki, 1992; Said, 1978) – one important reason why, as Lowan-Trudeau explores in Chapter 12 of this volume, we must think more critically about the cultural contexts in which particular knowledge-making traditions emerge and are deployed, and to what ends. In "chasing anthropology's discarded discourse" (Bruner, 2005, p. 4), tourism's imaginary of cultural authenticity similarly pins hosts in non-Western tourist-receiving parts of the world into a catalogue for guests' experiential consumption (Echtner & Prasad, 2003) as part of a complex global system that tangles symbolic agency, material capital, and host and guest desire (Caton, 2011; Hollinshead, 2009). In this way, touristic discourse and performance becomes its own mode of contexualized knowledge-making, with its own external and internal drivers, and its own set of consequences for destination people and places.

Erickson explores this process in detail in Chapter 3 of this volume, describing how tourism uses racialized others to naturalize whiteness and affirm it as the centre against which difference is measured. Tourism's systems of production and consumption of "difference" support whiteness as a privileged position that can shift across geographies and ingest cultural difference into its own being and thus have access to a cosmopolitan subjectivity not achievable by racialized hosts, who, within the logic of this system, must not move or hybridize, lest it undercut their task of signing in for pure exotic otherness.

If our fellow *Homo sapiens* have not escaped this gaze of mastery, then propinquity tells us it should be of little surprise that those imagined as more distant from us have fared worse. Reis and Shelton (Chapter 5) and Franklin and Colas (Chapter 9) both explore this idea in this volume. Through a sustained exploration of the social construction of *Canis familiaris*, the domestic dog, in the context of New Zealand, Reis and Shelton consider how eco-politically loaded human knowledge structures position species in floating and often contradictory ways – in this case, as companion, pet, or predator. Similarly, Franklin and Colas implicate place production for touristic consumption in abetting knowledge regimes that taxonomize species into categories like endemic, native, invasive, or feral. The complexity of dynamic ecosystems, and the educative potential they hold for tourists, is invisiblized by a system of knowing that refuses mobile and hybrid possibilities. And as both pairs of authors explore, knowing other species in such ways triggers particular moral frameworks for reasoning about them that, in turn, legitimate various forms of human domination – most profoundly, the power to protect or annihilate individuals, or entire populations(!), of species in particular regions of the world.

The quest to know the other may still be misguided, however, even when no overt agenda of dominance is in place. Hazel Tucker (2016) has recently drawn out the epistemological problem of empathy, arguing that the uncritical celebration of this form of emotional engagement in the tourism literature belies its problematic core. In trying to grasp the experiences and frames of reference of another, there is always the risk of projection or appropriation, but even deeper lies the questionable premise that identification with another is ever fully achievable. Surely any assertion of such is, on some level, an assertion of mastery. On the other hand, a world without empathy would strike most of us as even more disastrous, and Tucker argues in the end, following LaCapra (2004, p. 76), for an "unsettled empathy," which "takes one out of oneself towards the other without eliminating or assimilating the difference or alterity." For empathy to be ethical, she argues, we must remain "affectively unsettled . . . by empathy's failure to live up to its own promise" (Pedwell, 2012, p. 292, quoted in Tucker, 2016).

In the end, the other can never be fully known. This is what Levinas (1996) is getting at, when he discusses the irreducible otherness of the face, before which all consciousness staggers, pulling up ever short of a capaciousness that could assimilate it. Or what the seventeenth-century mystic poet Henry Vaughan (1650) meant when he said that there is in God a "dazzling darkness" and why his fellow mystic, ecumenical Catholic theologian Thomas Merton (1941), said, "the darkness is enough." Perhaps a moral gaze, then, is one which holds within it a degree of epistemic restraint. To welcome the other in its fullness is to admit its unknowability, to honour its mystery.

Pedagogy of the kindred

Perhaps we can go one step further. It is possible not only to relinquish the desire for epistemic mastery of the other, but to assume the exact opposite subject position: to receive the other as teacher. How much wisdom, creativity, and resourcefulness are afoot in the more-than-human world? Some human scientists have taken note of this, and the approach of biomimicry – human imitation of other creatures' problem-solving strategies – has given us everything from cultural-moment-defining gadgets like Velcro to improvements that substantially impact individual or collective human quality of life, such as more functional prosthetic limbs that take their inspiration from tentacles (Kau, 2010) or quieter high-speed trains, like Japan's Shinkansen bullet train, with its aerodynamic nose modeled on the kingfisher's beak (Technology Beyond 2035, n.d.).

But we can learn deeper lessons, as well, about what those in the arts sometimes call "the human condition," but which could perhaps more accurately be characterized as the condition of being alive. I'll never forget the first time I met a Joshua tree, face-to-bark: me, with dirty hiking boots planted on the ground, ponytail flying in the hot Southern California wind, it, towering several feet above me, spiky-tipped arms askew. I had waited a long time to meet one of these creatures, so named because its eye-catching branches reminded early Mormon settlers moving through the tiny eco-region where it exclusively grows of the biblical prophet Joshua, waiving frantically to call them toward the promised land. It wasn't until years later, however, that I learned how *Yucca brevifolia* acquire their famed appendages; the plant will branch after an existing stem has bloomed, but also when weevils have bored in and created damage to the stem. For the Joshua tree, flourishing through effective response to adversity is not a metaphor. Biologists define life as that which is self-reproducing, and social theorists have explored how it is in the nature of life to strive to exceed itself (Grit, 2014). But life also has other characteristics, and one of these is antifragility – not robustness, meaning sturdiness or resilience to perturbation – but the true opposite of fragility, *antifragility*, the capacity to *grow stronger* as a result of disturbance below the threshold of serious damage that would pose a threat to the organism's continuance (Taleb, 2012). Joshua trees offer a dramatic illustration of this principle of antifragility, and remind us that, as fellow living creatures, this is in our nature, too.

We can also learn things from how we relate to trees. As my fellow students and I lay on our mats, each right foot to each left knee, arms arrayed at a variety of angles, in *vṛkṣasana*, tree pose, my yoga teacher spoke about the forest as a space of moral encounter. In the forest, we suspend judgement. We take in the various forms around us, never expecting any two trees to have the exact same shape. We see in their forms the reflection of their biographies, the contingencies of warmth and light and water and encounters with other creatures, because this too is a property of life: to respond and adapt to conditions outside oneself. How disappointing it would be if all trees looked the same – how unstoried. Do we approach the diversity of human forms with the same grace? Our own form in the mirror?

And we can learn from other creatures something about the limits of our own perspectives, the ways our well-worn cultural logics can blind us from making important connections. Cooke explores this experience in Chapter 2 of this volume, where she follows Coyote into a Wal-Mart parking lot in Whitehorse, Yukon, to encounter droves of tourists camping in RVs, in the heart of a journey to experience "The North." To the tourists, the pavement, shopping carts, and glowing blue corporate sign behind them may as well be invisible: their articulated experience is one of being surrounded by "nature" (plants and non-human animals), against a backdrop of "scenery" (mountains and sky). Cooke reflects on her own initial response to the tourists – her incredulity at their perceptions of "experiencing nature" from a multinational corporate parking lot – and this gives her pause, as she considers the cultural understandings of "wilderness" that lie beneath both the tourists' mental erasure of the human-made elements of the scene and her own surprise that their campsite occurs to them as "nature." There is a shared imaginary of wilderness operating in this space – nature as something to be subdued and then protected, a perspective which, when enacted, dislocates those who have long lived *in* it in other ways. But Coyote perceives no such boundaries, darting in and out over dirt and pavement, hunting prey and scavenging tourist flotsam and jetsam alike. For Coyote, there is no dichotomy of nature and culture, only space and the possibilities it presents to sustain life, and the hazards it harbors for the same. Following Coyote, Cooke can read Yukon's wilderness tourism experience as being of a piece with the roads that have brought the tourists there and the parking lot in which she found them. They are part of the same assemblage of late corporate capitalist settler-colonial Canada, part of the same conglomeration of ideological and material forces that pit settlers against other peoples, and against other species, in a bid for dominance over a space to which settlers have no defensible exclusive moral right. Considering the way another relates to the same space the self occupies can open our eyes to the limits of our own moral perspectives.

Finally, a moral gaze looks not only *at*, but *around*. To see something in its fullness is to see it in the context of its relations – to see the sense in which it *is* its relations. In many other contexts, I have written about the paradox of self: that we are fundamentally both discrete and collective (Caton, 2014, 2017). Rickly, too, considers this theme in Chapter 4 of this volume, where she explores rock-climbing as a nature context in which individuals negotiate relationships with community in complex ways, using lifestyle climbing to differentiate themselves from the mainstream collective, and yet finding themselves ever still bound within important (even life-sustaining) human communities, albeit communities that are mobile and highly fluid in nature (see also Veijola, 2014).

Both Rickly and I have learned about this inevitable tension between individuality and collectivity from several decades of hanging around with humans, but biologist David Haskell (2017) arrived at the same conclusion by spending quality time with trees, or more specifically, listening to them. He means that literally. Haskell travels the globe with a set of high-tech audio gear, listening to the sounds of trees and their habitats, camping among them, climbing into their canopies, circling back to visit them across the seasons and over time. Returning to the balsam fir, Haskell explores it as an individual, growing "from a single embryo within a single seed, its DNA coding a unique genetic identity" (p. 45). When the tree's truck falls into the forest, Haskell notes, "this individual will pass away, a biological atom with a beginning and an end." And yet,

> [e]very needle and root is a composite of plant, bacterial, and fungal cells, a weave that cannot be unknotted. The singular fir embryo was planted by a bird whose feathers were a sheen of bacteria, whose gut was a microbial community, and whose context was a cultured society. Cracked open, germinated, the seedling's growth was possible only because no herbivorous moose swallowed the young tree into a four-chambered mash of digestive microorganisms. For the absence of moose, the fir owes its life to wolves, human hunters, and the mosquitoes that infect moose with nematode worms and viruses. . . [The forest seeds the sky with moisture, and the] air's chemistry aggregates the aromas of pine, spruce, and fir into particles that draw mist into droplets. These add to the dust, smoke, and exhaust of North America's air, and a fine rain descends. The fir tree's life is relationship. Tilting our heads away from the atom, it seems that life is not just networked; it *is* network.
>
> (Haskell, p. 45)

Haskell insists on life's dual character – that neither our individuality nor our collectivity diminishes the truth of its opposite. Our metaphorical expression of not being able to "see the forest for the trees" captures the difficulty that we have in holding both truths in view simultaneously. But this is a perceptual problem, not an ontological one. Life *is* of this dual nature, and so an honest gaze toward any individual must also be a gaze at the ecosystem in which that individual is embedded.

This notion underscores Mullins's critique of the Leave No Trace land management ethic, in Chapter 10 of this volume. As he argues, Western settler ideas of "wilderness" as pristine space, clear of all human use, interfere with both our ability to see life's connected, ecological nature, and to realize just and caring relations with our fellow humans, in this case, Indigenous Peoples who have a different ethic regarding how to engage with land and who have long called what are, to settlers, wilderness recreational spaces, home. Ignoring the relationality of all life thus ends up having moral consequences for our ability to build just relationships with specific others, in specific times and places.

Smith, in Chapter 11 of this volume, further adds the dimension of time to the exploration of relationships across species and the human moral potential that can be activated by these relationships. Specifically, Smith explores the "residual agency" of fossils – long-dead individual organisms that can touch human lives epochs later, the event of their presence offering up the potential to reconfigure human understandings and moral logics about the past, present, and future. While we may have lost all sense of biological connection with long-extinct critters like the ammonites Smith references in his discussion, we can return ourselves to a state of relationship with these creatures by engaging with them and allowing them to interrupt our current ways of thinking. Just as the fossil record's role in establishing the idea of evolution helped to reconfigure the story of earth in less humancentric terms, using cultural practices like geotourism as a gateway to encounter materially the fixity of death by holding one of these fossils in our hands may spur us to reconsider what responsibilities we might hold to act in ways that preserve life beyond our own species. In forging a new kind of relationship with the ammonite – a cultural rather than a biological one – we invite the fossil to become teacher.

And much closer to home, cultural tourism may also hold the potential to help us build stronger relationships with fellow members of our own species, from whom we can also learn valuable lessons. Higgins-Desbiolles and Akbar consider this idea in Chapter 1 of this volume, when they not only outline the challenges of Indigenous involvement in the tourism industry in Australia currently, but also explore the potential of Indigenous-led initiatives to create better codes and practices that resist the kinds of dynamics critiqued by Erickson (Chapter 3), discussed above. Through careful and intentional practices of self-presentation, land management, and hosting, the Yolngu Peoples, who Higgins-Desbiolles and Akbar engage with in their case study, have been successful in establishing community-led tourism that not only interrupts traditional industry dynamics of cultural commodification and representational control by tourism brokers from dominant social groups outside the community, but also shares with guests a different cultural perspective, the Yolngu's notion of *lirrwi*, or the layers of connection of all life on earth.

Wonderland

How, then, might we summarize the moral gaze? First, it might be thought of as one which recognizes the presence of the other. From such recognition, then, would follow not instrumental desire, but an intrinsic appreciation of the other's being, not a move for mastery, but a welcoming of mystery, a willingness to receive the other as teacher. But above all, the moral gaze would have to be a *relational gaze*. And for this reason, it would also have to be a *reflective gaze*, back at ourselves, for we too are embedded in life's network. Just as it was for Alice, the view returned to us in this gaze would be not simply a reflection of what is, but also a dream of something else in the making. Through this looking glass is indeed a wonderland – humans, balsam firs, root fungi, soil microbes, giant redwoods, Joshua trees, kingfishers, coyotes, fossilized ammonites of the past, and as-yet-undreamed moral possibilities for the future – all of us here together, being and becoming, on this very blissfully unlonely planet.

References

Baronov, D. (2004). *Conceptual foundations of social research methods*. Boulder, CO: Paradigm Publishers.

Berreby, D. (2005). *Us and them: Understanding your tribal mind*. New York: Little, Brown & Company.

Bruner, E. (2005). *Culture on tour: Ethnographies of travel*. Chicago: University of Chicago Press.

Caton, K. (2011). Thinking inside the box: Understanding discursive production and consumption in tourism. In I. Ateljevic, N. Morgan, & A. Pritchard (Eds.), *The critical turn in tourism studies: Creating an academy of hope* (pp. 121–134). London: Routledge.

Caton, K. (2012). Taking the moral turn in tourism studies. *Annals of Tourism Research, 39*, 1906–1928.

Caton, K. (2014). Between you and me: Making messes with constructivism and critical theory. *Tourism, Culture, and Communication, 13*, 127–137.

Caton, K. (2017). Sense of journey. *Proceedings of the Canadian Congress of Leisure Research*, Waterloo, Ontario, Canada, May 23–26.

Echtner, C., & Prasad, P. (2003). The context of Third World tourism marketing. *Annals of Tourism Research, 30*, 660–682.

Everett, S. (2008). Beyond the visual gaze: The pursuit of embodied experience thorough food tourism. *Tourist Studies, 8*, 337–358.

Fennell, D. (2012). *Tourism and animal ethics*. New York: Routledge.

Foucault, M. (1980). *Power/knowledge*. New York: Pantheon.

Frost, R. (1928). Tree at my window. In *West-running brook*. New York: Henry Holt.

Gadamer, H. (1975). *Truth and method*. New York: Sheed & Ward.

Gould, S. (2003). *The hedgehog, the fox, and the magister's pox: Mending the gap between science and the humanities*. New York: Harmony Books.

Grit, A. (2014). Messing around with serendipities. In S. Veijola, J. Molz, O. Pyyhtinen, E., Hockert, & A. Grit (Eds.), *Disruptive tourism and its untidy guests: Alternative ontologies for future hospitalities* (pp. 122–141). Basingstoke: Palgrave Macmillan.

Haskell, D. (2017). *The songs of trees: Stories from nature's great connectors*. New York: Viking.

Hollinshead, K. (2009). The "worldmaking" prodigy of tourism: The reach and power of tourism in the dynamics of change and transformation. *Tourism Analysis*, *14*, 139–152.

James, A. (2012). *Assholes: A theory*. New York: Anchor Books.

Kau, K. (2010). *Prosthetic arm*. Retrieved from www.coroflot.com/kaylenek/PROSTHETIC-ARM.

LaCapra, D. (2004). *History in transit: Experience, identity and critical theory*. Ithaca, NY: Cornell University Press.

Levinas, E. (1996). *Emmanuel Levinas: Basic philosophical writings*. Bloomington, IN: Indiana University Press.

Malkki, L. (1992). National geographic: The rooting of peoples and the territorialisation of national identity among scholars and refugees. *Cultural Anthropology*, *7*, 24–44.

Maoz, D. (2006). The mutual gaze. *Annals of Tourism Research*, *33*, 221–239.

McAlister, M. (2001). *Epic encounters: Culture, media, and U.S. interests in the Middle East since 1945*. Berkeley, CA: University of California Press.

Merton, T. (1941). *Meditations, December 23–30, 1941*. Retrieved from http://merton.org/ITMS/Seasonal/25/25-4Montaldo.pdf.

Morgan, N., & Pritchard, A. (2000). Privileging the male gaze: Gendered tourism landscapes. *Annals of Tourism Research*, *27*, 884–905.

Moufakkir, O., & Reisinger, Y. (2013). *The host gaze in global tourism*. Oxfordshire: CABI.

Nussbaum, M. (2010). *Not for profit: Why democracy needs the humanities*. Princeton, NJ: Princeton University Press.

Pedwell, C. (2012). Economies of empathy: Obama, neoliberalism, and social justice. *Environment and Planning D: Society and Space*, *30*, 280–297.

Picard, D., & Robinson, M. (2012). *Emotion in motion: Tourism, affect, and transformation*. Farnham: Ashgate.

Pine, B., & Gilmore, J. (1998). Welcome to the experience economy. *Harvard Business Review*, *July–August*, 97–105.

Said, E. (1978). *Orientalism*. New York: Vintage Books.

Scarpato, R., & Daniele, R. (2003). New global cuisine: Tourism, authenticity, and sense of place in postmodern gastronomy. In C. Hall, L. Sharples, R. Mitchell, N. Macionis, & B. Cambourne (Eds.), *Food tourism around the world* (pp. 296–313). Oxford: Butterworth-Heinemann.

Singer, P. (2009). *The life you can save*. New York: Random House.

Springsteen, B. (1978). Badlands. In *Darkness on the edge of town*. New York: Columbia.

Strain, E. (2003). *Public places, private journeys: Ethnography, entertainment, and the tourist gaze*. New Brunswick, NJ: Rutgers University Press.

Taleb, N. (2012). *Antifragile: Things that gain from disorder*. New York: Random House.

Technology Beyond 2035. (n.d.). *Biomimicry*. Retrieved from https://technologybeyond2035.wordpress.com/biomimicry-2/.

Tucker, H. (2016). Empathy and tourism: Limits and possibilities. *Annals of Tourism Research*, *57*, 31–43.

Urry, J. (1990). *The tourist gaze: Leisure and travel in contemporary societies*. London: SAGE.
Vaughan, H. (1650). The night. In *Silex Scintillans*. London: Elliot Stock.
Veijola, S. (2014). Towards silent communities. In S. Veijola, J. Molz, O. Pyyhtinen, E., Hockert, & A. Grit (Eds.), *Disruptive tourism and its untidy guests: Alternative ontologies for future hospitalities* (pp. 68–95). Basingstoke: Palgrave Macmillan.

Afterword

The moral nature of tourism has become far more complex than it was in the time of the early anthropologists and sociologists who studied encounters between hosts and their tourist guests far away from the hubs of the Western way of life. Today, attention is paid increasingly to the *ethics of being-with*, being-alongside, and engaging in mobile neighbouring with everyone and everything that exists. Agency is no longer attributed to human beings only – it extends to all forms of life and matter. Subsequently, *nature* is no longer a mere setting and a background for recreational tourist activities, or even a matter of scientifically measuring the impacts of tourism on natural environments. In short, the problems caused by tourism have become more and more *practical* and *philosophical*.

The book at hand expands the range of morally relevant agencies and activities in tourist settings, and thus changes the horizon of tourism research profoundly. First, it questions the white gaze and mind as the foundation of the tourist experience, upon which most of the tourism businesses and studies are based. Second, it valorizes the active role of parking lots, highways, cars, and windscreens in constructing a pristine and authentic tourist experience, for instance when the north is considered as a frontier and a gate to wilderness. Third, it draws attention to the images, artefacts, and practices of Indigenous cultures that are original and self-made, not mere merchandize produced on assembly lines by non-Indigenous operators. Fourth, it shows in detail the multiple roles that *other species*, especially animals – the loved, hated, forgotten, and eaten ones – play in tourism imageries, hospitalities, and activities. Last, but not least, it investigates the methodologies, which we use when we take a critical stance: when we want to learn the Indigenous ways of knowing, leave no trace on places that we visit, or increase tourists' interest in heritage and history. Even these worthwhile aims deserve a closer look, the book states. All the issues have an ethical undertone: where do we draw the line between morally right and morally wrong action? How can philosophical investigation into the nature of ethics change the ways in which we understand nature in tourism? How can we construct an approach that enables us as tourists, entrepreneurs, developers, and researchers to "relate more ethically to a more-than-human world," and what would "orient us in living and enacting better human-nature relationships through tourism"?

Tourism is, by definition, a double-faced phenomenon: it evokes fundamental human values that are ends-in-themselves and then puts them on sale. Jacques Derrida notes that when, for example, love, friendship, hospitality, or a gift gets paid for, it turns into a tool with only instrumental value. Tourism commodifies human values and desires – yet if it did not do that, seeing the world by travelling would require military interventions, caste- or estate-based networks, or particular institutionalized venues providing protection against (predominantly male) violence. (Belonging to a royal family or a presidential entourage might also be helpful.) There would be no relatively safe, institutionalized venues for tourists. Money, paradoxically, liberates us from cultural fundamentals – such as customs, especially those based on religion, that legitimize the unequal treatment of human beings on the basis of gender, ethnicity, class, or sexual orientation. Grand, grandiose, and humbler tours are available for more and more people, thanks to the highly globalized infrastructures of tourism. Thus, tourism is our inescapable and morally ambivalent guide, host, and guest when learning about the world – and about ourselves.

For ethics, which in traditional Western thought means philosophical studies of the foundations of morality, tourism is an endlessly inspiring phenomenon. One could ask, for instance, the following questions that link with the empirical world in numerous ways: does tourism promote *good life* through virtues, or *vices*? Does it give people *rights* that do not infringe on other people's rights? Does it *benefit all* and lead to common good or does it help only a select few while harming others? Does it state clearly and also follow up on its *duties*? Does it treat everyone in a *just* way so that in principle anyone could accept any role in tourism? What kind of *ethics of care* is it devoted to? And, finally, is it based on *ethical relativism*, according to which one cannot judge other cultures' moral norms from another culture's perspective?

Of course, tourism is not *one* actor, just like nature is not one entity. Yet, as an institutionalized arrangement of service-assisted encounters of people and places that are largely unknown to one another previously, it has an agential role in culture and society. In a parallel fashion, *one* tourist is not responsible for the behavior of all other tourists.

Or is s/he?

There would be no *one* tourist if there were no *other* tourists. Ontologically, a tourist is always already-with-other-tourists. Following Jean-Luc Nancy, the ethical, the social, and the ontological subsume one another because a human being cannot have engendered as one single being. Through another human being the social and thereby the ethical enter the scene. In this framework I could ask, "What is my duty as a tourist towards people I meet during my traveling?" In the framework of a world which is more-than-human, I could also ask, "What is my duty as one-tourist-among-many towards other species and the planet as a whole?"

However, in a social world such as tourism, founded on the opportunity to escape from the moral communities and norms of everyday life and to follow one's heart and desires, how can one address tourists (or even tourism entrepreneurs) as *a moral community*, or an ideological or political *movement*, without unintentionally introducing new forms of governance into the world already governed inside-out? The notion of a *tourist community* is thus perhaps a bit more intriguing paradox than what it appears at the outset. Moreover, tourism is deeply rooted in society as an ingredient of practically all forms of human inquiry and creativity. Hence, its moral aspects cannot be investigated as if they were exceptions or exits out of this world. A swimming pool next to the bar, the ropes securing a rock climber, and guards escorting an ancient neckless to a gallery on the other side of the world are still all confined to the planet Earth.

What tourism can do is show us "a portrait of our self," of what we really have become, a portrait similar to the secret painting of Dorian Gray in Oscar Wilde's famous novel. The portrait painted in the book at hand directs our attention to what is included in and excluded from the background and through what kinds of discursive frames the human subject in her/his environs, the tourist in a tourist destination, holds in front of her/him when s/he looks back at us.

Just like tourists, entrepreneurs are not alone. There is no *single* entrepreneur without institutionalized arrangements of making business. If an entrepreneur is rooted in a local community where tourism and hospitality companies operate and if one is also engaged in social activity – a hobby, a passion, science, or art that brings visitors together – tourism has a fair chance of becoming a living part of the local community. Entrepreneurs can lead the way toward "new institutions of tourism" (see Giovanna Bertalla, in this book) if their skills and capacity are directly linked to their own visions and ideas of a livable and just world, and if they do not simply go by the cut-and-paste business strategies of management guides for busy readers. Moreover, these circumstances can create respectful ways of being-with and being-alongside forms of life and matter other than humans only. Destinations become places, again. People, who are products of places, may realize that places are made not only by their people but also by their first inhabitants: land, sky, trees, plants, and animals.

Indeed, when reducing tourism to a mere issue of economic growth, there is no difference between elite and mass tourism in terms of the consequences. Rich people are often considered as role models among less wealthy people. Thus, also their lifestyle in holiday-making, which is unsustainable in a number of ways (for instance, using a private jet to treat the dear kitty with her favorite caviar or to get the poodle trimmed by someone he knows), inspires also masses to conspicuous consumption. Perhaps less money is spent per capita, but *en masse* the sum escalates. Interpreting vanity as luxury thus wastes the world's natural and human resources.

Individually, most people understand that we are just visitors in this world. But, certainly, when thinking seven generations ahead, as several Indigenous Peoples do and kindly advise others to do, we should realize that the vacation of the human species on the planet is winding toward its end, and that the destination that used to be so cool is about to become a huge insect hotel. In addition to the deadly viruses that they carry in their belly packs, mosquitos are much better travelers than we are, even if it is the human species that has assisted their heedless, devil-may-care journeying. They can soon spread anywhere as long as their pools are heated – thanks to globalized mobilities and all other human-made competitive creativities that have escalated global warming.

If distancing oneself from the particular problems of tourism leads to such scenes of dark tourism on a planetary scale, one may ask, "What point is there to investigate 'transformations necessary for just and sustainable tourism natures'?" (See Introduction.) From an ethical point of view, giving up on turning tourism into an asset in increasing the awareness of global problems is, of course, not a real option. Along with books, films, and other cultural artefacts, also tourist encounters with nature and other forms of life can help us notice the power relations embedded in the narratives we circulate about the world and about tourism. Which ones are violent and which ones are not? Who (position in society) tells what (choice of important topics), to whom (which positions and relations count), on which forum (which discourses dominate), and with what consequences to each stakeholder (public interest and justice versus private interest and exploitation)?

How do we *conference*, that is, convene to talk about important issues together? Meetings as ethical encounters can become walks into the woods, yet this time *together with* the path, the forest, the ants (careful where you step!), and the wind in the air.

Soile Veijola
University of Lapland, Finland

Index

Page numbers in italics indicate figures and those in bold indicate tables. Notes are indicated by page numbers followed by n.